ONE MONEY FOR EUROPE

Also by Michele Fratianni

LA LIQUIDITA INTERNAZIONALE, 1972
INFLAZIONE, PRODUZIONE E POLITICA ECONOMICA IN ITALIA, 1975
L'ECONOMIA ITALIANA 1974-75, 1975
L'ECONOMIA ITALIANA 1975-77, 1976
BANK CREDIT, MONEY AND INFLATION IN OPEN ECONOMIES (*co-editor*) 1976
LE ORGANIZZAZIONI ECONOMICHE INTERNAZIONALI, 1977
L'ECONOMIA ITALIANA 1976-78, 1977

Also by Theo Peeters

HET VERENIGD KONINKRIJK IN DE E.E.G. VOOR- EN NADELEN VOOR DE BELGISCHE ECONOMIE (*co-author*), 1970
DETERMINANTEN VAN DE INTERNATIONAL HANDEL IN FABRIKATEN, 1971

ONE MONEY FOR EUROPE

Edited by

MICHELE FRATIANNI

and

THEO PEETERS

First edition 1978
Reprinted 1980

Published by
THE MACMILLAN PRESS LTD
London and Basingstoke
Companies and representatives throughout the world

British Library Cataloguing in Publication Data

One money for Europe
1. Monetary unions – Congress
2. Money – European Economic Community countries – Congresses
1. Fratianni, Michele II. Peeters, Theo
332.4'566'094 HG3894

ISBN 978-1-349-04310-1 ISBN 978-1-349-04308-8 (eBook)
DOI 10.1007/978-1-349-04308-8

Contents

Preface

The signatories to the *Manifesto on European Monetary Union* published in *The Economist* of All Saints' Day 1975, met their critics and supporters in Leuven at the end of November 1977 to discuss the principal issues arising from the Manifesto's proposals. The proceedings of the conference constitute this book.

Those taking part in the conference were asked to consider the following points from the Manifesto: (i) the case for economic and monetary union, (ii) the properties of an inflation-proofed parallel currency, called the Europa, (iii) the types of exchange rate arrangements which are compatible with the Europa and conducive to the early adoption of monetary union, (iv) the advantages of the Europa mechanism over a stabilisation of existing national monies and (v) the institutional problems.

In Part I of the book, Herbert Christie and Michele Fratianni offer an overall view of the issues under consideration. They argue that a strong case can be made for both economic and monetary union in Europe, but leave open the question as to whether most of the benefits arise from economic union or from monetary union. The main questions then are not about the desirability of economic and monetary union in Europe but about the best ways to achieve it. Christie and Fratianni consider three alternative strategies: (i) the approach currently followed by the Commission of the European Communities with its emphasis on the snake arrangement and coordination of policies; (ii) the early introduction of a common currency; and (iii) the deferral of major steps in the monetary field until after economic union has been achieved. The current approach is manifestly not succeeding. The monetary-unification-first strategy has the advantage of relying on market forces in contrast to difficult and numerous political decisions to bring about monetary unification. The money-last strategy entails that all efforts initially be concentrated on eliminating barriers to the movement of goods, services, capital and labour. An increase in the degree of economic integration could facilitate the decision to adopt a common currency at a later stage.

Part II of the book deals with the Manifesto proposal and its critics. An early reaction to the Manifesto was that the proposed parallel currency was too good and, thus, would quickly drive national currencies out of circulation. The key issue in this respect appears to be whether governments are prepared to forgo the inflation tax. David Laidler does not think so, and gives the signatories of the Manifesto proposal a low political score. He believes that governments will go to great lengths to ensure that national monies remain, for example by requiring that taxes be paid in national money. Laidler himself favours either a currency reform or a money-last strategy. But suggestion of a currency reform poses the following problem: how can one fault the Manifesto proposal for lack of political realism and propose at the same time a change which would require a comparable political commitment?

Little progress was made on why governments prefer inflation taxation to explicit taxation. Governments can use their monopoly power to maximise tax revenues. The highly variable rates of inflation which have been experienced suggest that governments do not extract the maximum inflation tax. Rather they may fall back on it because 'legislated' tax is more difficult to raise. Indeed, as Benjamin Klein notes, 'the control of a nation's money supply . . . represents a very large potential tax that can be levied quickly and collected in a broadbased and efficient way, without short-run market or democratic tests'. From this Klein concludes that 'a single established money in Europe would eliminate whatever amount of competition between monies now exists and greatly increase the inflationary incentives. . .'.

On more theoretical grounds Klein, and to a lesser extent Laidler, argue that the Europa would face an almost insurmountable confidence problem. Klein finds no significant cases in history where a new money has rapidly displaced existing ones. Klein's discussants were quick to point out, however, that the historical evidence is not relevant to the Manifesto proposal, because the failure of new monies to emerge can be largely attributed to the actions of states in defending existing currencies so as not to lose seigniorage.

Vaubél discusses two aspects of the economics of parallel currency. First, competition between the Europa and the national currencies should lead to the formation of an optimum currency area. The Europa should assert itself first as a standard of value, then as a store of value and finally as a medium of exchange. In the end it will be an empirical matter whether the Europe of Nine or Twelve is a feasible currency domain. Currency competition is compared to language competition. Since the process by which 'inferior' languages are driven out by 'superior' ones is indeed slow, and new languages such as Esperanto have not been widely adopted, this comparison does not augur well for the quick achievement of monetary union.

Vaubél's second proposition is that a parallel currency avoids the temporary unemployment otherwise necessary to move from a high to a low rate of inflation. This depends on the acceptability of the parallel currency in the market place. If Klein is right in saying that the parallel currency will not be accepted rapidly, Vaubel's point loses most of its punch.

Triffin sees little value in pressing for an inflation-proofed Europa since governments do not seem to want such an innovation and he suggests that efforts be concentrated instead on promoting the adoption of a modified European Unit of Account. In his own words, this could be used initially 'as an alternative, not to national currencies, but only to foreign currencies and Euro-currencies already and increasingly used today as parallel currencies for international transactions'.

The current approach to monetary union stresses coordination of macroeconomic policies in general and monetary policies in particular. Could its chances of success be improved by eliminating positive feedbacks from exchange rate changes to the domestic price level? Basevi and De Grauwe think so and explain the implications of a rule designed to achieve it (the OPTICA rule) based on Purchasing Power Parity in the context of a two-country model. The rationale of the rule derives from evidence concerning 'overshooting' of the spot exchange rate when inflation rates diverge and monetary policy is accomodating. Thus under present arrangements large and sudden changes in exchange rates which are not warranted by PPP could be quickly validated through the incorporation of higher inflationary expectations into new wage and price settlements.

Some of the most interesting questions during the discussion of the Basevi-De Grauwe paper dealt with the dynamic properties of the rule. Its application might well reduce exchange rate fluctuations if expectations about the future value of the spot rate are of the error-learning type; but the rule is likely to introduce instability if expectations are formed rationally (This point, which was discussed at the conference, is formally developed in an unpublished paper by Giorgio Basevi, Paul De Grauwe and Alfred Steinherr.) In addition, there remains the need for accomodating changes in real exchange rates and for care concerning the choice of the base period and price index.

Finally, Michael Parkin tackles the intitutional problem. Is there a correlation between the design of monetary institutions and the performance of monetary policy? He finds weak evidence that the single-minded pursuit of price stability is associated with the achievement of a lower average rate of inflation than in comparable cases when no such objective is legislated. He finds strong evidence, however, that full independence of central bank policy is associated with a relatively low rate of inflation but not with a more predictable monetary policy. In that case monetary policy appears to be used primarily as an anti-inflation weapon and not to stabilise real output and employment.

Do we want the central bank of Europe to pursue a stable policy or to deliver a counter-cyclical Keynesian-type policy? The first could be set up immediately; the second would have to be delayed until the European Parliament was fully functioning. Parkin proposes a steady money supply growth rate as the objective. The existing central banks would then be left with secondary tasks such as bank regulation.

Polly Reynolds Allen summarizes the main points of agreement and disagreement and the unresolved issues of the conference. Provided that there is a will on the part of EEC Governments to move to a monetary union, she concludes that the introduction of a parallel currency, the Europa, of constant purchasing power offers a reasonable and promising means of moving to monetary union, with the additional benefit of reducing the costs of monetary reform.

In the epilogue Sarah Hogg sets the conference in its political context. She points out that the remarkable shift which took place early in 1978 towards greater enthusiasm for monetary union on the part of Europe's political heads makes the conference proceedings of immediate relevance to Europe's contemporary monetary problems and preoccupations.

MICHELE FRATIANNI
THEO PEETERS

Acknowledgements

The planning and execution of a conference is seldom the effort of one or two individuals. This conference was no exception. We thank the Belgian Ministry of Foreign Affairs, and in particular Minister R. Van Elslande, for financial support, Dirk Heremans for advice on the planning, the staff of the Centrum voor Economische Studien of the Katholieke Universiteit Leuven for the many details and last-minute organisational chores and Dale Larson compiling the index. We finally thank the editor of *The Economist*, London for permission to republish the All Saints' Day Manifesto.

M.F.

Th.P.

List of Participants

J.P. ABRAHAM, Facultés Universitaires Notre Dame de la Paix, Namur

P.R. ALLEN, University of Connecticut, Storrs

G. BASEVI, Università di Bologna, Bologna

J. BATCHELOR, The City University, London

F. BOYER de la GIRODAY, Commission of the European Communities, Brussels

H. CHRISTIE

H. DALGAARD, Danmarks Nationalbank, København

P. DE GRAUWE, Katholieke Universiteit Leuven

G. de MENIL, Ecole des Hautes Etudes en Sciences Sociales, Paris

M. EMERSON, Commission of the European Communities, Brussels

R. FLOC'H, Banque de France, Paris

A. FOURCANS, ESSEC, Cergy

M. FRATIANNI, Indiana University, Bloomington, and Katholieke Universiteit Leuven

J. HARBOORT, Adviser to the Belgian Senate, Tournai

I. HODAC, College of Europe, Brugge

D. HEREMANS, Katholieke Universiteit Leuven

S. HOGG, *The Economist,* London

E. KIRSCHEN, Université Libre de Bruxelles

B. KLEIN, University of California, Los Angeles

N. KLOTEN, Landeszentralbank in Baden-Wurttemberg, Stuttgart, and Universität Tübingen

P. KORTEWEG, Erasmus Universiteit, Rotterdam

D. LAIDLER, University of Western Ontario, London, Ontario

H. LANGOHR, INSEAD, Fontainebleau

R. MASERA, Banca d'Italia, Roma

J. MELITZ, INSEE, Paris

J.C. MOREL, Commission of the European Communities, Brussels

U. MOSCA, Commission of the European Communities, Brussels

G. MURPHY, Central Bank of Ireland, Dublin

J. NIEHANS, Universität Bern, Bern

D. O'MAHONY, University College, Cork
F. ONIDA, Università Commerciale Luigi Bocconi, Milano
M. PARKIN, University of Western Ontario, London, Ontario
T. PEETERS, Katholieke Universiteit Leuven
J.J. REY, Banque Nationale de Belgique and Université Libre de Bruxelles
P. SALIN, Université Paris IX-Dauphine, Paris
H.E. SCHARRER, Institut für Wirtschaftsforschung, Hamburg
A. STEINHERR, Université Catholique de Louvain, Louvain-la-Neuve
K. TAVERNIER, Katholieke Universiteit, Leuven
N. THYGESEN, Københavns Universitat, København
R. TRIFFIN, Yale University, New Haven and Université Catholique de Louvain, Louvain-la-Neuve
P. VAN DEN BEMPT, Commission of the European Communities, Brussels
J. van YPERSELE, Belgian Ministry of Finance and Université Catholique de Louvain, Louvain-la-Neuve
R. VAUBEL, Institut für Weltwirtschaft, Kiel
A. VERHEIRSTRAETEN, Katholieke Universiteit Leuven
J. VUCHELEN, Vrije Universiteit Brussel
M. WEGNER, Commission of the European Communities, Brussels
F. WOEHRLING, Commission of the European Communities, Brussels
G. ZIS, University of Salford, Lancashire

PART I:
AN OVERVIEW

1 EMU: Rehabilitation of a Case and Some Thoughts for Strategy

HERBERT CHRISTIE and MICHELE FRATIANNI

I. INTRODUCTION

The object of this paper is to restate the case of economic and monetary union in Europe (EMU); to indicate the extent of progress so far towards EMU; to outline alternative strategies to bring union about; and to indicate the main problems associated with each of these strategies.

Economic Union (EU) will be understood throughout the paper to mean a situation in which all barriers to the movement of goods and factor inputs between participating regions or countries have been removed. Monetary Union (MU), unless otherwise stated, signifies an area where one currency prevails and where a single institution is responsible for controlling the area's money stock. It will be noted that the U in EU and MU here stands for union and not unification.

EMU will be discussed in the context of the existing nine member country EEC. But the paper would require little modification if Greece, Portugal, Spain and other countries eventually became members too.

Ideas, like most phenomena in life, are subject to ups and downs. EMU has been no exception. It reached a high point in December 1969 when the heads of the member states meeting at the Hague decided to adopt it as the long-term goal of the EEC. The immediate consequence of the Hague decision was the establishment of the Werner Committee and, in due course, other *ad hoc* specialist committees to help to plan economic and monetary integration. An outcome of their work was a spate of directives, resolutions and Council decisions concerning the coordination of economic and financial policy. The machinery of coordination which was then created was ambitious and

---

We are grateful to P. Buffet, C. Cavanagh and H. Van Zonneveld for their comments on an earlier draft. For the views expressed and any errors remaining we alone are responsible.

extended over a large number of fields.[1] It provided for regular consultation between the Commission and the member states concerning short and medium-term economic policy. It sought to establish common guidelines at Community level for fiscal, monetary and other macro-economic variables. And it provided for annual reports on the convergence of the member states. Yet its achievements were disappointing.

The political will necessary for success was absent: there was little disposition on the part of the member countries to modify national policies, or even at times to forgo party political advantage, in the interest of wider Community objectives. Thus although increasing numbers of Committee meetings took place at all levels, in practice the process of coordination was a formality which did not seriously constrain the policies of the member countries. In particular the member countries did not always observe the Council's recommendations concerning the sort of conjunctural policies to be adopted or make much effort to comply with the monetary and budgetary guidelines which had been agreed. The Commission was never publicly critical of member countries in breach of Council recommendations; and the recommendations of the Marjolin and Tindemans reports, designed to advance EMU, were not followed up. There was a tendency for enthusiasm to wane, for consultation to become a substitute for collective action, and for lack of achievement to become self-reinforcing.

Many thought that the recurrent misfortunes of the snake arrangement, the drastic deterioration in the terms of trade following the jump in oil prices of 1973-74, and the subsequent recession, had dealt a fatal blow to the prospects of achieving EMU. Certainly many advocates of economic and monetary unification became less attached to the idea, which was perhaps an indication that their commitment to it was feeble or at least conditional on the persistence of a favourable phase of economic activity.

During 1977, however, there was a revival of interest in EMU. The Heads of State had it on the agenda for their meeting, which was in December: the Belgians said that they aimed to initiate practical progress towards it during their tenure of the Presidency of the EEC Council in the second half of 1977; and Mr Jenkins, the new President of the EEC Commission, has recently advocated an increase in momentum leading to the eventual introductio of a common currency.[2] This paper is intended as a contribution to the growing debate which these political initiatives have provoked.

II. BENEFITS AND COSTS OF EMU

Economic and monetary unification is analytically equivalent to a once-for-all jump in efficiency or, in terms of a neoclassical model, to a rightward shift in full-employment output. It follows that the case for EMU holds whether the current level of economic activity happens to be high or low. This economic argument has a parallel in the political field. EMU represents a once-for-all political change comparable in importance to the Roman conquest some 2,000 years ago. The case for changes such as this cannot depend on temporary phenomena such as the particular phase of the trade cycle.

II.1 Benefits

1. Increased mobility of goods and factors. The main economic benefit from EU would come from an improved allocation of resources as markets were enlarged. Consumers should benefit from the resulting increase in competition. Producers should be enabled to hold down their costs by the savings from freer trade and, eventually, by the exploitation of untapped economies of scale and possibilities of improved location. The distribution of new capital investment should be improved in that the changed system would establish pressure for an equalisation of real returns at the margin, both geographically and by industrial sector. The changed distribution of employment implied by the changes in production and investment should provide for enhanced levels of labour productivity and hence real wages; and workers would have increased opportunities to seek jobs in other countries of the Community.

2. Common currency. Benefits of the kind just outlined could be achieved by economic union without monetary union. The move to a common currency, however, promises benefits additional to those of EU. The benefits which the individual receives from a medium of exchange increase with the size of its transaction domain. Exchange-rate uncertainty and conversion costs reduce the usefulness of money and lower efficiency in the goods and asset markets. On these considerations alone the world is the optimum currency area (Tower and Willett, 1976, p. 8). In addition, a world of multiple currencies and variable exchange rates leaves an obstacle to financial integration, because exchange rate risks induce portfolio holders to diversify over assets denominated in different securities. As Kenen (1976, p. 28) put is, 'the store-of-value function [of money] is exploited most efficiently when all assets are denominated in a single currency'.

3. Risk pooling. A currency area achieves economies of scale in international reserves because external shocks tend to cancel each other out in accordance with the law of large numbers. Stated differently, the risk from output fluctuation is reduced whenever the correlation among individual countries' shocks is less than one (Laffer, 1973). It follows that two or more countries with output fluctuations less than perfectly synchronized would earn a seigniorage, by forming a MU, equal to the amount of international reserves saved. This saving results because 'the use of a common currency of a currency union by one member implies involuntary lending on the part of the remaining members' (Mundell, 1973, p. 121). A word of caution is here in order: unless the MU is using commodity money the saving in international reserves implies no saving of resources for the world (Tower and Willett, p. 12). The reserve saving would allow the MU to run higher temporary trade deficits than would be the case for the sum of the participating countries. While this feature might be welcomed by policy makers of the European MU in the sense that the correction of a trade imbalance could be postponed for a longer period of time, the risk for the world would be a higher rate of inflation.

Finally, the European currency could well become a key currency in the world and thus permit the external balance constraint to be further attenuated in the short run. As in the case of the economies-of-scale argument, the emergence of a European MU whose money would rival the dollar in the international money markets would effectively transfer resources from the rest of the world to itself. The world might not benefit.

4. Centralization vs. coordination of economic policies. MU and a multiple-currency-fixed-exchange arrangement differ from one another in the administrative efficiency with which aggregate demand is managed. This topic has been analysed in the theory of fiscal federalism and the following long quote from Wallace E. Oates[3] gives the flavour of what is at stake:

> The 'federal system' is envisioned as an *existing* and well-defined entity with a central government along side of a set of decentralised levels of the public sector. It is a single currency area in which the central government is presumed to have the power to create or destroy money, to undertake spending and levy taxes and to issue non-monetary debt; decentralized governments have only the fiscal prerogatives of expenditure and taxation (along, perhaps, with the power to issue bonds).
>
> Within the institutional framework, the thrust of the literature is that the central government must assume the primary responsibility for the stabilization function in the public sector. First, and most obvious, the central government exercises control over the size of the money supply. This must be so within a single-currency area, for the incentives for 'localities' to create money with which to acquire real resources from their neighbours would be irresistible, if individual local governments could create money, we would have essentially a fixed exchange-rate system with each jurisdiction possessing, for all practical purposes, an infinite stock of reserves. Each locality could simply print money and purchase goods and services from other jurisdictions with no effective budgetary constraint. The exercise of monetary policy must, therefore, rest with the central government.
>
> Second, the government of small and highly-open jurisdictions will tend to be highly restricted in the scope for an active countercyclical fiscal policy. The relatively high marginal propensity to import implies that injections of new spending into the local economy will rapidly dissipate themselves into flows of spending into other areas. As a result, the expenditure multiplier (the reciprocal of the sum of the marginal propensity to save and the marginal propensity to import) will tend to be quite small.

The controversy as to which country or countries in the Community should reflate at present well illustrates the case for a centralized economic policy as distinct from policy coordination. In Europe today several large countries have a depressed level of economic activity coupled with balance-of-payments deficits; and a few countries enjoy balance of payments surpluses and a large accumulation of reserves. It is quite obvious that asking the surplus countries to be the 'locomotives' of the reflation train is tantamount to enforcing the rules of the game of the fixed exchange rate system. The simultaneous achievement of internal and external balance in the absence of exchange rate changes implies an expansionary economic policy in surplus countries which have a relatively low rate of inflation, and either a neutral or an expenditure-increasing policy in deficit countries which have a depressed level of economic activity.

Policy coordination in principle aims at speeding up the adjustment process between surplus and deficit countries. One of its weaknesses is that in practice each country tends to hold back, waiting for other countries to take appropriate action first. Centralization of the classical macro-economic instruments would eliminate this impasse, provided the member countries agreed on the objectives of policy.

It should not be forgotten that neither policy coordination nor centralization are substitutes for needed adjustment. To illustrate, take the intractable case of inflation and surplus in one country and deficit and unemployment in another country. The intractability of this situation arises either because objectives of policy are inconsistent or because there is a shortage of instruments given the number of objectives (Swoboda, 1973). The two countries could accept, respectively, a higher rate of inflation and more unemployment to meet the external balance objective; or, the inconsistent objectives could be made consistent by deploying instruments other than expenditure-changing policies. The surplus country could appreciate its currency and simultaneously lower expenditures while the deficit country could depreciate its currency and reflate. In a currency area the exchange rate cannot be used to correct payments imbalances and thus an income transfer from surplus to deficit country would have to take place (it will be argued below, p. 23, that exchange rate changes are not effective in altering a net export balance). The advantage of a common currency area is that policies would be coordinated automatically in the sense that participating countries or regions would accept the principles of the fixed-exchange rate system (Swoboda, 1973, p. 141).

To summarize, the administration of aggregate demand of a number of regions or states linked together by fixed rates of exchange is more efficient if policy instruments are centralised rather than coordinated. This conclusion holds so long as participating regions or states agree on the objectives to be pursued. If they do not, as is the case now in Europe (with surplus countries reluctant to reflate for fear of rekindling inflation and to appreciate their currencies for fear of damaging export industries), the issue of the relative efficiency of administering aggregate demand at the centre versus policy coordination loses relevance.

Making the administration of aggregate demand more efficient is not at all the same as increasing the wisdom of the decision eventually taken. Thus if wrong judgements are made concerning the appropriate level of aggregate demand, the gain in the efficiency of decision-taking will make matters worse. In this sense the efficiency gain is double edged.

5. Benefits of MU to a small open economy. The benefits of a MU are positively related to the openness of an economy. This is so for several reasons. First, the smaller economy tends to produce a less diversified range of output with a relatively large concentration of traded goods. External shocks – such as a sudden change in world demand – have a larger impact on the small undiversified economy than on a bigger country with a high incidence of non-traded goods. As already said, the formation of a MU lowers these risks through pooling Second, to the extent that changes in world prices or in the exchange rate affect a large proportion of items in the domestic price index, price movements inside the country are heavily influenced by external disturbances. Third, the low degree of diversification of the country's output tends to reduce the price elasticities of exports and imports so that the changes in domestic economic activity necessary to correct external imbalances are necessarily large (Tower and Willett, 1976, p. 40). Fourth, the small open economy cannot alter international prices of traded goods and assets. This implies that expenditure-switching policies (i.e. altering the relative price of traded to non-traded goods) are not an effective means of correcting balance of trade deficits, which require instead changes in domestic absorption. It also implies that any attempt on the part of the monetary authorities to raise the domestic supply of money above the amount which individuals and firms demand leads inevitably to a balance of payments deficit, a loss of reserves and a return to the initial stock of money.

Finally, the small economy with its modest currency size faces a higher probability that collusive behaviour among speculators will alter the value of the exchange rate.

II.2 Costs and Risks

6. Temporary costs due to reallocation of resources. As consumers, all residents of the Community stand to gain from a freeing of factor and product movements; but, as producers, some would lose, namely those unable to survive the resulting intensification of competition. The presumption is, however, that the real resource costs of increased competition would be temporary. These costs would take the form of local underutilisation of productive capacity and labour while production patterns were altered and resources transferred to new activities. To see how this might work in practice it will be useful to consider some of the consequences in greater detail.

If present plans are successful, indirect tax structures and rates will eventually be the same in all EEC member countries, VAT and excise taxes on traded goods will eventually be paid in the country of origin and not, as at present, in the country of destination, and fiscal frontiers will be abolished. Simultaneously, impediments to the free movement of capital and labour will be phased out. What would be the cost of these changes, assuming for the moment that each country kept its own currency and exchange rate?

Clearly the process of equalising indirect tax structures and rates will benefit some consumers and producers and not others within each country, depending not only on the tax rates at which equalisation takes place and the relevant price elasticities, but also on the consequential direct and other tax changes made by Governments anxious to avoid changes in their total tax revenues. It is impossible to predict without additional knowledge who will gain and lose from these domestic changes. The pattern of international trade and capital movements will also be affected in unpredictable ways. The consequential real resource transfers between member countries, and between member countries and non-members, will, however, be damped by offsetting movements in exchange rates during this transitional phase and therefore may not be very big after all. The whole process will be spread over a number of years and against the background of other events may not be particularly noticeable.

An alternative to the gradual equalisation of indirect tax structures and rates would be the early abolition of fiscal frontiers without an equalisation of taxes. A sudden change of this kind, even if announced and prepared some years in advance, would cause a certain amount of disruption, since the timing of consequential changes would necessarily be bunched. For example, some customs men would have to be redeployed, together with their support staffs. Those private firms which at present earn their living by facilitating the transit of goods across administrative frontiers would have to change the nature of their businesses. To the extent that the abolition of frontiers caused new trade channels to be created, old channels would suffer. For example, there would probably be a greater tendency to by-pass traditional channels such as specialised importers and firms established as international hauliers, and instead to buy direct in the country of origin and transport in own vehicles. This could even apply at the level of the final consumer. For example, when considering the purchase of a consumer durables, consumers living within reach of international frontiers would be more likely to compare prices internationally if they were certain that there would be no complications or delays at the border, even if they crossed it outside office hours, and that they could easily bring their purchases home in their own cars.

Abolishing exchange control would in principle, through its once-for-all effect on exchange rates, have a once-for-all effect on wages and prices. In practice controls would be phased out so as to minimise disturbance and speculation and, if the operation were entirely successful, the consequences of abolition would be scarcely preceptible against the background of other changes. There would be some risk however of speculation and hence of temporary instability in the capital markets. And as exchange control is regarded by some member countries as a normal instrument of economic management, its loss would be preceived by some policy makers as a cost of progress towards EMU.

Restrictions on the movement of capital are so complex in some member countries that banks and private firms have to employ specialist staffs to cope with them. These specialists together with their counterparts in the public sector who administer the controls would have to be redeployed if the controls were abandoned[4]

A further relaxation of restrictions on the movement of labour might well lead to increased international migration both of highly skilled workers and of unskilled workers, although the continued existence of linguistic and cultural differences within the Community would ensure that the international movement of workers, at least within the nine existing member states, was unlikely to be extensive. There could however be problems if international differences in social security provisions promoted the international movement of labour by attracting indigent immigrants to the countries with the most generous welfare systems. In this context the enlargement of the Community to include Greece, Portugal and Spain could create problems.

In sum, at the macro-economic level the costs and risks of freeing the movement of factors and products, harmonising indirect taxes and abolishing fiscal frontiers are less than might have been thought, because exchange rates would adjust so as to limit the extent of the consequential changes in the flow of goods and services and capital. At the micro-economic level the costs would essentially be the same as those of a successful competition policy. In addition, those who earn their living from the administration of the present system would have to be redeployed, this being the counterpart to the gain from the reduction in adminstrative complexity.

7. Enforcing national standards. If there were no border controls, the international movement of all goods and services would become much easier than it is now. Since the present controls are used to enforce national regulations of various kinds a consequence would be that these regulations would become harder to enforce. In particular a wide range of trade restrictions of various kinds, collectively known as non-tariff barriers to trade, would be weakened if there were no border controls. Those who at present benefit from these barriers to trade would lose.

If frontier controls were abolished, individual member countries could retain their separate laws governing the possession of goods (e.g. pornography), their use (e.g. vehicle inspections for motor cars) and conditions of sale (e.g. specified medicines to be obtainable by prescription only). An increase in the random checks carried out within each member country could, at least to some extent, make up for the loss of control over border traffic. But national administrations would find it somewhat harder than at present to impose product standards more stringent than those of their neighbours. In the extreme case without checks the laxest standards which any member state applied to itself would apply *de facto* throughout the Community. To reduce any adverse effects on the member countries which at present have the highest standards, without at the same time sacrificing any of the benefits to be obtained from the weakening or abolition of non-tariff barriers, it would be necessary to ensure, before border checks were abolished, that the laxest standards in use were sufficient, or that they were raised during negotiation so that they became sufficient, to safeguard the health and safety of the consumer and protect the environment from pollution. If the matter were carefully handled, it is almost certain that the costs of abolishing fiscal frontiers and border checks would be heavily outweighed by the ensuing benefits.

8. Loss of national control over the money stock. One of the main features distinguishing monetary union from economic union of the kind just described is the loss of national control over monetary policy. It follows from this that all regions or countries in the union will necessarily have the same *ex post* rate of inflation. Any discrepancy between a region's *ex ante* rate of inflation and the common rate of inflation will be accompanied by movements in real resources, since exchange rates will no longer be available as a means of making the necessary adjustment. Thus the creation of a monetary union would introduce new risks of high unemployment in its more inflation-prone member states. The risk here derives from the possibility that workers would demand equality of nominal wages rates (or nominal wage increases) in a situation where labour productivity rates (or labour productivity growth rates) were unequal. Thus the workers whose productivity (or its rate of growth) was lowest would be in danger of pricing themselves out of the market. Eventually no doubt the force of this would come to be widely appreciated and reflected in wage settlements. But the lesson might not be learned at once and, if unemployment increased, the cause might not immediately be perceived to be an unrealistically high level of money wages.

In the case of both large and small countries a loss of national control over monetary policy implies a loss of control over the national rate of inflation in the long run. In the short run, however, the costs of joining a monetary union are relatively higher for a large country. This is so because the small open economy is likely to be more exposed to world trade and thus to be a price taker in the traded goods market as well as in the asset markets. Changes in the exchange rate are quickly reflected in equivalent changes in domestic costs and prices, with the consequence that exchange rates are no longer useful as a tool of economic policy.

An independent monetary policy (i.e. a policy of flexible exchange rates) gives the country the ability to determine its own rate of inflation. The relative importance of international trade and inter-country financial flows tends to be lower the bigger is the country concerned. Monetary policy, or alternatively exchange rate policy, is more effective in influencing the real sector of the economy in the short run, though in the long run these real effects tend to disappear. In summary, it is the relatively higher leverage of economic policy in large countries that accounts for the perceived asymmetry of costs between large and small countries.

It is sometimes stated that member states joining the monetary union would no longer face a balance-of-payments constraint. While it is true that a region of a union neither adjusts the value of its money in relation to the value of the money of other regions nor experiences changes in foreign exchange, regional current account imbalances exist and are of a higher order of magnitude than countries' current account imbalances[5]. The question is then: how does a region cope with such imbalances? As a member of the union it faces the consequences of the union's balance of payments. Consider the case of a union deficit which causes a loss of international reserves (if the regime is one of fixed exchange rates) and thus a reduction in the growth rate of the union money stock. Interest rates in the union at first will tend to rise while inflation will tend to fall. These phenomena influence to different degrees all regions of the union. More specifically, suppose further that a given region enjoys a current account surplus both vis-a-vis the other regions of the union and the rest of the world. Interest rates in that region would tend to rise less than in the rest of the union; similarly, the *ex ante* rate of inflation in the region will tend to rise more than in the rest of the union. The law of one price must eventually prevail throughout the union. Thus, the temporary discrepancy in interest rates would induce private capital to move out of the surplus region. The discrepancy in inflation rates will eventually reduce the current account surplus. The adjustment process between regions of the union is therefore qualitatively similar to that implied by the gold standard.

9. Regional imbalances and public transfers. The above process may not be adequate to complete the adjustment. Differences in productivity may persist among regions; the price of labour in the deficit regions may not fall, relative to wages in surplus regions, to reflect lower levels of productivity; and private capital flows rather than performing an offsetting role to trade flows, might accentuate trade imbalances. It is a feature of modern welfare states that public finances act in the direction prescribed by the adjustment process of the gold standard with net transfers going from high productivity central regions to low-productivity peripheral regions. This transfer may well create a serious welfare problem in the sense that capital is flowing in the 'wrong' direction (Johnson, 1972). To summarize, regions within a union suffer from payments imbalances which are corrected partly by the same adjustment process as the union experiences in correcting its payments imbalances vis-a-vis other unions and partly by the redistributive role of public finances[6]. Redistribution away from the richest regions is necessary to maintain the monetary union and the net benefits it generates. Such redistribution should be taken into account explicitly. Rich regions are understandably reluctant to commit themselves to a big programme of transfer payments, while poor regions fear that regional aids, as they exist in the Community, are too weak to be relied upon to counter high levels of unemployment. Thus there would be a real risk in giving up national policy instruments at a time when the process of monetary unification was creating new stresses within the member states and before there were adequate Community instruments to replace the former national instruments.

In sum, there are two kinds of cost in passing to a monetary union from an economic union. One is that of achieving common rates of inflation throughout the Community. It is usual to think of these costs in terms of the temporary increase in unemployment necessary to bring down the rate of inflation in the most inflation-prone countries (not from temporarily high levels such as exist at the moment but from more sustainable levels). Against this, however, there would have to be set any temporary decrease in unemployment in the least inflation-prone countries if they had to increase their inflation rates. There would be some such offset if the common inflation rate were above that of the least inflation-prone country.

The second kind of cost is that of sacrificing the freedom to determine economic policy on a national scale. The extent of the loss here would depend on the degree of economic integration existing immediately before the monetary union was established, for the greater was the degree of integration, the less would have been the national room for manoeuvre in any case. This cost is perceived to be high by large countries.

The risks which the move to monetary union would entail arise from the fact that macro-economic policy would be facing new obstacles. The biggest risks would be those of pressure for the equalisation of nominal wage rates and consequently of a tendency towards higher unemployment. But there would also be significant risks that the new central institutions would be unable to cope adequately with structural unemployment or with unsynchronised fluctuations in national activity rates. The introduction of the new currency would carry risks on its own; in particular there would be risks that control over the main monetary aggregates would be diminished, at least temporarily. And there would always be some risk that the common currency would be mismanaged, which would have more serious consequences than the mismanagement of any single national currency.

III. EMU AND REPRESENTATIVE GOVERNMENT

The foregoing discussion suggests that the net benefits of EMU promise to be considerable, although not necessarily spread evenly between small and large countries or between high performance and low performance areas. Moreover, it is encouraging to note that the USA, which contains within its borders states with economies fully as different from one another as are the member countries of the EEC, is a continent-wide EMU of long standing which successfully maintains high living standards and a remarkable degree of political and economic stability. The fundamental question which remains however is: why is there so much resistance in Europe against monetary unification if the case for EMU is so overwhelming?

The answer follows from the proposition that in a representative democracy well-organised pressure groups have a disproportionate influence on public policy. These pressure groups include marginal producers and workers who stand to lose by what amounts to an increase of competition, monopolistic industries which fear an erosion of their positions, national monetary institutions and bureaucracies whose power and livelihood depend on the existence of fiscal frontiers, exchange controls, and impediments of various kinds to the movement of goods and capital. These groups tend to generalise and exaggerate their fears that they will lose individually from EMU and conclude that union would be against the national interest.

The benefits of EMU are diffuse and affect consumers in a general way. Each consumer perceives that his likely gains from EMU are small relative to the opportunity cost of lobbying for monetary union. The affected industries and bureaucracies find themselves in the oppostite situation: the opportunity cost of exerting pressure on the government is low relative to the expected temporary loss of income they would suffer following the implementation of EMU. The political market place is characterized by an uneven distribution of participations costs with the unorganised individual bearing a disproportionately high share of these costs. Bureaucrats enjoy a double role, affecting both the demand for EMU and supply of it. With an electorate which is uncertain about the merits of EU or MU, the activity of bureaux can determine the final outcome. This can be done by raising information costs to citizens. In sum, the present failures of EMU can be well explained by the modern economic theory of representative government as formulated by Downs (1967) and Breton (1974)[7]. A successful strategy for economic and monetary unification needs to take this into account.

In Part V of the paper, which deals with the choice of strategy, it is assumed that a policy of small steps, each of which is designed to weaken the points of resistance of the various pressure groups, has a lower probability of success than a strategy which entails a large jump. This in turn implies that politicians should by-pass the resistance of the bureaux and pressure groups and seek to convince the electorate directly of the net benefit of an EMU.

IV. PROGRESS TOWARDS EU

IV. 1. Abolition of trade restrictions

Tariff barriers were abolished by July 1, 1968 between the six original member countries and by July 1, 1977 between the nine. At those same dates the common external tariff was adopted by the six and by the nine. On July 1, 1977 too, free trade was established between the EEC and EFTA in respect of most industrial products.

The situation as regards non tariff barriers is much less satisfactory. Some traditional forms of non tariff barrier, in particular quantitative restrictions, were phased out along with tariffs. There has been some progress, too, in harmonising product standards which hamper trade. But more than 50 of the Commission's proposals for harmonising product standards have yet to be adopted by the Council. And many sophisticated types of non tariff barrier remain. Indeed, if the number of complaints is a reliable guide, non tariff barriers have become more numerous in recent years. Complaints to the EEC Commission about such barriers numbered about 70 in 1970, 93 in 1972, 114 in 1974 and are now at an annual rate of about 300.

The policy of harmonising indirect taxes has been partially successful in that all the member countries have adopted VAT. But VAT structures and rates differ from one member country to another and little progress has been made in the direction of equalisation throughout the EEC. International differences in excise taxes are even greater than differences in VAT. Thus border checks are still necessary, and, although procedures have been simplified, it remains the case that international transactions require more administrative effort and hence have higher costs than equivalent domestic transactions.

The proportion of the member countries' total trade which was with other member countries increased rapidly after 1958. But this rise subsequently slowed and, as the following figures show, there has been some decline since 1972.

Table 1.1 *EEC intra-trade as a percentage of total EEC trade in volume terms*

	The Community of Six		*The Community of Nine*		
	1958	1970	1970	1972	1976*
Imports	33.8	48.4	48.8	53.6	51.8
Exports	30.7	48.9	50.4	51.9	51.5

* First three quarters

The recent decline does not seem to have been caused by the entry of the three new members at the beginning of 1973, but rather by events external to the EEC itself. In particular, the rapid increase in each way trade with the OPEC countries and agressive selling within the EEC by Japan and other countries has reduced the share of intra-trade in total Community imports.

It is as interesting to relate the volume of intra-trade to GNP as to relate it to total trade. The volume of exports by member countries to other member countries rose from 9.2 per cent of Community GNP in 1970 to 10.4 per cent of it in 1972 and 11.3 per cent in 1975. By this measure the mutual interdependence of the member countries has continued to increase in recent years.

IV. 2. Abolition of restrictions on the movement of capital

External transactions on current account have been largely free of exchange controls for some time. The exceptions are that in some cases export receipts have to be repatriated within a specified time limit, imports may not be paid for in advance, and residents of France, Ireland, Italy and the UK are subject to tourist allowances and restrictions concerning the import and export of banknotes.

The numerous controls used by the member countries to restrict international capital movements fall into three main categories:

Controls of a structural kind intended to check the entry of foreign capital into sensitive sectors of the economy, to limit the proportion of the nation's savings which is invested abroad and to diminish the scope for tax evasion. These controls mainly affect movements of long term capital.

Controls intended to benefit the balance of payments. These cover long and short term capital movements.

Controls intended to influence domestic liquidity. In particular these controls aim to prevent access to foreign credit being used to frustrate the effects of a tight domestic monetary policy.

The stringency of the controls, particularly the two latter categories of control, has varied to some extent with the state of the European economy. But restrictions concerning the holding of foreign bank accounts, the granting of short term credits of foreigners, and the issuing of foreign liabilities in domestic capital markets have generally been stringent, capital exports being particularly tightly controlled by Denmark, France, Ireland, Italy and the UK. Germany does not have any exchange control and Belgium and Luxembourg are also very liberal.

The existence of controls does not guarantee their success. Two questions are of relevance. First, have controls been effective in slowing down the process of financial integration? Second, has the potency of controls been increasing over time. In his recent survey on financial integration, Kenen (1976) concludes that exchange controls have achieved their objective of preventing a higher degree of market integration and that 'the process of financial integration has slowed down in recent years' (p. 23). An examination of the evidence leads to the following conclusions. The interest parity theorem holds quite well for short-term maturities in the Eurocurrency market (see, for example, Marston (1976)). It does not perform as well when tested against domestic rather then Eurocurrency rates. The deviations between the covered domestic interest rate and the dollar rate increase dramatically during so-called speculative periods. For example, during 1976 the interest differential against the belgian franc, the pound and the lira was systematically positive for long periods of time with values in the order of several hundred basis points. While it is true that Eurocurrency markets enjoy lower transaction costs, higher mobility of funds and less thinness than their domestic counterparts, it is generally acknowledged that exchange controls in the UK and Italy and the two-tier exchange rate system in Belgium were responsible for preventing domestic arbitrageurs from responding to apparent profit opportunities. Exchange controls were thus effective in fulfilling their objectives when the pressure on the domestic currency was particularly high.

The observation that exchange controls bite at intermittent intervals in the short-term funds market, and our poor knowledge of how exchange controls affect the movement of longer term funds, make it difficult to generalize as to whether controls have become tighter or not in the recent past. But, however the evidence is read, there does not seem to be any willingness in the Community to abandon exchange controls as an instrument of economic policy.

IV.3. Freeing the movement of labour

The free movement of persons, which is one of the basic principles of the common market, already applies to all employees. Restrictions still apply to the self employed, however, for there is still not a right of free establishment or freedom to provide professional services such as the services of lawyers and architects. The most recent evidence of progress in this field was that on December 20, 1976 the Council directive of June 16, 1975 came into effect. It provided for rights of establishment, freedom to provide professional services and the recognition in each member country of formal qualifications in medicine obtained in other member countries.

IV. 4. Conclusions concerning progress so far

The main successes so far have been the abolition of tariff barriers and the removal of obstacles to the free movement of labour. On none of the other main issues has progress been impressive since EMU was adopted as the target in 1969. Indeed in recent years progress seems to have slowed and the will to progress seems to have faltered. There is still a very great deal to be done if EMU is to be reached.

In part the lack of recent progress may be attributed to a preoccupation with other matters, in particular the energy crisis, the slow rate of economic growth and the high and rising level of Community unemployment, not to mention the accession to the Community of the UK, Ireland and Denmark. These are factors which would have caused the member countries to become more conscious of their mutual interdependence and thus more willing to concert their policies. The fact that the outcome seems to have been a slowing and a weakening of progress towards EU, rather than the reverse, raises doubts as to whether the commitment to MU as an objective has been wholehearted.

V. ALTERNATIVE STRATEGIES

To qualify as a viable strategy, any course of action has to provide for the freeing of factor and product movements among the member countries, the establishment of a common currency, the convergence of economic policies and performance so that a common inflation rate is achieved throughout the Community, and the institution of a mechanism for ensuring that all the member countries share the benefits of unification. The main alternatives differ from one another only in the order and manner in which these four requirements are satisfied and in the length of time over which they are spread. The strategies to be discussed are the existing approach, the early establishment of a greater degree of monetary integration and the deferral of monetary unification until after a large measure of market integration has been achieved. To avoid duplication, the discussion of the second and third of these alternatives will be restricted to the main points on which they differ from the existing approach. In any case the three strategies constitute three roads all of which lead to Rome. Some of these roads are more tortuous than others; some roads are for fast riding, others are strewn with pebbles. All of them, however, merge into a single road before Rome is reached.

V. 1. The existing approach

As has emerged from the preceeding section of this paper, the Commission has from the beginning been seeking to advance all the main elements of economic and monetary integration simultaneously. Since the preceding section also gives some indication as to what remains to be done, what obstacles remain to be overcome, and what the main advantages and disadvantages are of continuing on the present course, the coverage of these questions here will be brief.

a. Coordination and convergence. As the economic interdependence of the member countries grows, the national interest of each of them in a greater coordination of policies will increase also. Thus if the Commission maintains its pressure for a coordination of policies, the machinery of coordination may come to be taken more seriously. Apart from the problems discussed in Section II, there is some question as to whether it will ever be possible to coordinate economic policies successfully if the member countries continue to operate without a common framework of analysis. The problem is best illustrated by considering what would be involved in achieving a common rate of inflation. There is a preliminary problem of deciding which of the many available cost and price indices is to be the target variable. But the main difficulties arise after that.

According to one school of thought, the first step, having chosen the target rate of inflation, would be for each of the member countries to adopt appropriate targets for its money stock. These targets would have to be determined on the basis of reliable estimates of the demand for money and the long run rate of growth of output and, all being well, they would ensure that the target inflation rate was eventually attained. The commitment of pre-announced and binding monetary targets would have to be understood to hold for a number of years so that each country not only reached the target rate of inflation but demonstrated its willingness and ability to maintain that rate.

According to another school of thought, there is a distinction to be drawn between demand and cost inflation. Where resources are underutilised, as they are at present, inflation is largely caused by the pressure of organised labour for higher wages, plus extraneous pressures such as the rise in oil prices at the end of 1973. Money has little, by way of an independent role in this system for it is increased by the authorities more or less automatically to whatever extent is necessary to achieve a tolerable combination of employment levels, inflation rates, external deficits and currency depreciation in the foreign exchange markets. A government which subscribes to this doctrine will be reluctant to accept pre-announced and binding monetary targets; it will value the achievement of such targets as are set less highly than the successful negotiation of an incomes policy.

In the presence of such conflicts of doctrine, the creation of EMU becomes difficult, even though all member countries may be able to achieve a common measured rate of inflation at least for a time. Thus, faced with a real prospect of entering into a monetary union, some countries may baulk, fearing that their *ex ante* inflation rate will not for long remain as low as the common inflation rate and that they will lose real resources in consequence.

b. Integration of markets. It is only because there are differences in indirect tax structures and rates within the Community that fiscal frontiers continue to exist between the member countries now that tariffs have been eliminated. Harmonising indirect taxes is, however, extremely difficult and virtually no progress at all is being made towards achieving it.

Attempts to harmonise indirect taxes commodity by commodity have shown that each member country is strongly attached to its own rates and reluctant to change them in the interest of European harmonisation. The rates in force embody hard-won compromises between the wishes of competing power groups, and politicians are unwilling to disturb the agreed compromises. Even if this sort of consideration did not impede harmonisation, commodity by commodity, however, there is a deeper difficulty. Inter-member-country comparisons show that indirect taxes account for very different proportions of government revenue. Thus harmonising the structures and rates of indirect taxes would alter budgetary revenues and require consequential changes in other taxes, government expenditures or public sector surpluses and deficits. The unwelcome nature of such consequential changes reinforces the reluctance to harmonise commodity by commodity.

In sum, the present approach is fraught with difficulties and, at least for the foreseeable future, its chances of achieving worthwhile progress are negligible. There must be serious doubt as to whether it could ever succeed.

Non tariff barriers may have increased in recent years much as they did in the 1930s and for the same reasons as applied in the 1930s, namely that businessmen and governments were seeking to preserve stability in domestic markets at a time when economic difficulties and high unemployment were proliferating internationally. Even if the economic environment were somewhat improved, however, non tariff barriers would be difficult to dislodge. The position is typically that the abolition of any particular barrier would confer a small benefit on each of a large number of consumers, whereas its retention would continue a large benefit to each of a small number of producers or distributors. The smaller group, each member of which stands to lose substantially, has usually been the more cohesive and effective in pressing its case. Thus individual barriers are difficult to dislodge and new types of barrier seem to come into existence as fast as old ones are eliminated.

The ostensible justification for many of the current non tariff barriers to trade is consumer or environmental protection of one kind or another. But the barriers at issue are very varied. For example cases currently being examined by the Commission include:

i. Dutch regulations on the import of pharmaceutical products;
ii. new German provisions restricting the quantity of harmless bacteria permitted in mineral waters;
iii. quantitative restrictions on the resale of wines imported into France;
iv. restrictions on the import of Italian cherries into the United Kingdom;

v. Belgian provisions requiring a certificate of origin for the import of alcoholic beverages;
vi. Italian regulations submitting imports of precious metals to a double hall-marking procedure, and requiring a representative domiciled in Italy;
vii. Belgian rules giving priority to materials of Belgian origin in the award of certain public contracts;
viii. the requirement in Denmark, France, Italy and the Netherlands of an agent established on national territory for the type-approval of imported motor vehicles;
ix. a Calabrian regional law making the grant of aid conditional upon the purchase of Italian-made buses;
x. licenses for the import of mutton and potatoes into Denmark.

It is evident that such cases have to be dealt with individually, they cannot be grouped together and dealt with collectively. Thus combatting non tariff barriers is in practice a slow and difficult process.

It is difficult to assess the extent to which such devices restrict trade; hence it is difficult to assess their quantitative importance in terms of resource mis-allocation. But it is clear that if the free movement of goods is to be delayed until non tariff barriers to trade have been abolished by mutual agreement case by case, then the persistence of such barriers will postpone the achievement of the objective indefinitely.

The prospects of eliminating exchange controls is all the more remote in that what is at issue is much more than the freeing of intra-EEC flows of capital. There is no common ring fence of exchange control round the Community in the way that there is a common external tariff. Moreoever, some member countries have no restrictions on exports of capital to non-member countries and would be reluctant to introduce such restrictions. Thus in practice permitting free outflows of capital to other member countries would mean permitting free outflows to countries such as the USA as well. The prospect that such outflows, or the devaluation of the exchange rate necessary to prevent their taking place, might be very big is one factor inhibiting the introduction of freer capital movements within the EEC. Policy makers must, however recognise that Eurocurrency markets have already brought about a great deal of capital market integration in Europe through the substitution which they permit between domestic credit instruments and Eurocurrency credit.

In any case the habit of controlling the volume and direction of inward and outward capital movements is long established and will be hard to break. Substantial progress on this front will require a complete change of attitude on the part of the more restrictive member countries and their implementation of the Community's existing regulations.

c. Redistribution. Unless the operation of market forces causes the benefits of economic and monetary unification to be spread more or less evenly, there is a case for redistributing income on a Community-wide basis to ensure that no region or social group is a major loser. Redistribution here should be understood as that amount of net transfers among regions or States which will ensure the viability of MU. The basic argument here is that transfers have to be on a scale sufficient to prevent the weakest regions from seceding from the union. In the words of the MacDougall Group Report (p. 60):

> The need for redistribution between member states arises partly because the process of economic integration, which may confer net gains in the aggregate, does not necessarily raise the economic welfare in all areas. The changing pattern of production and exchange that characterises an integrating Community typically brings gains to some but losses to others. To make integration acceptable to all participants may thus require an explicit redistributive mechanism to divide the gains from integration in a politically acceptable way. Failure to attend to this matter may at the least result in a stagnation of the integration process, and at the worst result in secession and dissolution.

Moreoever, transfers to the less developed areas of the Community would be spent mainly on goods and services produced by the other areas, so the most developed parts of the Community might well find that such transfers were in their own long run commercial interest. Thus, even if there were no disposition to try to narrow the present distribution of income per head on egalitarian grounds, the Commission is likely to be drawn into more far-reaching policies of regional distribution than it has contemplated so far.

d. Conclusions concerning the existing approach. The present approach relies primarily on administrative decisions to achieve its objectives. Its strength is that its procedures ensure that each step is considered in a thorough and leisurely way before it is taken and that risks are kept to a very low level. These are considerable advantages.

Yet it is clear that something is fundamentally wrong. Progress is so slow as to be imperceptible, although Heads of State have on several occasions since 1969 reaffirmed that EMU remains the Community's objective. Such political impetus as is exerted from the top seems to be dissipated and the wider interest lost to sight in a hundred and one points of niggling detail. Lobbies fight successfully to hold their ground; the outcome is stalemate. As the economic theory of representative government suggests, the present strategy plays into the hands of those who stand to gain most from the preservation of the status quo.

The most promising way to reinvigorate the existing programme would be to introduce into it a greater reliance on market forces. This is the central feature of both of the strategies which remain to be discussed. The alternative strategies respectively introduce monetary unification and the freeing of factor and product movements at an early point.

Either of these would involve a big political step. But once one or other of these political steps was taken, market forces could be relied upon to accomplish a very large part of what remained to be done.

V.2. Options which put the emphasis on monetary integration

a. Locking Exchange Rates. The construction of the Bretton Woods system was largely motivated by the desire to promote integration. The fixing of rates of exchange was to facilitate the integration of the goods market by ensuring that, allowing for differences in transport and other costs, a single price would prevail throughout the world for any given tradeable good. It also ensured that the costs which come with the uncertainty of forecasting the relative price of monies were kept to a low level. A regime of truly fixed rates implies that the rate of inflation will be approximately equal in all the participating countries. The fixed-rate arrangement also implies that a country's monetary policy in the long run cannot be independent of the world price level which, in turn, is largely dominated by the hegemonial role of the key currency.

The case for a return to fixed rates of exchange is extremely weak for the following reasons. First, the claim that such a system eliminated uncertainty in the exchange markets does not correspond with experience, for there have been long stretches of exchange rate stability interspersed by large jumps in parities. During the Bretton Woods era uncertainty about parity changes was never eliminated; on the contrary, forecasts of the timing and size of parity changes turned out to be 'guesstimates' of how long central banks could support disequilibrium exchange rates.

Only the existence of a single currency ensures that rates of exchange are permanently fixed. So long as multiple currencies coexist and national authorities retain the option of parity readjustment, economic operators will not be convinced of the fixity of the relative price of monies.

Second, a fixed-exchange-rate arrangement with multiple currencies does not eliminate the socially unproductive use of resources which goes in exchanging one currency into another.

Third, the implementation of a rigid set of exchange rates in the Europe of the Nine of 1977 (where inflation rates of 4 per cent coexist with inflation rates of 20 per cent) is bound to create dramatic balance-of-payments crises which will either further strain the union or bring about a general misallocation of resources, of which unemployment will be the most visible and politically sensitive aspect.

Finally, the fixed-rate system cannot be sustained without one currency reaping the benefits of the hegemonial currency. In the Bretton Woods system this currency was the dollar and the Europeans resented the implicit exploitation by the USA which this represented.

To summarize, while the imposition of fixed rates of exchange would certainly mean enormous adjustment costs for high-inflation countries and grant quasi-seigniorage gains to the pivot-currency country, the benefits of the arrangement would be minimal. Exchange rate risks could not be eliminated so long as government retained the right to break the cartel, and exchange costs would persist.

b. The Snake. Most of the difficulties raised against the fixed-exchange-rate regime also apply to the 'snake' arrangement. As in the Bretton Woods system, the snake currencies fluctuate within prescribed margins. As in the Bretton Woods era, the central banks of the snake currencies intervene in foreign exchange markets to maintain the value of their currencies within the prescribed margins.

Within the snake the weak-currency countries obtain credit from strong-currency countries, with FECOM (European Monetary Cooperation Fund) acting as a clearing house just as in the Bretton Woods system short and medium-term credit was extended to countries with balance-of-payments deficits. The snake arrangement also resembles the Bretton Woods system, in that the commitment to the rules of the snake cartel agreement is far from being solid: some countries have joined and left the snake at will, others have remained but have altered their parity values. As the IMF-instituted Special Drawing Rights subsidize the activity of borrowing by keeping the interest rate on these assets below market rates, so the settlements of balances through FECOM constitute a policy of potentially subsidizing borrowers.[8] Unlike the Bretton Woods system the snake countries float vis-a-vis a large number of important countries, a safety valve of some importance.

The success of the snake arrangement will ultimately depend on the ability of the participating countries to follow consistent policies. If such policies are not pursued, strains will develop which will either result in additional parity changes or in quantity adjustments, in other words unemployment and unused capacity.

If the snake experiment constitutes a serious effort to coordinate monetary policies around a *de facto* pivotal DM, then further encouragement ought to be given to that experiment. But then the emphasis should clearly be moved from exchange rate management to inflation rate management so that potential new members of the snake clearly understand what the fee is for joining the club.

c. A Common European Currency. The economic advantages to be derived from the adoption of a common currency have been summarized in Section III. In the immediately preceding discussion it has been argued that a common European currency is superior to fixed or quasi-fixed multiple currency exchange rate systems. One possible disadvantage is that individual member states would forfeit a potential adjustment mechanism by adopting a common currency, namely the possibility of regaining external balance and full employment by altering exchange rates. However, such a strategy is advantageous only to the extent that, and for the period during which, workers do not obtain full compensation for the cut in real wages which has come about as a result of the devaluation. The effectiveness of a devaluation therefore depends in large part on the persistence of a degree of 'money illusion' among workers, and empirical evidence suggests that in recent years this has been significantly reduced in many countries.[9]

Another claim – based on the idea of a negative relationship between inflation and unemployment – is that a flexible exchange rate system permits a country to choose a given inflation level and, as a consequence, a corresponding level of unemployment. Individual member states would, it is claimed, lose the possibility of determining their preferred level of unemployment following monetary integration. There is now, however, ample empirical evidence that in the long run employment is independent of inflation, although not disclaiming that in shorter periods an acceleration of unanticipated inflation may temporarily lower the measured rate of unemployment. Inflating is no way to achieve prosperity; on the contrary, to the extent that the goal of lower unemployment, even for brief periods, requires that the government inflate in a manner which is not expected, inflation becomes a cost to society. Economic agents adjust to a variable inflation rate by using resources, including their time, and these resources are no longer available for alternative uses.

While a single currency is widely perceived as desirable, there remains controversy concerning the form and quality of this single currency and the timing of its introduction (see Vaubel (1974)). As to the form, while many existing currencies are eligible as the future money of Europe, there are convincing arguments for the creation of a new currency (OPTICA Report '75, pp. 27-8). As to the quality, the new currency should have a yield at least as good as that of the strongest European currency. Indeed some economists claim that European monetary unificiation offers a unique opportunity for a monetary reform, in other words to launch an inflation-proofed currency (see *The Economist's* 'The All Saints' Day Manifesto').

One mechanism of issuing the new currency, Europa, is described in the All Saints' Day Manifesto. Suppose that one Europa is defined to be initially equal to one EUA and that central banks or, better, a European institution, are empowered to issue these new assets. Since transactions in Europe are entirely on a voluntary basis, the quantity of Europas in circulation will depend exclusively on the desire or lack of it to hold the new currency. The purchase of Europas would occur at a price determined by the market, in the case of non-indexed Europas, or determined by a commitment of the member states in the case of price-indexed Europas. (For further discussion, see Chapter 2 of this volume, which shows how an inflation-proofed currency would be issued by an Euroagent and then sold to the ultimate buyer through the central and commercial banking system.)

It is particularly important to note that the commitment to a constant purchasing power currency amounts to the elimination of the inflation tax. The Euroagent which issues the new currency acquires national currencies which constitute claims on central banks. These claims depreciate at a rate equal to the rate of inflation. However, the Euroagent issues liabilities which are inflation proofed. The loss in the value of the assets relative to the liabilities must be charged to the Treasuries of the member countries. This, in turn, implies that governments will have to collect additional taxes to replace the loss of revenue from the inflation tax.

The European money supply would not be affected by this arrangement and would still depend solely on the issuing policies of the European central banks. On the other hand, the money supply in pounds, deutschmarks, etc., would be altered by conversions between Europas and national currencies.

Exchange rates would be flexible both between national currencies and between each national currency and the Europa. The advantage of this arrangement is that the cost of adjusting to a common inflation rate (an event which occurs when all national monies disappear) will not be as drastic and sudden as when rates are locked at a given date.

To summarize, the Europa could be introduced alongside national currencies and, since it would be more stable and reliable than national currencies, it would eventually displace them. The process of displacement would bring about monetary unification by relying on market forces. Far fewer political decisions would be needed once the parallel currency had been decided upon than would be the case if the present programme of policy coordination were continued; and since flexible exchange rates would prevail throughout the transition period, the temporary unemployment would be avoided which would otherwise ensue if the rates of inflation of the Community's countries were adjusted downwards abruptly.

An indexed Europa would discourage competitive devaluation and inflation among the member countries, and make it impossible for governments to use inflation as a way of augmenting their tax receipts. The proposal would, however, be difficult for the more inflation-prone countries to accept. The reason is that the currencies of such countries would be the first to be displaced by the Europa. Thus the central banks of such countries would find their central functions becoming rapidly obsolete. During the transitional period interest rates on deposits in national currencies would have to rise to high levels to offset the attractiveness of the new currency. It would be absurd to protect the existence of the national currency on a long-term basis where the stated objective is to have it superseded by the single Community money. In any case one of the most important questions would be what form the Community's new monetary institutions should take.

d. The 'minimal' monetary union. While a discussion of the institutions which would take charge of the Community's monetary policy is beyond the scope of this paper, it may nonetheless be useful to set out some guiding administrative principles of a monetary union evolved from the present system with minimal institutional changes. These are that national central banks transfer control over international reserves, exchange rates and creation of the domestic monetary base to the union's monetary authority.[10] The latter might be nothing more than a Board of Governors of the Community's central banks which would use one of the national central banks to executive its policy objectives (in the same way that the Board of Governors of the Federal Reserve System uses the Federal Reserve Bank of New York as its executive arm). The suggested changes are consistent with a monetary union having one or more currencies, provided the relative values of these currencies were irrevocably fixed.

Under this arrangement national central banks would transfer their net claims on foreigners (international reserves), on governments (public debt) and on domestic banks (borrowings and rediscounts) to the union's authority, in exchange for reserve certificates. National central banks could no longer take independent action to alter the size of their assets which would be constituted primarily by the union's reserve certificates. Against these certificates they would continue to issue claims held by national banks and the public in the form of deposits and paper money. The integrated balance sheets of the national central banks and of the union's monetary authority would constitute the Community's monetary base. Changes in the latter could be effected exclusively by the union's authority, although national central banks could retain a small degree of autonomy in the administration of the discount window and reserve requirements.

The union's authority could buy or sell securities issued by any member country, crediting or debiting the appropriate national central banks. Thus, a purchase in the open market of, say, Italian government bonds would imply an increase in the assets of the Banca d'Italia. Bank reserves in Italy would expand; bank deposits and bank credit would rise by a multiple of the change in bank reserves. For a given demand for credit, interest rates in Italy would fall relative to interest rates in the rest of the union. For a given demand for money, the price level in Italy would rise relative to the price level in the rest of the union. Capital and trade flows would ensure that the stimulus spread throughout the union. There are, of course, the important considerations of time lags. The greater the integration of the securities markets the more immediate would be the diffusion of the monetary stimulus across the union. Capital movements between countries of the union would bring about lower interest rates across the union. A lower degree of substitution between securities would slow down the transmission of the monetary stimulus from the target country to the rest of the union.

In the long run any attempt on the part of the union's authority to control the distribution of the money stock in the union would fail regardless of the degree of integration in the securities markets. This is so because the integration of the traded goods markets would eventually force newly injected money to flow out of the target country through a current-account deficit.[11] In essence, the union's authority could not pursue a regional or country-level monetary policy. The relevant domain of monetary policy would be the union.

Balance-of-payments imbalances of member states would affect the amount of reserve certificates held by national central banks. A surplus vis-a-vis a non-union country would imply an inflow of international reserves which the national central bank would transfer to the union's authority in exchange of reserve certificates. A surplus vis-a-vis a union country would imply a transfer of reserve certificates from the deficit to the surplus country central bank. 'It is essential that the means of settlement be the same for external and intra-union deficits. Otherwise, there would be an incentive to distort the direction of trade and capital flows'.[12]

It needs to be emphasised that the principles just enunciated concern the regional distribution of the money stock in the union and, in particular, the settlement of inter-country imbalances. Nothing has been said about the conduct of the union's monetary policy, for that will depend on the type of monetary constitution the Community adopts.

V. 3. Options which put market integration first.

If market integration were put first, member countries would jointly announce that from some future date, say five years from now, fiscal frontiers would be abolished and that by then all remaining restrictions governing the intra-EEC movement of capital and labour would have been phased out. Each member country would retain the fiscal and monetary instruments which it has now, and its own currency and exchange rate. Everything would go on much as before in fact, except that the market forces making for the economic integration of the member countries would have been greatly reinforced. It would not be too much to expect that within a decade or so the member countries' mutual interdependence would have become as great as that of the regions within a single country at the moment. Thus the way would have been prepared for the adoption of a common currency in the 1990s.

The effect of this strategy on labour markets would not be very great, given the extent of the international labour mobility already possible within the Community. The abolition of exchange control would, however, cause a a once-for-all devaluation of the currencies most subject to controls and have secondary effects on retail prices. In any case, the effects, which are perhaps of greatest analytical interest, would be in the product markets.

If the full benefits of free trade within the EEC are to be achieved, all barriers to the free movement of goods and services will have to be abolished. Fiscal frontiers *inter alia* will have to be eliminated; in other words the indirect tax adjustments which at present take place when goods pass from one member country to another will have to cease. This would eliminate the considerable real resource costs of operating the present system, open up new trade channels in the way discussed on p. 9 above and undermine existing non tariff barriers such as those listed on p. 19 above.

There would have to be some prior harmonisation of indirect tax structures and rates if the abolition of fiscal fronteirs were not to result in unfair competition and a worsened allocation of real resources in the Community. To explain why this should be so, it will be necessary to begin by explaining some features of the present system of tax administration.

Indirect taxes are levied on imports and not on exports. This is the so-called destination principle of taxation; it ensures that the indirect taxes levied on imported goods are the same as those levied on home-produced goods. The implicit assumption is that all indirect taxes are fully shifted forwards (and no other taxes are shifted forwards), so that taxes do not affect competition between home and foreign suppliers.

VAT is administered as a tax on sales, less a rebate of the tax paid on purchased materials. To see the implications of this, suppose that the wheat sold by a farmer for 100 has value added by a miller who sells the resulting flour for 120, and by a baker who uses the flour to make bread to a value of 150. Suppose, too, that a VAT of 10 per cent is now imposed and shifted forwards. The result would be that the farmer, the miller and the baker would charge 110, 132 and 165 respectively; and they would pay to the tax authorities 10, 2 and 3 respectively. Some groups, however, are exempted from the payment of VAT, farmers being one such group. Suppose, therefore, that the farmer was exempted from VAT. In this case the three prices would be 100, 132 and 165 and the three tax payments would be zero, 12 and 3. Thus the effect of exempting the farmer would be fully offset by the way the tax was levied on the miller; the final consumer and the baker would be completely unaffected.

Having disposed of these preliminaries, it is time to turn to the existing approach to the abolition of fiscal frontiers. Its central feature is that all indirect tax structures and rates should be made equal or nearly equal as a preliminary to the abolition of fiscal frontiers.[13] Its rationale is that if taxes were equal then the taxes levied on imports in their country of destination would exactly equal the tax rebates granted them in their country of origin; the fiscal frontier would have become no more than a wastefully expensive mechanism for allocating tax revenue between the countries concerned. The difficulties inherent in implementing this approach were explained above (p. 19) and it will suffice here to repeat the earlier conclusion that this approach is making hardly any progress and that it is unlikely ever to succeed.

An alternative approach takes as its starting point the fact that the abolition of fiscal frontiers would be at least partially offset by exchange rate changes. The objective of this approach would then be to make maximum use of exchange rate changes to minimise the adverse effects on competition and resource allocation of abolishing fiscal frontiers within the Community. If this second approach were to be adopted, a preliminary change in the present method of tax administration would be required. This change need apply only to cross border transactions which are not sales to final buyers. Reverting to the example, suppose that the farmer were an exporter from a country where the rate of VAT was zero. Then a mechanism would be required which ensured that the miller, the importer, did not pay VAT on the value added by the farmer as well as paying it on the value added by himself.[14] If such a mechanism existed, the VAT paid by the miller and the baker would be 2 and 3 respectively and the price to the consumer would be 155 and not 165 as before. Thus when fiscal frontiers were abolished, and the origin principle substituted for the destination principle, the price to the consumer would change, even in cases where the importer was not the final buyer. It is consumers' reactions to these changes in price which cause exchange rate changes. These reactions constitute the mechanism central to the whole strategy.

The switch from the destination principle to the origin principle would thus change the relative prices of domestic and imported goods. The balance of trade of the countries with the lowest indirect tax rates would tend to increase at the expense of that of countries with higher indirect tax rates; and there would be an accomodating adjustment of currency values, the currencies of the countries with the lowest indirect tax rates tending to appreciate relative to the currencies of the countries with higher tax rates. In the simplest possible case a new equilibrium might even be envisaged in which the exchange rate adjustment exactly offset the differences in indirect tax rates (Fratianni and Christie (1977)).[15] In this simple case, there would be no immediate changes in trade patterns, employment patterns or price levels, though the capital account would be affected. Each member country's net budgetary receipts would change only in so far as the new indirect tax revenues from its exports differed from the loss of indirect tax revenues on its imports. Disturbance would be minimised if the appropriate exchange rate adjustment could be accurately forecast, for then central bank intervention might even be used to bring it about quickly. In the longer term trade flows would have to change as indeed they would with any scheme which led to increased international specialisation of efforts.

The conclusion that changes in indirect taxation could be exactly offset in the short run by changes in exchange rates needs to be qualified in two main ways. The first arises because there are differences from one country to another in the number of VAT bands and the goods to which each band applies and differences too in the coverage and rates of excise duty. Since exchange rate changes provide an equal percentage adjustment across the board they would not provide an exact offset to a change from the destination principle to the origin principle in these circumstances. Stated somewhat differently, the change in exchange rates would reflect differences in the mean values of the distributions of tax-inclusive prices in the member countries. To the extent that the distributions of tax-inclusive prices differed, some sectors would gain and others would lose. States which tax certain commodities considerably more than other states would inevitably face strong pressure from the affected industries to lower taxes to the level of the lower-tax countries. The lobbying process would induce a tendency towards equilisation of indirect taxes in Europe. The alternative to such a 'market' solution would require that taxes be harmonized before the change from destination to origin principle.

The second qualification arises because of trade with non-member countries. If the switch from the destination principle to the origin principle applied to trade with non-member countries as well as with member countries, in principle an exchange rate change could compensate for the weighted average difference in VAT rates (appropriate weighting being applied in the calculation of the average to allow for the fact that trading partners are of unequal importance). But if the switch to the origin principle applied to intra-EEC trade and the destination principle continued to apply to trade with non-members, there would be a distortion in that trade with non-members would be affected by the exchange rate change but not by the indirect tax change. The way in which this might work has been explored formally (Fratianni and Christie (1977)). Further work would be required to quantify its practical importance.

The two approaches to the abolition of fiscal frontiers differ in the anticipatory tax harmonisation which they require and in the constraints which they impose on national policy. Both approaches set constraints on the distribution of indirect tax rates; hence, for example, both constrain the extent to which alcohol can be penalised and milk favoured. The first option sets the more stringent constraint in that it requires a near equalisation of indirect tax rates.

This implies changes from the present indirect tax revenues and from the present balance between direct and indirect tax revenues, and it prevents indirect tax rates from being used to alter the level of aggregate demand or the balance between the public and private sectors. The second option requires a near equalisation of the distribution of indirect-tax-inclusive prices but not an equalisation of the level of indirect taxation. Thus it does not imply any significant changes in the balance between direct and indirect taxation and it does not exclude changes in the level of indirect taxation from time to time.

The second option could only be an intermediate solution in that MU would require the near equalisation of tax rates implied by the first option. If MU were scheduled for the near future, the detour implied by the second option might not be worth making. But if MU is a distant prospect, the second option has very definite attractions, justifying a more elaborate analysis of its likely benefits and costs.

VI. SUMMARY AND CONCLUSIONS

The net benefits of economic and monetary unification promise to be considerable and the accompanying risks acceptable. Thus on economic grounds there is every reason to continue to pursue EMU as the objective. But progress so far has been disappointing. The main successes have been the abolition of tariff barriers and the removal of obstacles to the movement of labour. On no other main issue has progress been impressive.

The main obstacle to further progress at the moment is said to be the nature of the national responses to the problems of slow growth, rapid inflation and high unemployment which the majority of member countries face. Moreover, as often happens at times of economic difficulty, protectionist sentiment is strong. Pressure groups, which have a disproportionate influence in European democracies, have had no difficulty in winning the battle against those who would benefit from further market integration. The benefits of EMU are diffuse, the costs localised.

At present reliance is placed primarily on administrative decisions. Thus consensus is required for the implementation of each step along the road towards EMU. Consensus means acceptance of the lowest common denominator, with the consequence that progress is likely to be extremely slow.

There are three main strategies which might be used to achieve EMU. The first is to continue the existing approach, the second is to implement some form of monetary unification at an early date, and the third is to work for the early abolition of fiscal frontiers and other barriers to factor and product movements, leaving monetary unification to the end.

The three approaches, while sharing a common final objective, differ in the manner and speed with which the goal is reached. All alternatives foresee the birth of a monetary union at some stage. To the extent that a single currency will facilitate uniform wage bargaining, efficiency wage rates (i.e. wage rates adjusted for productivity levels) will rise in the periphery of the

Community, thus creating there a higher unemployment rate than existing at the centre. Regions within a union might suffer more from balance-of-payments disequilibria than when these regions were separate currency areas. In other words, the implementation of EMU might accentuate regional imbalances. To make EMU politically viable a federal fiscal system of income redistribution would have to be simultaneously implemented.

The strategy which emphasizes the early introduction of a new currency alongside existing national currencies has the advantage that market forces, in contrast to political decisions, would be relied upon to bring about monetary unification. Once the initial political decision to issue a new currency is taken, individuals participating in market transactions would decide the fate of that currency. The degree of acceptance of the latter would depend on the relative rates of return of the national and Community's monies. A new and stable currency would be an attractive asset to holders of national currencies. This conclusion would apply *a fortiori* if the new currency were to be indexed to the general price level of the Community.

The existence of a parallel currency is consistent with a system of flexible exchange rates so long as national currencies remain in the system. It follows that the parallel-currency approach avoids the temporary losses of employment which instead occur whenever exchange rates are locked to one another in a fixed relationship.

The third option is to plan for the abolition of all barriers to the intra-EEC movement of goods, services, capital and labour. It is argued in the paper that if this were properly prepared, its initial effect would be to bring about a realignment of exchange rates without there being any dramatic disturbance of flows of trade.

The longer term effect promises to be a significant increase in the degree of European integration, with consequential changes in trade and capital flows of the kind associated with the elimination of tariffs.

A strategy of continuing exactly as at present has little to commend it for it is manifestly failing. There is thus a need for a credible alternative which will create a new sense of urgency and purpose in all concerned. The innovations which it seems most promising to pursue are the taking of fewer and bigger political steps and the placing of greater reliance than in the past on market forces as distinct from administrative decisions, each involving the need for compromise.

The early introduction of a parallel currency would be the fastest and surest way to EMU. Failing that, the early abolition of barriers to factor and product movements would yield considerable benefits in itself and prepare the way for MU. Either course of action would be far better than the present reliance on policy coordination.

NOTES

1. An extensive apparatus had already been built up: it included the Monetary Committee (established in 1958), the short term conjunctural Policy

Committee (1960), the medium term Economic Policy Committee (1964), the Committee on Fiscal Policy (1964), and the Committee of Central Bank Governors (1964).

2. Refer to his 1977 Jean Monnet lecture delivered at the European Institute of Florence, subsequently published in Lloyds Bank Review of January 1978.
3. Commission of the European Communities, *Report of the Study Group on the Role of Public Finance in European Integration*, Brussels, April 1977, Volume II, p. 284 (Referred from here on as the MacDougall Group Report).
4. For example, the Exchange Control Department of the Bank of England employs 750 people. This is far from being the full extent of the administrative cost of regulations. There are 250 banks, authorized for foreign exchange dealings, which carry responsibilities delegated to them by the Bank of England. Stock Exchange members too play a part in ensuring that exchange control regulations are not violated, and many firms and individuals constrained by the controls employ specialist advisers to help them minimise the effect of the controls on their affairs. *See Blanden* (October 14, 1977).
5. Cf. MacDougall Group Report (1977), Table 4, p. 33.
6. Cf. MacDougall Group Report (1977), pp. 32-5.
7. A lucid discussion of these issues can be found in Rowley and Peacock (1975, esp. ch. 6). See also Grubel (1973, pp. 111-12).
8. See Vaubel (1977).
9. See, for instance, Chapter 1 of Commission of the European Communities (19
10. This is the proposal advanced by Allen (1976).
11. Ibid, pp. 32-7.
12. Ibid, p. 15.
13. A variant of this would be to apply equalisation in the first instance only to goods imported direct by final buyers, at the same time raising duty-free allowances. This would, however, raise in relation to foreign goods sold direct to final buyers all the same problems as would a policy of total equalisation.
14. One way in which this might be done is for the importer to begin by reconstituting the import cost, including the VAT paid in the country of origin as part of this cost, as if it were made up of tax and value added in the same proportions as a domestic invoice of the same amount. In other words an accounting rule would be applied to invoices covering imports from EEC member countries before VAT was calculated on them. In the example the miller would for tax purposes treat the farmer's invoice as if the farmer's value added were 90.91 on which VAT of 9.09 had been paid. From this point onwards everything could continue the normal way.
15. The proposition that changes in exchange rates could offset changes in indirect taxation had been recognised by several people. Its earliest appearanc in the literature seems to have been in the European Coal and Steel Community Report (1953). It also appears in Reddaway (1958), Krauss (1968), Johnson and Krauss (1973).

REFERENCES

Allen, P.R., 'Organization and Administration of a Monetary Union', *Princeton Studies in International Finance*, No. 38 (Princeton, N.J., 1976).

Basevi, G., Fratianni, M., Giersch, H., Korteweg, P., O'Mahony, O., Parkin, M., Peeters, Th., Salin, P., and N. Thygesen, 'The All Saints' Day Manifesto for European Monetary Union', *The Economist,* November 1, 1975.
Blanden Michael, 'The Case for Easing Exchange Controls', *Financial Times,* October 14, 1977.
Breton, A., *The Economic Theory of Representative Government* (London: Macmillan, 1974).
Commission of the European Communities, *Report of the Study Group on the Role of Public Finance in European Integration* (Brussels, April 1977).
Commission of the European Communities, *Fourth Medium-Term Economic Policy Programme* (Brussels, October 8, 1976).
Commission of the European Communities, *OPTICA REPORT 1975, Towards Economic Equilibrium and Monetary Unification in Europe* (Brussels, January 16, 1976).
Commission of the European Communities, *OPTICA REPORT 1976, Inflation and Exchange Rates: Evidence and Policy Guidelines for the European Community* (Brussels, February 10, 1977).
Communauté Economique Européenne, *Rapport du Comité Fiscal et Financier* (Brussels, 1962).
Council of the European Communities, *Interim Report on the Establishment by Stages of Economic and Monetary Union,* Supplement to Bulletin 7 -1970.
Downs, A., *An Economic Theory of Democracy* (New York: Harper and Row, 1957).
European Coal and Steel Community, *Report of the Problems Raised by the Different Turnover Tax Systems Applied within the Common Market* (Brussels, March 5, 1953).
Fratianni, M. and H. Christie, 'Exchange Rates, the Price Level and the Switch from the Destination Principle to the Origin Principle', typescript, November 1977.
Grubel, H.G., 'The Theory of Optimum Regional Associations', in H.G. Johnson and A.K. Swoboda (eds.), *The Economics of Common Currencies* (London: George Allen and Unwin Ltd., 1973), pp. 99-113.
Jenkins, R., 'European Monetary Union', *Lloyds Bank Review,* January 1978.
Johnson, H.G. and M.B. Krauss, 'Border Taxes, Border Tax Adjustments, Comparative Advantage, and the Balance of Payments', in M.B. Krauss (ed.), *The Economics of Integration* (London: George Allen and Unwin Ltd., 1973).
Johnson, Harry G., *Theoretical Problems of the International Monetary System* (Amsterdam, North Holland, 1972).
Kenen, Peter B., 'Capital Mobility and Financial Integration: a Survey', *Princeton Studies in International Finance,* No. 39 (Princeton, N.J., 1976).
Krauss, M.B., 'Tax Harmonization and Allocative Efficiency in Economic Unions', *Public Finance,* 3, 1968, pp. 367-71.
Laffer, Arthur B., 'Two Arguments for Fixed Rates', in Harry G. Johnson and Alexander K. Swoboda (eds.), *The Economics of Common Currencies* (London: George Allen and Unwin Ltd., 1973), pp. 25-9.
Marston, R.D., 'Interest Arbitrage in the Eurocurrency Markets', *European Economic Review,* January 1976, pp. 1-13.
Mundell, Robert A., 'Uncommon Arguments for Common Currencies', in Harry G. Johnson and Alexander K. Swoboda (eds.), *The Economics of Common Currencies* (London: George Allen and Unwin Ltd., 1973),

pp. 114-32.
Reddaway, W.B., 'The Implications of a Free Trade Area for British Taxation', *British Tax Review*, March 1958, pp. 71-9.
Rowley, C.K. and A.T. Peacock, *Welfare Economics, a Liberal Restatement* (London: Martin Robertson and Co. Ltd.), 1976.
Swoboda, Alexander K., 'Policy Conflict, Inconsistent Goals, and the Co-ordination of Economic Policies', in Harry G. Johnson and Alexander K. Swoboda (eds.), *The Economics of Common Currencies* (London: George Allen and Unwin Ltd., 1973), pp. 133-42.
Tower, Edward and Thomas D. Willett, 'The Theory of Optimum Currency Areas and Exchange Rate Flexibility', *Special Papers in International Economics*, No. 11 (Princeton, N.J., May 1976).
Vaubel, R., 'The Next Steps in European Monetary Integration: OPTICA 1975 and OPTICA 1976', paper presented to the Conference on US-European Monetary Relations, Washington D.C., March 17-18, 1977.
Vaubel, R., 'Plans for a European Parallel Currency and SDR Reform: the Choice of Value-Maintenance Provisions and "Gresham's Law" ', *Weltwirtschaftliches Archiv*, 1974, Heft 3, pp. 194-228.

PART II:

THE ALL SAINTS' DAY MANIFESTO AND ITS CRITICS

2 The All Saints' Day Manifesto for European Monetary Union

We, the undersigned, concerned at the lack of progress towards the goal of European monetary union to which the governments of the member countries of the European Community have repeatedly committed themselves, and at the harmful consequences of the inflation which we are experiencing, present this manifesto to the public in the belief that our proposal offers the best way of achieving a monetary system which will be not only European-wide in scope but stable as well.

This manifesto, then, is a statement of purpose based on what we consider to be sound economic analysis and at the same time in accord with the political aspirations of our time. Our emphasis on the use of market forces stems from our conviction that it is difficult to bring about a monetary union by official edict or by the establishment of grandiose insitutions, no matter how well intentioned. On the contrary, we are convinced that it is for the people themselves to decide whether they want monetary union or not and that the only satisfactory way they can be given the opportunity to do so is by the introduction of a parallel stable money, as we explain below, which they may accept or reject as they wish. We believe they will accept it but we believe equally that they must accept it freely.

LESSONS FROM EXPERIENCE

Proposals for monetary integration appeared in the Werner report which set full economic and monetary union as a target to be achieved in three stages over a period of 10 years. The recommendations of the report were adopted as a goal of the European Community in March, 1971. Monetary union was identified with (1) total and irreversible convertibility of currencies; (2) elimination of margins of fluctuation in exchange rates; (3) irrevocable fixing of parities; (4) elimination of restrictions on capital movements; and (5) co-ordination of aggregate demand policies.

As in most endeavours which try to alter radically the course of events, the Werner report suffered from an excess of idealism. It overestimated the

---

This chapter and parts of the subsequent paper by Theo Peeters *et. al.* appeared in *The Economist*, London dated November 1, 1975 (All Saints' Day).

willingness of governments to depart from national decision-making because it underestimated the costs associated with a fast resetting of ultimate targets and the policy strategy necessary to meet such targets. We are aware that governments have different priorities with respect to the goals of high employment and inflation and that they have tried over the years to trade the achievement of one goal against the other. To the extent that wide differences of opinion remain about the scope and even the existence of such a trade-off, we must conclude that a common policy of the member countries is not feasible. Fixed rates of exchange necessarily imply *grosso modo* a common rate of inflation for participating countries. Therefore, the premature implement tion of a rigid exchange rate regime, in the absence of monetary policy co-ordination, is bound to lead to balance of payments crises; in turn, these crises will either destroy the union or bring about a general misallocation of resources, of which unemployment will be the most visible and politically sensitive aspect.

The Werner approach concentrated political attention on exchange rate unification. It provided, therefore, intellectual justification for the 'snake' arrangement, instituted by the Community in March 1972. The snake scheme is essentially tantamount to the formation of a cartel where each member retains the right of opting out of the system. The opting-out provisions were necessary because of the failure to implement a system of quotas based on credible money supply targets. It is hardly surprising that it did not stand up fully against some of the strains it had to face.

A major weakness of the earlier approach based on co-ordinated decision-making is its non-automatic nature and its reliance on political discretion. Monetary unification, if it is to succeed at all, must be brought about by a gradual process. From a political point of view, it is necessary to proceed gradually so that nationalist feelings are not provoked by sudden losses of what are perceived to be national powers. The earlier approach, although gradual, was discretionary: the co-ordination of economic, monetary and exchange rate policies was based on an infinite series of painful compromises and concessions. It maximised political friction for minimal economic results. From an economic angle the case for gradualism and automaticity is the case for market processes.

The lesson we draw from the foregoing is that an approach to monetary unification which is based on co-ordination of policies will fail because it involves the locking of exchange rates without monetary reform. The approach we advocate is radically different in that it achieves monetary unification through monetary reform based on the free interplay of market forces.

THE CASE FOR A SINGLE STABLE MONEY

Money has a comparative advantage in transmitting information and in reducing uncertainty. The introduction of money in a barter economy frees resources which were previously absorbed by economic agents in finding 'appropriate' exchange rates between goods. The case for a monetary union is similar to the case for a monetary rather than a barter system. But the single money, which will eventually replace separate national currencies, has to possess purchasing power stability.

That a single stable money is better than multiple currencies (even if they are stable) as a medium of exchange is obvious from the fact that socially unproductive transactions between currencies are entirely eliminated. In its role as a store of value, a single currency with stable purchasing power would serve the community better than the existing arrangement of many currencies. Most importantly, it would eliminate exchange risks which are generated primarily by uncertainty as to how much money each central bank will supply in relation to the demand for this money. We believe it inappropriate to suggest that these risks may be eliminated by forward operations. The forward markets, beyond three months, are simply not that well developed and, even if they were, the resources devoted to them could be entirely freed by a single currency.

The aspect of multiple currencies which is probably most costly to society is its impairment of the efficiency of money as a unit of account or standard of value, since there is no common standard of value in a multiple-currency-flexible-exchange-rate system.

The objection that a single money is not necessary and that a fixed exchange rate between multiple currencies would perform equally well is only partly correct. It is true that currency transaction costs are reduced, but that is all. The more important disadvantages of multiple monies, the creation of uncertainty and the impairment of the efficiency of money as a unit of account, still remain. Experience with fixed exchange rates has been one of long stretches of little exchange rate flexibility interspersed by large jumps in parities. Uncertainty about parity changes has never been eliminated. Fixed exchange rates are inferior in this respect to flexible rates, and, in turn, flexible rates are inferior to a single stable-valued monetary system.

COPING WITH IMBALANCE

The main argument against monetary union is that it would be likely to result in an unwanted combination of unemployment and inflation in some or all members of the union. This argument derives from the negative relationship which is thought to prevail between unemployment and inflation. The studies undertaken in the 1950s and 1960s, which showed that this kind of relationship seemed to hold, have now been corrected. More recent studies indicate that, in the long run, employment is independent of the rate of inflation. We urge governments to accept the conclusion which follows from this, namely, that monetary policy, whilst influencing the rate of inflation, cannot reduce what has come to be called the 'natural' rate of employment, i.e. the rate of unemployment which is determined by labour market conditions, taxation policy, and a variety of structural and institutional factors. Accordingly, any attempt to drive the rate of unemployment below the 'natural' rate by means of expansionary monetary policies will be self-defeating and will engender a process of accelerating inflation. Since the rate of unemployment is not, in the long run, related to changes in the price level, a monetary union cannot be regarded as a cause of unemployment.

We recognise that the tendency for labour and capital to move to the central highly-developed areas from the peripheral areas may be accentuated by a monetary union. The reason is that wages in the peripheral low-productivity areas may be increased to the level of those in the high-productivity areas while productivity differentials remain unchanged. Consequently, unit labour costs in the peripheral areas may become so high that firms which previously were viable may no longer be able to pay their way and the prospect of a satisfactory return on new investment may disappear. Should that happen, capital would tend to move to the high-productivity areas and thereby attract labour to move from the peripheral to the central areas.

In Europe regional diversity is highly, and in our view rightly, valued. We consider, therefore, that monetary union should not be permitted to encourage the movement of labour and capital to the central developed areas at the expense of the peripheral and less developed regions. For this reason we look upon a vigorous regional policy as an integral part of monetary unification in the European Community. We regard it as essential that such a policy should concentrate on eliminating the causes of regional imbalance by raising productivity levels in the poorer areas and that income transfers to alleviate the consequences of low productivity should be used as an interim measure only.

The transition to a European monetary union would not, of course, be without difficulties. The higher a country's rate of inflation is, the greater these difficulties would be. For a country with a rate of inflation as high as that in the United Kingdom the transition might involve a recession lasting for several years. It is not surprising that many people consider this too high a price to pay for monetary union, especially as the teaching of two generations of economists has been that domestic demand management policies can be relied upon to achieve any desired level of employment.

In the long run the need to reduce high inflation rates is virtually inescapable so that ultimately the consequences of bringing inflation under control have to be borne whether a country joins a monetary union or not. The introduction of a new stable money that is not subject to inflationary expectations will, however, minimise the transitional costs.

A COMMON EUROPEAN MONEY: THE EUROPA

Monetary reform to fight inflation will become more urgent the longer the current inflationary situation lasts. The launching of a new common European money, the Europa, offers a unique opportunity of carrying out this monetary reform while at the same time setting the pace for monetary integration. The most radical approach would be to replace the existing national currencies by a stable European money in one drastic move. We rule this out because it violates the principle of gradualism and would not give the people any choice in the matter. Moreover, it would produce a severe stabilisation crisis in most countries.

The approach we advocate offers both gradualism and automaticity, and is based on monetary reform and on the free interplay of market forces. We propose the launching of a parallel European money of constant purchasing power, issued in accordance with a European monetary treaty, that would circulate along with the existing national currencies.

The presence of a stable European money will compel governments to replace the implicit tax now existing on holders of money with explicit taxation. With money keeping a constant purchasing power, the issuer earns seigniorage on each Europa which is equal to the real rate of interest on perfectly liquid and riskless assets minus the costs of issuing, replacement and policing against forgery; if the money loses its value, an additional burden is imposed on the holders of money which is equivalent to a tax. In the absence of money illusion, this inflation tax is equal to the difference between the nominal and the real rate of interest, i.e., the expected rate of inflation. To eliminate the inflation tax on the holders of Europas is to offer them a purchasing-power guarantee.

To propose a Europa of stable purchasing power is to invite the question why a problem which proves so difficult in the case of the national monies should be so easy to solve in the case of the parallel money. The answer is twofold. One, it makes a great difference from what position one starts. It is much easier to prevent inflation than to eliminate it. This is the reason why many times in history the creation of a new money has been preferred to a stabilisation of the old money; this is also the reason for linking European monetary unification with European monetary reform. Two, during the transition period (i.e., the period during which national monies and Europas co-exist), it is easier to achieve a constant purchasing power of Europas than of national monies. This is so because, while the purchasing power of a national money depends on how the public reacts to changes in its supply, the purchasing power of a parallel money can be stabilised with absolute precision if the issuer administers the exchange rate of the Europa vis-a-vis the national monies directly through currency conversions.

The adoption of the Europa requires one major political decision on the part of each national government: to permit their residents to use and to hold Europas in competition with national money. The fate of the Europa, however, will be determined in the market place by the economic operators.

INFLATION-PROOF EUROPA

The mechanism for maintaining a stable Europa, while it circulates alongside national monies, can be rather simple. Its essence is to keep the price level of a representative commodity basket constant in terms of Europas. The commodity basket can be defined as the weighted sum of the national commodity baskets used to calculate the national consumer price indices. The weights ought to reflect the relative share of each country in community GNP, intra-community trade, etc. The Europa itself is expressed in terms of a (weighted) basket of national monies.

Europas will be exchanged against the basket of national monies at a variable exchange rate that would be implied by the maintenance of a constant purchasing power of the Europa. As a practical guideline, the exchange rates between national monies and the Europa would be adjusted according to a crawling peg formula. The timing of the crawl would depend on that of the publication of the relevant price indices. This would amount to adjusting the exchange rate between the Europa and each of the national monies by a weighted average of inflation rates of consumer prices expressed in national monies.

When the Europa has ultimately replaced national monies, its supply should be controlled according to a monetary rule that would continue to guarantee its purchasing power stability.

THE EUROPA SOVEREIGNTY

Initially, we envisage that the central banks would issue the Europa against national monies only. In that way it would not add to the total community stock of money. Only at a later stage would it be issued through rediscounting of bills and other loans to the banking system, through open market operations or through financing of community expenditures. To the extent that the issue of a stable Europa will raise the demand for real money balances, such additions to the money stock can be absorbed without a simultaneous fall in the demand for national monies.

Will monetary policy be more conducive to long-run stability in the monetary union than in the existing arrangement? The answer to this important question depends on the type of institution or institutions which will eventually replace national monetary authorities. Whatever the details of the arrangement, it would be wise to keep in mind one guiding principle: we must give the monetary authorities the same independence from political control and the same responsibility to the rule of law we have accorded the judicial system. It follows that the new institution or institutions should be removed from the jurisdiction of treasuries, and monetary authorities should be appointed or elected for long periods of time, if not for life. The purpose of these two features is to assure a longer time horizon than can be found in other branches of government.

SUMMARY

We recapitulate the principal propositions emerging from the document.

1. It is difficult to envisage a monetary union created by official edicts and legalistic structures. It must evolve in the market place.
2. The benefits of a monetary union are qualitatively similar to the benefits accruing to a society as it moves from a barter to a monetary arrangement.
3. The case for a monetary union is not a case for fixed exchange rates in a world of many monies. It is rather a case for the replacement of all national monies with one common unit of account, medium of exchange and store of value.
4. The single money (Europa) which will replace national monies must have stability of purchasing power.
5. Our vision of monetary union differs from other visions in that we do not emphasise labour and capital mobility but rely on structural policies to correct possible regional imbalances.
6. There are no unemployment costs in monetary unification in the long run. The abdication of the national monopoly to print money has consequences only for the national rate of inflation, not for the long-run rate of unemployment.
7. The cost of monetary unification is transitional and results from the temporary loss of employment as the country adjusts its inflation rate to the union inflation rate.
8. The adoption of the Europa presupposes the political will to harmonise inflation rates among countries. It also presupposes that national governments will be willing to replace the inflation tax with explicit taxation. We thus call for a full-fledged monetary reform.
9. In the period when the Europa and national monies will coexist, the quantity of Europas will be solely determined by the desires of those who want to hold it. Conversions between Europas and national monies will occur at variable ratios.
10. To preserve the benefits of the monetary reform, i.e., the benefits which derive from a stable-valued money, monetary authorities should be given the same independence from political power and the same responsibilities to the rule of law we have accorded the judicial system.

SIGNATORIES

Giorgio Basevi, Università di Bologna, Italy
Michele Fratianni, Indiana University, U.S.A. and Katholieke Universiteit Leuven, Belgium
Herbert Giersch, Institut für Weltwirtschaft an der Universitat Kiel, Federal Republic of Germany
Pieter Korteweg, Erasmus Universiteit, Rotterdam, Netherlands
David O'Mahony, University College, Cork, Ireland
Michael Parkin, University of Manchester, United Kingdom
Theo Peeters, Katholieke Universiteit Leuven, Belgium
Pascal Salin, Université Paris-IX-Dauphine, France
Niels Thygesen, Københavns Universitat, Denmark

The Inflation-proofed Europa: How it might work

THEO PEETERS, PAUL DE GRAUWE and ROLAND VAUBEL

The objective of this note is to show how the inflation-proofed Europa (₤) would work in relation to the existing European unit of account (EUA) which was introduced in March 1975 by the Community for the European Development Fund and the European Investment Bank. For that purpose we present a simulation exercise from March 10 1975 to September 10 1975 and an illustration of a possible issuing mechanism of the ₤.

1. The value of the inflation-proofed Europa: A Simulation from March 10, 1975 to Septeptember 10, 1975

The inflation-proofed Europa is defined in terms of the European unit of account. EUA in turn is composed of a basket of European currencies weighted to reflect shares of GNP, trade, etc. (Table 1, col. 1). On March 10, 1 EUA = 1 ₤, the value of which in national currencies is given in col. 5.

Table 2.1: *1 EUA = 1₤ on March 10, 1975*

Currency	Amount of Currencies in basket (1)	Sterling Exchange Rate on 10.3.75 (2)	Sterling Value of Currency Amounts (3) = (1): (2)	Currency Weights (4) = (3): Σ(3)	Value of ₤ in each currency (5) = (2). Σ(3)
DM	0.828	5.607	0.1477	27.4	3.02
FF	1.15	10.20	0.1127	20.9	5.50
£ sterl.	0.0885	1.0	0.0885	16.4	0.539
Lira	109.0	1536.0	0.0710	13.2	825.0
Hfl	0.286	5.763	0.0496	9.2	3.11
Bfr/Luxfr	3.80	83.24	0.0457	8.5	44.9
Dkr	0.217	13.24	0.0164	3.0	7.14
Irish £	0.00759	1.0	0.0076	1.4	0.539
			Σ=£0.539		

The EUA's value in terms of national currencies changes as a result of the weighted average movements of the market exchange rates in col. 2. (For comparison between March 10 and September 10, see Tables 2.1 and 2.2.) As an example, the Ɇ has depreciated over that period against the EUA by 4.6 per cent. The lira, however, has appreciated vis-a-vis the EUA by 3.3 per cent.

Table 2.2: *EUA on September 10, 1975*

Currency	Amount of Currencies in basket (1)	Sterling exchange Rate (2)	Sterling Value of Currency Amounts (3)	Currency weights (4)	Value of Ɇ in each currency (5)
DM	0.828	5.455	0.1518	26.93	3.075
FF	1.15	9.295	0.1237	21.94	5.240
£ sterl.	0.0885	1.0	0.0885	15.70	0.5637
Lira	109.0	1415.0	0.0770	13.66	797.6
Hfl	0.286	5.585	0.0512	9.08	3.148
Bfr/Luxfr	3.80	81.40	0.0467	8.28	45.89
Dkr	0.217	12.62	0.0172	3.05	7.114
Irish £	0.00759	1.0	0.00759	1.35	0.5637
			Σ=£0.5637		

In the inflation-proofed Europa the amounts and weights of the national currencies in the basket are further adjusted on the basis of past inflation rates as measured by percentage changes in the national consumer price indices (CPI, Table 2.3).

Table 2.3: *Ɇ on September 10, 1975*

Currency	Increase in CPI from Jan. to July (1)	Amount of Currency in Basket (2)	Sterling Exchange Rate on 10.9.75 (3)	Sterling Value of Currency Amounts (4)=(2): (3)	Currency weights (5)=(4): Σ(4)	Value of Ɇ in each currency (6)=(3). Σ(4)
DM	3.12	0.854	5.455	0.1566	26.20	3.260
FF	4.73	1.204	9.295	0.1295	21.66	5.56
£ sterl.	15.55	0.1023	1.0	0.1023	17.11	0.5977
Lira	5.02	114.0	1415.0	0.0806	13.48	845.7
Hfl	4.35	0.298	5.585	0.0534	8.93	3.338
Bfr/Luxfr.	5.19	4.00	81.40	0.0491	8.21	48.65
Dkr.	3.29	0.224	12.62	0.0177	2.96	7.542
Irish £	12.13	0.00851	1.0	0.00851	1.42	0.5977
				Σ=£0.5977		

The weighted average inflation rate in Europe (₠ Sept. 10/EUA Sept. 10) over the six month period is equal to 6 per cent. If markets exchange rates were not to change over the relevant period, the ₠ would offer a lower purchasing power guarantee in the high inflation countries than a fully indexed national money; and conversely a higher guarantee for the low inflation countries than a fully indexed national money. But in practice, the purchasing power of the ₠ in a particular country depends on the relationship between the country's rate of inflation and the rate of depreciation (appreciation) of the domestic currency relative to other European currencies. If a currency has depreciated more (appreciated less) than would be warranted by purchasing power parity, than the ₠ would offer increased purchasing power in that country, regardless of the relative rates of inflation. This would mean that in at least one other country the currency had appreciated more (depreciated less) than indicated by purchasing power parity, and that the ₠'s purchasing power had declined in that country. If exchange rates exactly followed purchasing power parity, than the purchasing power of the ₠ would be constant in all countries, regardless of rates of inflation. (We are indebted to Polly R. Allen for this point and for drawing our attention to an error in an earlier version of this note.)

It is assumed that Consumer Price Indices are only published six weeks following the month in question (i.e. on the 10th). Alternatively one could consider the case of the CPI being published on the 10th of the following month and that the inflation adjustment would be spread over a month. For the example of March 10 to September 10 period this means using inflation rates for the January to July period. (For Ireland, which only publishes quarterly data, twice the February-May rate has been used.) In practice, the specific arrangements would naturally depend upon the choice of an adequate price index and the timing of its publication.

The formula for calculating the EUA can be expressed as follows

$$\text{EUA} = \sum_{i=1}^{8} a_i/r_i$$

where a_i equals the amount of national currency in the basket and r_i represents the exchange rate of sterling against the other national currencies on a particular date.

$i = 1, 2, \ldots, 8$ where $1, 2, \ldots$ stands for DM, FF, £, Lira, Hfl, Bfr/Luxfr., Dkr., Irish £.

The formula for calculating the inflation proofed Europa can be expressed as follows:

$$₠ = \sum_{i=1}^{8} a_i\,(1 + \pi_i)/r_i$$

where π_i is the inflation rate in terms of the national consumer price index over the relevant period.

2. The ₠ issuing mechanism: how it affects the balance sheets of the banking system

To illustrate how the ₠ might be issued, we start with simplified balance sheets of the British commerical banking system and the Bank of England. The example can of course be repeated for the banking system of the other member countries. The day before the introduction of the Europa the following balance sheets hold:

A	Bank of England – March 9		L
Domestic assets	100	Currency	150
Foreign assets	100	Commercial bank reserves	50

A	Commercial Bank – March 9		L
Reserves	50	Deposits	400
Other assets	350		

Two cases are considered. In the first case we assume a 100 per cent reserve requirement on Europa deposits, an assumption which allows to reduce the mechanics of the conversion to its essentials. In the second case, we take into consideration a more realistic, though more complicated, conversion scheme.

a. 100 per cent reserve requirement on Europa deposits. At the time of the introduction of the ₠ (March 10) it is assumed that enough pounds are converted into ₠100. The conversion occurs with the aid of a financial intermediary which acts as a clearing agent. Such an intermediary is called for convenience the Euro-agent. The sale of pounds for ₠ 100 affects the balance sheets of the British banking system, the Euro-agent and the banking systems of the other member countries. The exercise that follows ignores the effects of the transaction on the latter.

The conversion process can be sketched as follows. First, the commercial banking system issues Europa deposits for the account of its customers in the amount of ₠100, and reduces these customers' sterling accounts by £53.9. The commercial bank now has an open position in Europas, and therefore runs not only an exchange risk but also an inflation risk (because the Europa has a value-maintenance guarantee). In order to cover its Europa position it will first have to buy ₠100 worth of national currencies in the proportions implied by the ₠ formula. Assume, for example, the banking system obtains the sterling funds necessary to purchase the different national currencies, by reducing its reserves at the Bank of England by 10 per cent of the £53.9, and by discounting bills for the balance. It then transfers this basket of currencies to the Bank of England in exchange for a Europa deposit of ₠100. By doing so the commercial bank has now covered its Europa positions. This is shown in its balance sheet as of March 10.

The Bank of England, subsequently, transfers the basket of currencies implied by Ɇ100 to the Euro-agent which in turn credits the account of the Bank of England. This transaction is shown in the balance sheet of the Bank of England and the Euro-agent as of March 10. (Note that all figures in the T-accounts are converted into £ and that the underlying data are those given in the tables of Section 1. Furthermore, figures are rounded to the nearest decimal.)

Finally, we want to show how the Europa would affect the relevant balance sheets six months after its introduction. The value-maintenance provision of the Europa implies that governments would have to compensate the Euro-agent for the losses he has incurred. In particular, each country would guarantee the Euro-agent a payment equal to the amount of national currency in the basket times the domestic rate of inflation.

A — Bank of England – March 10 — L

A		L	
Domestic Assets	148.51	Currency	150
Foreign assets	100	Commercial bank (£-account)	44.61
Euro-Agent (Ɇ100)	53.9	Commercial bank (Ɇ-account)	53.9
		Euro-Agent	53.9

A — Commercial Bank – March 10 — L

A		L	
Reserves (£)	44.61	Deposits (£)	346.10
Other assets	301.49	Deposits (Ɇ100)	53.9
Reserves (Ɇ100)	53.9		

A — Euro-Agent – March 10 — L

A		L	
Bundesbank (DM 82.8)	14.77	Bank of England (100 Ɇ)	53.9
Banque de France (FF 115)	11.27		
Bank of England (£8.85)	8.85		
Banca d'Italia (Lira 10,900)	7.10		
Nederlandsche Bank (Hfl 28.6)	4.96		
Banque Nationale de Belgique (BF-LF 380)	4.57		
Danmarks Nationalbank (Dkr 21.7)	1.64		
Central Bank of Ireland (Irish £0.759)	0.76		

A — Bank of England – Sept. 10 — L

A		L	
Domestic assets	148.51	Currency	150
Foreign assets	100	Commercial bank (£-account)	44.61
Euro-Agent (Ɇ100)	59.8	Commercial bank (Ɇ-account)	59.8
Inflation correction (claim on Treasury)	1.38	Euro-Agent	53.9
		Euro-Agent	1.38

A	Commercial Bank – Sept. 10		L
Reserves (£)	44.61	Deposits (£)	346.1
Other assets	301.49	Deposits (₤100)	59.8
Reserves (₤100)	59.8		

A	Euro-Agent – Sept. 10		L
Bundesbank (DM 85.4)	15.66	Bank of England (100₤)	59.8
Banque de France (FF 120.4)	12.95		
Bank of England (£10.28)	10.23		
Banca d'Italia (Lira 11,490)	8.06		
Nederlandsche Bank (Hfl 29.8)	5.34		
Banque Nationale de Belgique (BF-LF 400)	4.91		
Danmarks Nationalbank (Dkr 22.40)	1.77		
Central Bank of Ireland (Irish £0.851)	0.85		

b. A more realistic example with fractional reserve ratios. We start again with an amount of sterling deposits being converted into ₤100. Assume the original reserve ratio on sterling deposits to be 1/8 (12.5 per cent) and that, after the conversion, the commercial bank maintains this ratio on both its sterling and Europa liabilities. (This is a necessary assumption if one wants to avoid cases of net credit contraction or expansion.)

It follows that the bank would reduce its sterling reserves by 1/8 against pound deposits and increase Europa reserves by an equivalent amount against Europa deposits.

The difference between the present and previous conversion scheme is that the Treasury now is supposed to provide for the bulk of the 'cover' on Europa liabilities of the commercial bank. This is done by issuing Europa-denominated government securities. How could this work? Initially, as in the previous scheme, the commercial bank buys the basket of national currencies in the exchange markets. In this case, however, the commercial bank purchases national currencies by reducing its sterling reserves by £6.7 (so as to maintain a reserve ratio of 12.5 per cent) and by selling pound-denominated government securities to the Bank of England. Subsequently, the commercial bank transfers the equivalent of £6.7 worth of the currency basket to the Bank of England, in exchange for a reserve credit of ₤12.5. The bank transfers the remainder of the currency basket to the Treasury which then issues Europa-denominated securities, while transfering the basket of currencies to the Bank of England. These operations, in fact, amount to a transformation of a sterling-denominated debt (previously held by the commercial bank) into a Europa-denominated debt.

Assuming that the Bank of England acts as the Treasury agent, the balance sheet may look as follows, after the conversion.

A		Bank of England – March 10	L
Domestic assets	100	Currency	150
Foreign assets	100	Commerical Bank (£-account)	43.3
Sterling debt retired	47.2	Commercial bank (Ɇ-account)	6.7
Euro-Agent	53.9	Outstanding Ɇ-Treasury bills	47.2
		Euro-Agent	53.9

A		Commercial Bank – March 10	L
Reserves	43.3	Deposits (£)	346.10
Sterling assets	302.8	Deposits (Ɇ100)	53.9
Reserves (Ɇ)	6.7		
Ɇ-assets (U.K. Treasury bills denominated in Ɇ)	47.2		

After six months, and assuming the same inflation rate as before, the balance sheets look as follows.

A		Bank of England – Sept. 10	L
Domestic assets	100	Currency	150
Foreign assets	100	Commercial bank (£-account)	43.3
Sterling debt retired	47.2	Commercial bank (Ɇ-account)	7.5]
Euro-Agent	59.8	Outstanding Ɇ-Treasury bills	52.3]
Inflation correction (claim on Treasury		Euro-Agent	53.9
	1.38	Euro-Agent	1.38

A		Commercial Bank – Sept. 10	L
Reserves (£)	43.3	Deposits (£)	346.1
Sterling assets	302.8	Deposits (Ɇ100)	59.8
Reserves (Ɇ)	7.5] 59.8		
Ɇ-assets	52.3]		

The balance sheet of the Euro-agent remains unchanged with respect to the previous example.

The willingness of the Treasury to issue Europa-denominated bills is essential for normal banking operations to develop. This would not involve an additional risk or burden for the U.K. Treasury apart from the inflation payment attributable to the presence of £ in the basket. The burden of the inflation correction for the other currencies falls on the respective Treasuries via the Euro-agent.

It can be expected that the private sector would issue debt in Ɇ, thus increasing the size of the market for Ɇ financial assets and permitting banks to diversify between public and private debt. The issuers of debt in Ɇ will pay an interest rate which in equilibrium, *ceteris paribus,* will differ from the interest rate on debt in pounds by approximately the expected rate of inflation.

The monetary authorities and the Treasury in each country can control the conversion of national money into ₠ by altering the nominal rate paid on debt in national money as compared to the real interest rate paid on ₠-denominated bills.

Exchange rates will also be affected as national money is converted into ₠. Expected inflation rates will be a predominant factor in this respect. But at the same time exchange rate adjustments offer an additional protection against the prospect of a national money being driven out of circulation by one swift move.

3 Difficulties with European Monetary Union

DAVID LAIDLER

I. INTRODUCTION

It is now two years since the authors of the All Saints' Day Manifesto (Basevi *et al.*, 1975) advanced their proposals for European Monetary Union. The Manifesto itself, and subsequent writings by at least one of its authors (Parkin, 1976) make it clear that they envisage themselves as planning, not for some distant time in the future, but for the present. Their scheme is one that they would have implemented immediately in 1975, and presumably one that they would implement now had they the power to do so.[1] Given the renewal of interest within the EEC Commission in the goal of monetary union, it is of particular importance that the goal itself, and the methods that have been proposed to achieve it, be subject to critical scrutiny and debate. This paper seeks to contribute to such a debate. The Maifesto's authors have claimed that there is no case to be made against immediately moving towards European Monetary Union (EMU). It is my contention that there are serious problems involved in such a move, particularly an *immediate* one. To proceed towards EMU without a thorough analysis of these problems is to risk its failure. Whether one opposes or supports EMU, one can agree that a botched attempt at achieving it is something to be avoided. The arguments that follow stop far short of being a blanket condemnation of all aspects of the case put by the proponents of EMU. Rather they are advanced in the hope of tempering political enthusiasm for EMU by a little economic realism.

II. COMMON GROUND

To begin with, there is no dispute that, *ceteris paribus,* it would be more efficient for the trading system of the EEC (or of the whole world, for that matter), to use a common currency rather than a collection of national currencies. The existence of a multiplicity of currencies between which exchange rates are not rigidly fixed *does* introduce an extra element of risk into foreign trade; that risk can be mitigated by the activities of speculators

---

I am grateful to Michele Fratianni, Peter Howitt, Pieter Korteweg, Michael Parkin and George Zis for comments on an earlier draft.

in specialized foreign exchange markets, but such markets *do* consume real resources; even if exchange rates are rigidly fixed, there *are* extra transactions costs involved in moving between currencies; and so forth. I agree with all this. I would also immediately concede that there is no case to be made for maintaining a system of national currencies whose exchange rates one for another are rigidly fixed for all time. A group of nations which had moved to such a system could only gain by moving to a single currency. The case *against* a single currency is thus the case *for* maintaining some degree of exchange rate flexibility.[2]

Given the undoubted gains from having a single currency, any case against it must rest on the proposition that the move from a degree of exchange rate flexibility to a common currency does not leave the other things equal, but rather generates more than offsetting losses elsewhere. Let it be noted then that I agree with the proponents of EMU on one important issue concerning the losses to be expected from it, an issue that involves two propositions, one true, and one which I regard as false. The true proposition is that exchange rate flexibility permits different countries to sustain different inflation rates, and the one which I believe to be false is that this in turn will permit them to sustain different unemployment rates. From these two premises it is frequently argued that, given that different nations have different 'tastes' vis-a-vis inflation and unemployment, or a different capacity to combine them, EMU would force sub-optimal inflation-unemployment combinations on the nations participating in it.

Parkin (1976) has argued convincingly that whether or not one accepts the second premise of this chain of reasoning depends upon one's view of the causes of inflation. The premise is consistent with an institutional approach to explaining the causes of inflation, or with one based upon the Phillips-Lipsey theory of the relationships between excess demand, unemployment, and inflation. It is inconsistent with a belief in a 'natural unemployment rate' whose value is independent of (or positively related to) the anticipated inflation rate, and with a belief in the proposition that in the long run the actual and anticipated inflation rates are equal to each other. Since I agree with Parkin that these two propositions do seem to be consistent with a considerable amount of empirical evidence, I also agree with him that the foregoing commonly advanced argument against EMU is invalid.[3]

The final opinion that I share with the proponents of EMU may be put as follows. Monetary union is seen by many people on both sides of the debate as one part of a much more fundamental economic and political union that might be achieved within the EEC. The arguments for and against such a union range far beyond economics, and in my view, issues concerning EMU are trivial when viewed in such a context. If the aim is to turn the EEC into a federal state, then there is an extremely strong case for regarding a common currency as an important institution for that state to create. This paper is not the place to go into the pros and cons of forming a United States of Europe. Suffice it to say that in what follows I will in no way quarrel with those who argue that EMU should be one of the ultimate goals of those seeking to create such an entity, nor will I have anything to say in support of those who oppose EMU because they are opposed to a broader union. I *will* quarrel with the view that, given that EMU is a desirable ultimate goal, now is a good time to begin to move towards it, and that the means proposed in the All Saints' Day Manifesto promise an easy path towards its realization.

III. THE CASE AGAINST THE ALL SAINTS' DAY MANIFESTO

My basis for arguing that it is undesirable to move towards EMU *now* would be the observation that rates of inflation within the EEC are currently (Autumn 1977) extremely disparate, ranging from a low of 4 per cent in Germany to a high of 19 per cent in Italy. The authors of the All Saints' Day Manifesto recognize, indeed take as a starting point for their own proposals, that this fact precludes any rapid approach to monetary union through an orthodox sequence of events beginning with the harmonization of inflation rates, proceeding to the fixing of exchange rates between national currencies, with these in turn ultimately being replaced by a common currency. They recognize that it is politically impossible, not to mention economically undesirable, to get the low-inflation countries to drive their inflation rates up to the levels prevailing in Britain and Italy, and equally impossible and undesirable for those high-inflation countries to endure the transitional unemployment that would have to accompany a rapid diminution of their own inflation rates. However, those authors do claim that their proposals, which involve the issue of a parallel European currency, enable such problems to be bypassed.

As Parkin (1976) has noted, our knowledge of the economics of parallel currencies, particularly detailed empirical knowledge, is rather meagre, although Vaubel's work (1978) promises to make an important contribution here; any arguments about this matter must be tentative. Nevertheless, let me assert immediately that I am not convinced of the economic viability of the proposals advanced in the All Saints' Day Manifesto.

The proposals are simple enough. A European Central Bank is to be set up to issue a new currency called the Europa. Each member government of the EEC is to permit its nationals freely to use the Europa as a means of exchange, store of value and unit of account, in short as money, as and if they see fit. Initially the Europa is to be put into circulation only by means of the new European Bank offering to exchange it in unlimited quantities for a basket of the national currencies of EEC members.[4] In order to ensure that the purchasing power of the Europa remains constant, the price at which it is exchanged against this basket will be adjusted at regular intervals in proportion to the change in the purchasing power over goods and services of the various currencies that make it up over the interval in question. It is claimed that to introduce a new currency in this way will ultimately drive inflating national currencies out of circulation. The Europa will thus naturally evolve as the only European currency. At that stage, the authors of the Manifesto recognize that Europas will have to be issued in accordance with some rule about the behaviour of their nominal quantity outstanding that will enable the constancy of their purchasing power to be maintained. In short, the scheme is claimed to combine the advantages of ensuring the achievement of a common European currency, with those of ridding European countries of inflation by way of what amounts to a currency reform; and all of this is to happen as a result of voluntary choices made by private agents, rather than being imposed by any governmental authority. As the Manifesto puts it, 'The adoption of the Europa requires one major political decision on the part of each national government: to permit their residents to use and to hold Europas in competition with national money. The fate of the Europa, however, will be determined in the market place by the [sic] economic operators.'

In fact, much more is required of national governments if the scheme is to be viable and successful. First, and fundamentally, if national currencies are to be driven from circulation, then national governments must cease issuing them. If the Manifesto's scheme cannot guarantee that, it cannot guarantee to achieve either of its ultimate goals. The basic difficulty here may be put as follows. There is no better incentive to make a national authority cease to issue its own currency than that there ceases to exist a group of willing holders of such a currency. One cannot generate revenue from issuing money which has no willing holders. Now it is true that the introduction of a purchasing power guaranteed substitute currency would make the private sector of any economy less willing to hold an inflating national currency; the authors of the Manifesto seem – I say seem because they are not completely explicit on this matter – to believe that this very fact will force the national authorities to cease issuing it.[5] However, their proposal makes the new European Bank a willing holder of the inflating national currency that will replace the private sector. From the point of view of any national monetary authority, it does not matter who holds its currency. It can extract revenue from anyone who does. (Although the revenue that can be extracted from the European Bank will come in the form of falling real indebtedness, rather than as a current flow of goods and services.) Thus the scheme proposed in the text of the Manifesto does not encourage national authorities to give up issuing their own currencies.

We may pursue this matter from another angle. The European Central Bank is expected to issue a purchasing power guaranteed liability, and take in exchange for it the depreciating liabilities of national central banks. That of course is a recipe for making a continuous loss on its operations, that loss being equal to the inflation tax levied by national governments on the European Bank's holdings of their liabilities. The question arises as to how that loss is to be made good. Two possible schemes come to mind. First, it could be made good by national governments in proportion to the Bank's losses from holding particular national currencies. Second, it could be shared among the EEC countries according to some other formula. The first situation would of course require a conscious decision on the part of all national monetary authorities to give up a part of the revenue that they earn from issuing money and the second would require a conscious decision on the part of some national monetary authorities to permit themselves to be taxed by others. In either instance, the decision in question would have to be taken as part and parcel of the agreement to participate in the setting up of the European Bank that would issue the Europa. To ask that national governments make such a decision is to ask them to go far beyond simply permitting their own nationals to hold and trade in Europas, which the text of the Manifesto claims is the only step required of them to make the scheme viable. In fact, the paper by Peeters *et. al.* shows that the authors of the Manifesto have considered this problem, and have opted to have each national bank compensate the European Bank in proportion to the latter's holding of each national currency. The absence of any discussion of this issue from the text leaves the unwary reader ignorant of the extra, and serious, commitment that must be made by national authorities to surrender part of their revenue from money creation even before the scheme can be implemented.

The device for putting Europas into circulation by standing ready to trade them against national currencies at a price set by the Bank (though varying over time) lies at the root of the above difficulties. It also causes another problem Suppose that some argument is reached about who is to pay the tax levied by national central banks upon the European Bank, and suppose that the Europa does begin to circulate widely. Its price in terms of national currencies is supposed to be fixed with reference to the behaviour of some general price level measured in terms of those currencies. Once the Europa is circulating widely, what exactly will be the meaning of a price level measured in terms of a national currency? If the market were left free to determine cross rates between the Europa and other currencies this would not be a problem, of course, but it is of the essence of the scheme proposed in the Manifesto that such rates are to be set by the European Bank. There is a discomforting aura of indeterminacy about the way in which the scheme will work at this point. At some stage, and long before other currencies are driven out of circulation, some other means must be found for controlling the issue of Europas, but the Manifesto does not tell us what it will be.

The problems discussed so far, namely the requirement that National Monetary Authorities make a prior commitment to surrender some revenue from money creation, and the indeterminacy of the transition from national currencies to a common one, both arise from the institutional arrangement whereby unlimited quantities of Europas are to be traded at a stated price against national currencies. If the Europa is to be purchasing power guaranteed, an alternative mode for its issue would be at a fixed price against warehouse receipts for a selected commodity, or bundle of commodities. Such a mode of issue would tie down the price level of the chosen commodity bundle in terms of the Europa, regardless of the quantity issued. As to its price in terms of other currencies, that could either be left to respond to market forces, or it could be fixed in some other way. In either event that would be a decision to be left to the discretion of national central banks. Given that the price of goods in terms of the Europa was fixed, they would be able to decide whether or not to intervene in the market for Europas with their own currencies and they would have no obligation to make good losses made by the European Bank on any holding of their liabilities.

In current circumstances we can immediately rule out the feasibility of national central banks each adopting a fixed exchange rate against a constant purchasing power Europa. If they were able and willing to do that, they would be able and willing to do it vis-a-vis each other's national currencies. The first step in what might be termed the conventional path towards EMU could then be taken immediately, and without resort to any such device as the Europa. Only a scheme in which market forces predominate in determining the Europa's price in terms of national currencies is viable if the aim is to get it into circulation now. However, when markets are permitted to determine the relative prices of different currencies, Gresham's Law ceases to operate. Bad and good monies can continue to circulate together indefinitely when their relative prices are free to vary. Thus, to issue the Europa in the way I have just envisaged would add one more to the number of EEC currencies, albeit a constant purchasing power one, but it would not necessarily advance the establishment of a single European currency.

However, I would go further than that, and argue that more harm than good would be done in present circumstances by issuing the Europa in this way. I readily concede that Parkin's arguments, about how a lower rate of inflation could be achieved without any transition costs if agents moved to striking bargains in terms of a constant purchasing power currency, are formally correct.[6] Indeed they are ingenious. However, they completely ignore an institutional factor of great importance, namely that economic agents pay taxes to national governments. The laws and accounting conventions whereby tax liabilities are computed are currently set out in terms of national currencies. As the debate about inflation accounting attests, the difficulties involved in devising a new set of conventions are enormous, and provide what I would conjecture to be more than adequate incentives to ensure that, with current inflation rates, national currencies would remain the dominant unit of account even in the presence of the Europa. That in itself would help preserve them as means of exchange and stores of value; and why should governments who have an interest in maintaining their abilities to raise revenue from money creation alter the legal framework that helps maintain that ability? In short, I find it difficult to believe that a constant purchasing power Europa would become a widely used unit of account (or means of exchange at least in intra-national transactions) and hence cannot give much practical weight to Parkin's arguments about the advantages that would accrue if it was so used.

However, I have no difficulty in believing that the Europa could become a much sought after store of value. There is no need to dwell on the attractions of a riskless zero real rate of return security for residents of such countries as Britain and Italy. This would lead to two interrelated problems. First, to the extent that the introduction of Europas reduced the demand for national currencies, it would reduce the revenue accruing to the monetary authority at any rate of inflation. For a given public sector cash requirement, taxes and other borrowing would have to increase. Second, because the Europa would offer a far higher real return than otherwise comparable securities, its presence would put upward pressure on the interest rates, both real and nominal, at which the private sector could borrow. Neither of these effects is desirable given the current acutely depressed state of real economic activity; nor does it seem to me to be helpful to argue, as does Parkin, that they could be offset by expansionary fiscal policy, with the increases in already inflated public sector borrowing requirements and depressing effects on an already depressed private sector that that would entail.[7]

In short, I am not convinced that there is any means, in the current circumstances, whereby the approach to European Monetary Union can be eased by the issue of a European currency to circulate alongside national currencies. The scheme proposed in the All Saints' Day Manifesto glosses over the extent of the prior agreement required to implement it and is not fully worked out; alternatives either are not viable, or will fail to lead to the voluntary disappearance of national currencies, while themselves having unfortunate side effects. In the next section of this paper I shall deal with the case against a rapid approach to EMU by other, more orthodox, means.

IV. THE QUESTION OF AN EARLY CURRENCY REFORM

It has already been argued that it is not viable to approach EMU by way of first establishing fixed exchange rates amongst national currencies and then phasing these currencies out, if a rapid establishment of a common currency is what is required. There is one alternative that does, however, appear to be viable at first sight. The authors of the All Saints' Day Manifesto recognize, correctly, that the transitional unemployment costs associated with rapidly reducing the rates of price increase in high inflation countries can be avoided by a currency reform. Indeed, their scheme for a parallel currency was supposed to provide the same advantages as such a reform. We have seen that there are other problems associated with that scheme, but the basic insight remains valid: why not then establish EMU by a once-and-for-all currency reform? Instead of issuing the Europa as a parallel currency, why not establish it as a substitute currency?[8]

Now of course such a step would require a great deal of national governments. Each one would have to agree to give up the right to issue its own national money – except perhaps on the Scottish model of a 100 per cent reserve requirement with convertibility on demand; each one would have to agree to declare the Europa legal tender domestically; each one would have to subscribe to whatever arrangements were made to ensure that the nominal rate of expansion of the new currency was compatible with long-term stability in its purchasing power; and so on. All this would be extraordinarily difficult to arrange. Indeed many would argue that it would be politically impossible to do so in the present climate. However, Parkin has warned us against confusing arguments to the effect that certain things *will not* happen with arguments to the effect that they *ought not to* happen.[9] For an economist to fail to recommend an economically viable policy on the grounds that it is not politically acceptable at a particular time is to help ensure that the policy never will become politically acceptable. Let us therefore discuss this option on its economic merits.

There is much to recommend a quick approach to EMU by way of a currency reform. The inflation expectations whose inertia underlies the real stagnation that accompanies any significant reduction in an inflation rate must, by their very nature, be specific to a particular currency. If that currency ceases to exist and is replaced by a new one, then the formation of expectations must also start afresh. That is the essence of the case for tackling inflation by way of a currency reform. Although the case is broadly correct, it fails to get to grips with certain transitional problems that would arise from introducing a new currency in the contemporary European context. Inflation, though it has been severe, has been far from catastrophic over the last few years. In hyperinflations long-term contracts, whether in labour markets or capital markets, seem to vanish. Though in the last few years the period for which wage bargains have been struck has shortened, and although the long end of the capital market has seen its activities curtailed, there would nevertheless be a major problem as to what to do about the terms of contracts that had been struck in terms of a depreciating unit of account, with due allowance having been made for expectations about its depreciation, if that unit of account was suddenly replaced by a new one of constant purchasing power. If a three-year consumer loan, denominated in sterling, bears a nominal interest rate of 20 per cent, what would be the appropriate rate in Europas? And what about the terms of a 25-year fixed interest mortgage? I am not suggesting that problems such as these are insuperable, of course, but I am suggesting that the costs of dealing with them, or those imposed by failing to deal with them, must be offset against the benefits of tackling moderate inflation by way of a currency reform. They would not, after all, arise if EMU was achieved by a sequence of events that involved, as a first step, the gradual harmonization of national inflation rates at a desirable level.

However, it is not the costs that a currency reform imposes upon the private sector that raise the most serious questions about the desirability of achieving EMU by such a means. Rather it is the constraint that it imposes upon the public sector. An excessively rapid pace of monetary expansion does not occur fortuitously in a modern economy. It arises because the government, having difficulty in meeting its budget constraint by other means, resorts to generating revenue by money creation. A currency reform that is not accompanied by measures to make it possible for the public sector's budget constraint to be met by other means is going to fail, and having failed reduces the chances of any future reform being successful. If EMU is to be achieved by such a route, then, it had better be achieved at the first attempt.

To the extent that inflation itself is a major contributor to the government's fiscal problems, a currency reform itself will make a major contribution to the government's ability to meet its budget constraint without resorting to further inflation. Such was the case with the Weimar hyperinflation where lags in tax payments interacted with rising prices to produce enormous falls in the real value of government revenue, which in their turn forced the government into further money creation. To the extent that a currency reform coincides with other changes that affect government finance, there is also reason to suppose that it will be successful. Such was the case with China in 1949 where the accession of a new government resulted from the end of the Civil War, the financing of which itself had been the major cause of the previous regime's resorting to the printing press.[10] However, in contemporary Europe, neither of the above conditions seems to hold. Money creation is funding deficits, but a currency reform will not do anything to reverse those deficits, nor does a move to EMU promise to do anything in and of itself to reduce them.

If a currency reform is to be an effective means of rapidly approaching EMU in current circumstances, and if the danger of the Europa itself becoming an inflating currency is to be avoided, the governments of individual EEC countries must either find an alternative source of revenue to money creation, or cut down on their expenditures. We have already noted above the depressed state of the real economies of EEC members, and have commented on the undesirability of any rapid contraction of fiscal policy in current circumstances – however desirable it might be in the long run to shrink the share of government in the economy. These consideration are relevant here, because unless it is argued that currency reform and EMU will, because of their effects on the 'animal spirits' of the private sector, generate a boom there, the fiscal restraint that would have to go along with such measures could only serve to depress further what are already excessively depressed economies. Thus, though EMU through currency reform is a viable alternative to gradualism in monetary policy under a given currency, and cannot be opposed on narrow monetary grounds, its adoption in current circumstances might require the abandonment of gradualism in fiscal policy, and that is much harder to defend.

Even if the foregoing objections to EMU were irrelevant, if national finances were already in order and national inflation rates harmonized at low levels, it would be wrong to pretend that all objections to a rapid movement to EMU would have disappeared. It could, and should, still be argued that monetary union would better be achieved after, or simultaneously with, fiscal union rather than prior to it. I have discussed the issues involved here elsewhere (Laidler (1976)) and there is no need to go into the arguments in elaborate detail here. It will suffice to describe them briefly. The first argument is somewhat esoteric; it rests on the simple proposition that money creation, being a source of revenue to its issuer, is, from the point of view of the promotion of economic welfare, best analysed and regulated as part of the overall system of taxation of an economic entity. Such a viewpoint leads at once to the conclusion that monetary union should go along with fiscal and political union rather than being regarded as a separate and prior goal.

The other arguments are of more practical importance, but lead to the same conclusion. These arguments rest on the belief that economies are subjected to what are usually termed 'real shocks' as well as to nominal shocks, and on the belief that, in the short run, variations in the quantity of money influence real as well as nominal variables. Though it is readily admitted that there is nothing that can be done with monetary policy to offset the effects of real shocks in the long run, it nevertheless follows from the foregoing assertions that the nature of the transition from one real equilibrium to another can be influenced by the behaviour of the quantity of money, and would differ depending upon whether a particular country enjoyed domestic monetary autonomy combined with exchange rate flexibility, or was a member of a currency union.

To see why this might be so, consider the response of an economy to a shock which requires a change in the level of real wages relative to those ruling elsewhere in the currency union to which it belongs. If the economy is a member of a currency union, its price level is given, so it is money wages that must adjust to accommodate such a shock. Under domestic monetary autonomy an alternative means of adjustment would involve exchange rate and price level variations. If we apply to these alternatives Hicks' (1974) distinction between 'fix' and 'flex' price markets, and if it is agreed that the labour market has far more 'fix' price characteristics than does the foreign exchange market, then it can be argued that the adjustment involving exchange rate and price level changes is likely to be smoother, and less characterized by variations in real income and employment, than that which requires the burden of adjustment to fall upon money wages.

Now this amounts to saying that even if the process of transition to a common currency is costless, there are certain disadvantages to be offset against the admitted advantages that a country gains from belonging to a currency union. These arguments are not however a blanket objection to a particular country ever joining a currency union under any circumstances. Moreover, whatever force they may have is weakened if there exists other means than monetary autonomy and exchange rate variability to cope with the real income and employment consequences of whatever real shocks might fall upon a particular economy. We do not often hear it argued that geographical regions of particular nations would be better off to abandon the national currency and adopt their own, even though real shocks do impinge differently upon different regions. The reason for this is surely that an individual nation is a fiscal union as well as having a common currency. Individual countries typically do make provision within their fiscal systems for interregional transfers of resources to take place, both on a long-term basis, and on a short-run basis in response to specific difficulties. And this is not to mention the fact that individual regions do have their representatives in the national legislature to help ensure that their particular problems are known about, and responded to.

With fiscal and political union then, there are created a set of institutions, which provide an alternative to those associated with monetary autonomy, for dealing with some of the economic problems that arise for particular regions within the union. Thus the case for maintaining separate currencies is severely weakened by the creation of such institutions – indeed positive arguments in favour of a currency union, that need no elaboration here, arise from the creation of such a union. It is, after all, easier to devise and implement a common fiscal policy when there is but one unit of account and means of exchange for the whole fiscal union.[11]

V. CONCLUSIONS

The conclusions that seem to follow from the arguments presented in this paper are easily summarized. First, it would be desirable to aim for EMU as and if fiscal and political union are also achieved, rather than to attempt to achieve this aspect of European unification earlier. I would argue for this position even if every member of the EEC had already achieved full employment and price stability. However, I would concede that in such circumstances there is considerable scope for argument about this conclusion. I would be much less willing to give up ground on the proposition that, given the current wide disparity of inflation rates between the countries of the EEC, and given the depressed state of the real economies of those same countries, the side effects of attempting to achieve an early monetary union in present circumstances make that course of action economically undesirable.

NOTES

1. See Parkin (1976), p. 4.
2. The arguments of the preceding paragraph have been made in greater detail in Laidler (1976).
3. It should be noted that Sumner (1976) contains the fullest account of the issues dealt with in the preceding paragraph.
4. On this see the final section of the Manifesto as printed in *The Economist.*
5. See the penultimate section of the Manifesto as printed in *The Economist.*
6. See Parkin (1976), pp. 13-15.
7. Ibid, p. 15.
8. It is worth noting that the authors of the Manifesto considered this possibility and rejected it on the grounds that it would create a stabilization crisis in most countries. Perhaps they had in mind the arguments advanced below.
9. See Parkin (1976), p. 4.
10. The examples of Weimar and China are not chosen at random. They are the examples of successful currency reforms cited by Parkin (1976).
11. One need only remind the reader of the difficulties of implementing the Common Agricultural Policy of the EEC under floating exchange rates in order to convey to him the weight of this argument.

REFERENCES

Basevi, G., Fratianni, M., Giersch, H., Korteweg, P., O'Mahony, D., Parkin, M., Peeters, T., Salin, P., and Thygesen, N., 'A Currency for Europe: The All Saints' Day Manifesto for European Monetary Union', *The Economist,* November 1, 1975.

Hicks, J.R., *The Crisis in Keynesian Economics* (Oxford: Blackwell, 1974).
Laidler, D., 'Concerning Currency Unions', paper presented at the Fourth University of Paris-Dauphine Conference on International Monetary Economics, Fort-de-France, Martinique, November 1976. University of Western Ontario Research Report 7618 (mimeo).
Parkin, M., 'Monetary Union and Stabilisation Policy in the European Community', *Banca Nazionale del Lavoro Quarterly Review*, September 1976, pp. 3-21.
Sumner, M.T., 'European Monetary Union and the Control of Europe's Inflation Rate', in Parkin, J.M. and Zis, G. (eds.), *Inflation in the World Economy* (Manchester: Manchester University Press, 1976).
Vaubel, R., 'Strategies for Currency Unification, the Case for a European Parallel Currency and the Economics of Currency Competition', mimeo (Kiel: Institut für Weltwirtschaft, 1978).

COMMENT ON LAIDLER

Pascal Salin

One year ago I had the pleasure to comment on David Laidler's paper against currency unification.[1] I have renewed pleasure in discussing the same arguments against currency unification and, more precisely, against the parallel currency approach. I am no more convinced now by his criticisms than I was the first time. The reasons for my dissatisfation will be explained in six points:

1. Laidler says that he does not see why the issue of a new purchasing power guaranteed currency by the means suggested by the Manifesto will give national governments any incentive to cut down or cease the issue of their own depreciating currencies. 'If the Manifesto's scheme cannot guarantee that, it cannot guarantee to achieve either of its ultimate goals.' In fact there are two reasons why a stable parallel currency would have such an influence. First, it is likely that people with the highest inflationary expectations would shift from national currencies to the Europa, thus exerting less pressure on national monetary authorities to create more money (in case the authorities would not behave in an independent manner).

Second, national monetary authorities, fearing the competition of the Europa, might be induced to create less national money.

Even if there was no effect of Europa creation on national monetary policy, this would not undermine the scope of the plan. The goal of the Manifesto is to offer Europeans an alternative, so that one inflation rate – that of the Europa – is zero, and rational economic decisions can be taken all over Europe without giving any consideration to the rate of depreciation of the other currencies. The existence of the Europa would thus meet the definition of monetary union given in the OPTICA 1975 Report: 'Monetary union would be an institutional organization among countries aiming at economic union, such as to minimise the inefficiencies inherent in the use and control of money within the union.' [2]

The only difficult problem in the Manifesto scheme is the following: at which point will the European authorities have to decide to shift from one system – issuance of Europas against national currencies – to another system – for instance to issue Europas by open-market techniques – and how to guarantee a stable purchasing power in this final stage?

2. Laidler is certainly right in saying that the Maifesto scheme does not imply only that the national authorities allow the free circulation of Europas but

that they accept to pay for the real losses incurred by the Euro-agent, since it will hold claims in depreciating national currencies and will issue purchasing-power-guaranteed liabilities. Such payments by the national authorities to the Euro-agent were an integral part of the Manifesto.

On the other hand, Laidler indicates that there can be other systems for distributing these losses among countries since any criterion corresponding to a given idea of what is 'fair' can be worked out.

It can also be imagined that the Euro-agent could invest its liquid assets in short-term interest-bearing assets and thus be reimbursed for at least a part of the depreciation of the national currencies. The remaining part would have to be paid by national authorities.[3]

If a central bank accepts to pay for the depreciation of its own currency, it would follow that the inducement to create money would diminish. This is one more reason why the existence of Europas would induce slower creation of national currencies.

3. Laidler writes 'Once the Europa is circulating widely, what exactly will be the meaning of a price level measured in terms of a national currency? If the market were left free to determine cross rates between the Europa and other currencies this would not be a problem, of course, but it is of the essence of the scheme proposed in the Manifesto that such rates are to be set by the European Bank. There is a discomforting aura of indeterminacy about the way in which the scheme will work at this point.'

This sentence seems to have two different meanings. One, which is not questionable, refers to the shift from one system to another in creating Europas (see 1. above). The other one seems to imply that there would be indeterminacy when the exchange rate between the Europa and national currencies is not perfectly flexible. That would be the case if the Euro-agent had a discretionary quantity policy for issuing Europas, while maintaining an exogenously determined price for the Europa (determined by cross rates between national currencies and inflation rates). However, in the Manifesto the supply curve of Europas is infinitely elastic, so that an exogenous price cannot cause any indeterminacy.

However, things might be different in a system where Europas are created by open-market techniques, or similar techniques. The Euro-agent becomes an European central bank and makes monetary policy, which implies that the supply of Europas is no longer infinitely elastic. In such a case there can be an excess demand for Europas. The only solution to this problem might be to change the definition of the Europa. The holders of Europas could be compensated for depreciation losses. If the Euro-agent issues too many Europas in relation to the demand, it would have to reimburse individuals for the inflation tax. In fact, one cannot imagine a system whereby a given institution would both create money against various types of assets and offer total convertibility in terms of other currencies at an exogenously determined price.

4. Laidler proposes another system to issue Europas, namely against com-

modities. Three objections can be opposed to this proposal. First, it implies an additional quantity of money in Europa, while the mechanism described in the Manifesto implies that an European parallel currency is created inasmuch as national currencies are bought and 'destroyed' by the Euro-agent. The creation of Europas against commodities would thus be inflationary in terms of national currencies (the same amount of money would have to finance a smaller number of transactions, since part of them would be financed by Europas).

Second, the scheme amounts to the Manifesto scheme as regards the payment of depreciation allowances by national authorities. Let us assume, for instance, that the Euro-agent buys 10 kilos of corn and sells 10 Europas. However, the Euro-agent is not interested in holding corn, which it cannot use. It will sell it against, say, 10 Francs (at that time 1 kilo of corn = 1 Franc = 1 Europa) and it can invest the 10 Francs. One year later, 1 kilo of corn is worth, say, 2 Francs. To keep the purchasing power of its assets, the Euro-agent must be reimbursed by national authorities for the inflation tax, for instance, by that authority which issues Francs.

This scheme does not allow the Euro-agent to fix the exchange rate between the Europa and national currencies, no more than in the Manifesto scheme. In fact, Laidler admits that flexibility would be necessary, for he says that 'when markets are permitted to determine the relative prices of different currencies, Gresham's Law ceases to operate'. In fact, it was also the case in the Manifesto, as we have seen in 3. above: Gresham's Law does not operate when the elasticity of supply is infinite and the relative price of currencies is exogenous. It would not be the case in Laidler's proposal. With prices exogenously determined (for instance if they were fixed) the Euro-agent would have a discretionary policy to issue Europas. It is the reason why Laidler concludes that exchange rates would have to be flexible (endogenous). This does not imply that they would have to be in the Manifesto scheme, since the issuance policy would not be the same, i.e. the exchange rate between the Europa and national currencies can be exogenously determined.

Third, Laidler is wrong when he writes that 'bad and good monies can continue to circulate together indefinitely when their relative prices are free to vary', since 'can' does not mean 'will'. In the Manifesto – as in Laidler's system with flexible prices and Europas issued against commodities – the 'inverse Greshan's Law' would work: good monies drive out bad monies.

Now, Laidler's scheme could be recommended when the Europa circulation is so wide that Europas can no longer be issued against national currencies, since the mere concept of a price level in terms of national currencies would no longer have meaning. It would then be quite similar to a gold standard, the respective advantages of a gold standard or a commodity standard being of a second-order importance.[4] Finally, even in that stage, there are no fundamental differences between such a system and a system where the Europa is issued against assets with a reimbursement provision.

5. One can share Laidler's doubts that governments would not accept payment

of taxes in Europas. However, this does not mean that Europas would not be used, since it is possible to pay taxes in national currency on transactions paid in Europas by going through the exchange markets. Although I admit that this implies transaction costs, a scheme cannot be rejected on the sole grounds of practical difficulties as Laidler himself admits.

6. Laidler argues that national government, losing the inflation tax because of their obligation to reconstitute the value of the assets held by the Euro-agent, would have to increase other taxes, an outcome which is deflationary. This conclusion is unwarranted on several grounds.

To begin with, people bear the inflation tax. Therefore, they would pay more 'explicit' taxes to the government, but would gain as holders of money.

Second, it may be wrong, at least in some cases, to say that 'inflation is a major contributor to the government's fiscal problems' and that the budget constraint is the main cause of inflation. In fact, the inflation tax is not very large in comparison with other taxes and there are other reasons for governments to favour inflation.

Third, the present state of affairs cannot be invoked as an argument against a rapid disappearance of inflation. If the government does not want to adjust at once to a non-inflationary situation, since it could have a deflationary influence, it can borrow (possibly abroad) to compensate for its loss of the inflation tax, without increasing other taxes. Moreover, the present depressed state of affairs is not linked to insufficient total demand.

Similarly, Laidler believes that nominal interest rates would increase if the inflation tax was to disappear. This result is not certain if present nominal rates are equal to the sum of the real rate, the expected rate of inflation and a risk premium. If there are Europa-denominated assets (with the same real rate of interest as national assets) why would the expected risk on national assets be increased? In fact, if Europas have a stabilizing influence, the risk premium would be lower and the nominal rate could fall.

Thus, I cannot accept Laidler's assertion, according to which 'the scheme proposed in the All Saints' Day Manifesto is technically flawed.' It must also be added that, when discussing the alternative of a currency reform, he rightly puts the discussion on economic grounds and does not rely on the argument that national governments would not accept the reform. But he previously accepted this argument when he said that the Manifesto scheme would not work since it would imply a guarantee from the governments or central banks, or when he said that governments would not abandon the right to extract an inflation tax.

NOTES

1. David Laidler, 'Concerning Currency Unions', Fort-de-France, Fourth Paris-Dauphine Conference on Money and International Monetary Problems, November 1976 (to be published in E.M. Claassen and P. Salin, eds., *Currency Areas and Exchange Rate Regimes*).

2. 'Towards Economic Equilibrium and Monetary Unification in Europe', Brussels, Commission of the European Communities, Report by a group of independent experts II/909/75-E final, January 16, 1976, p. 2.
3. This part would be low if the nominal interest rate in each country reflects not only the real interest rate and the expected rate of inflation, but, moreover, the payment of a risk premium (because of inflation).
4. If some commodities are not durable goods, contrary to gold, they have to be exchanged against national currencies, with the consequences we have seen.

4 Competing Monies, European Monetary Union and the Dollar

BENJAMIN KLEIN

Since I am going to criticise the All Saints' Day Manifesto (see p. 37-43 and the attempt to achieve European monetary union by the creation of a parallel European currency, I should explicitly state at the outset that I am very sympathetic to the major thrust of the proposal. First of all, it represents an increased understanding and awareness that we must move towards a more predictable monetary framework. In addition, it clearly recognizes the economic forces that exist in favour of the establishment of a single unified currency within an interdependent trade area such as the European community.

Unfortunately, however, much of my previous work on competing monies suggests that large-scale voluntary public adoption of a new parallel currency such as the proposed Europa is highly unlikely. Although the intended reliance on market forces rather than government edicts to determine the quantity of this new money is consistent with the spirit of my earlier work, the Manifesto greatly simplifies and thereby misunderstands the nature of the competitive process in the market for monies. In particular, important analytical distinctions between monetary stability and monetary predictability, between interest bearing and non-interest bearing money, between money used as a medium of exchange or unit of account and money used as a store of value, and between a dominant domestic money and an international money, are either ignored or blurred. This incomplete theoretical analysis leads to faulty empirical conclusions and policy recommendations.

Advocates of this proposal for a new competitive money believe that because the Europa is to be price indexed and hence inflation-proofed, it will quickly drive the European national currencies out of circulation. Historical evidence suggests this will not be the case. On the contrary, monetary confidence and hence new dominant monies evolve very slowly in the market place and are not easily substitutable once established. The Manifesto basically confuses the inflation problem and the problem of achieving monetary integration. The benefits of a monetary reform establishing rules of money supply growth which would produce a stable price level are, I believe, enormous. But this

I am grateful to Lynne Schneider for research assistance and to the Foundation for Research in Economics and Education for financial support. Useful comments on an earlier draft were made at a seminar at the Federal Reserve Bank of St Louis.

does not imply that European monetary union can be readily accomplished by the introduction and market adoption of a new currency with these characteristics.

I. INFLATION COMPETITION: STABILITY vs UNCERTAINTY

When considering competition between alternative monies it is crucial to distinguish between the mean and the variance of the inflation, or the average level of inflation and the predictability of inflation, in terms of the alternative monies. In the international context in which we are discussing these issues, competition between monies does not occur primarily on the basis of the average inflation rates of the different monies but on the basis of the variance or predictability of these inflation rates.

If it were a low inflation rate rather than a highly predictable inflation rate that was the driving competitive force in this market, we would expect gold, with its significant increase in real purchasing power over the past seven years, to be an important, if not dominant, competing money. This is, of course, far from the reality of the current situation. In fact, the high volatility of the real exchange value of gold over the recent past has demonetized it to such an extent that gold is now essentially just a commodity like any other internationally traded commodity. A fundamental determinant of a money's liquidity services is the predictability of its future exchange value in terms of real goods and services. Gold is now highly illiquid in this regard, and therefore not a major competing money.[1]

The reason the average inflation rate does not appear to be an important competitive force is because much of the money stock, broadly defined, yields a competitive rate of interest. Demand is therefore invariant to the anticipated inflation rate. This leads us to our second important distinction between interest bearing money and non-interest bearing money. It is only currency and bank reserves, i.e. high-powered money, which do not yield interest and therefore may be expected to possibly be demand-sensitive to varying inflation rates.

Recent empirical work indicates that in the United States bank deposits can usefully be assumed to be paying implicit competitive interest (see Klein, 1974b) and I would expect this also to be the case for liabilities issued by banking institutions located in the highly competitive financial centres of Europe. Euro-dollar deposits, for example, have essentially zero high-powered money backing and yield a market rate of interest.[2] We, therefore, should expect such dollar denominated deposit holdings to be totally invariant to the US inflation rate. Dollar price uncertainty and not the level of the dollar inflation rate is what is theoretically relevant as a determinant of demand.

Although short-term dollar liabilities have at times, especially during 1973-4, yielded negative *ex post* real rates, this was due to an unanticipated dollar inflation, i.e., it was produced not by inflation but by inflation uncertainty.[3]

The Europa's promise of a zero ex post real return represents a benefit to holders not because it promises no inflation, but because it promises no unanticipated inflation. That is, for the large interest-bearing element of the money stock it is the predictability of the proposed Europa's inflation rate and not the promise that the inflation rate is zero that is important for potential holders.

It is this type of competition between market interest bearing monies on the basis of inflation predictability that I originally outlined in my 'Competitive Supply of Money' article (Klein 1974a). I assumed there that alternative monies paid a competitive interest rate and were therefore completely hedged for the expected inflation rate in terms of the various monies. But the real demand for a particular firm's money output was assumed to be a positive function of the consumer confidence in the money, measured by the degree of future price predictability in terms of the money. I also assumed that all money producing firms were price takers in a perfectly competitive market for monetary services. In the context of this theoretical framework any increase in price uncertainty, created for example by an unanticipated increase in money, produces an increase in the real implicit price of monetary services and drives the individual firm's demand to zero. This implied a new type of Gresham's Law, namely that 'high confidence or strong monies will drive out low confidence or weak monies'. What it means for a currency to be 'strong' in this framework is not a low average inflation rate, but a low degree of uncertainty around that expected mean rate.

The empirical evidence for the existence of this inflation uncertainty competitive mechanism is generally weak. One difficulty in isolating the effect is that the two distinct elements of inflation, its average rate and its predictability, are generally highly positively correlated. This is, however, not always the case, as the recent experience with gold clearly indicates.

The recent international experience with the dollar may also provide some evidence for the price uncertainty competitive effect. The acceleration of the dollar inflation rate in 1965-6 (when dollar price level uncertainty was still low by historical standards) does not appear to have significantly reduced the international demand for dollars. Rather, it appears to be the increase in dollar price uncertainty, espcially the increase in long-term price uncertainty in the later 1960s, that influenced the international demand for dollars. The evidence regarding the much greater substitution away from dollars to marks for use in long-term contracts compared to the substitution from dollars to marks as a reserve asset is also evidence for the recent rise in long-term relative to short-term dollar price level uncertainty.[4]

Another major difficulty in establishing the existence of the inflation uncertainty competitive effect is theoretical. As indicated above (Klein 1974a), in a perfectly competitive money supply framework a currency such as the Europa could be expected to drive the demand for other (price uncertain) monies to zero. But in the real world where money supplying firms do not face perfectly elastic demand schedules for monetary services, an increase in price predictability has theoretical ambiguous effects on the demand for money.[5] If we assume that the monetary service flow is proportional to the real stock of money held, then the predicted relationship between price uncertainty and money demand is related to the price (interest) elasticity of demand for money. Since the domestic demand for money is generally interest inelastic, the predicted relationship is positive, which is what we, in fact, find to be the case for the US over the last century (when price uncertainty is measured by variability) and for Brazil over the postwar period.[6] Only in the German hyperinflation experience has this effect been measured as zero.[7]

The competitive (or negative) effect has not, as yet, been systematically measured because we have concentrated our estimates on domestic money demand functions. The international demand for monetary services from alternative monies is likely to be much more interest elastic than the domestic demand and therefore we would expect to find this competitive effect.[8] The Europa, however, is intended to compete not only in the international money market, but also to replace monies used domestically. In each separate national market the fact that the Europa supposedly will have zero price uncertainty is not sufficient to drive out of existence the established dominant monies. In fact, because the established monies have interest inelastic demands, theoretical and empirical results suggest that increased price uncertainty will actually increase money demand.[9]

II. COMPETITIVE CURRENCIES

The fact that the proposed Europa will have a zero inflation rate may appear to be an important competitive factor in dislodging these national monies. Since national currencies, as opposed to deposits, are non-interest bearing and individuals holding them are paying an inflation tax, we would expect this element of monetary demand to be sensitive to alternative inflation rates. We therefore would also expect some switching by individuals in an inflationary environment to an indexed currency such as the proposed Europa. Unfortunately the degree of competition that is assumed to exist by the signers of the Manifesto is far from an accurate description of the real world.

For example, Fratianni and Peeters, in a memo written for this conference, state that: 'It is clear that a national currency that is subject to an inflation tax cannot co-exist with an inflation-proofed Europa.' This proposition, however, is not so clear. It depends upon the implicit assumption that alternative monies are perfect substitutes, which must be determined empirically.[10] And, on the contrary, the historical evidence I am aware of suggests the exact opposite conclusion.

The switching by the public to a new medium of exchange appears to be highly inelastic to the currency's inflation rate. Even in the extreme cases of the post-World War I hyperinflations or in the moderately rapid but decades-long Latin American inflations, individuals did not switch to competing currencies. Although in these cases individuals often drastically reduced their real holdings of the inflating currency, competing currencies were not held as alternative media of exchange.

One might want to argue that in certain cases competing currencies do not develop because of government regulations prohibiting their existence. Yet it is difficult to believe that legal restrictions, including legal tender requirements, are really very effective competitive contraints.[11] There is much historical evidence in other areas that price controls and trade restraints are, in general, evaded at least partially, even if attempts are made to enforce them strictly. In any case, the evidence suggests that there was no significant black market pressure towards substitute media of exchange. Cagan (1950, p. 101) notes that of the seven hyperinflations he studied, only for 1923 Germany did substantial amounts of unauthorized currencies issued by local governments and private organisations circulate. But, unbelievable as it may seem, these illegal substitute currencies were denominated in the hyperinflating unit! Also, Barro's (1972) estimates of the fraction of transactions conducted without domestic money during hyperinflation, that is conducted with a substitute money *or by barter*, are quite low. For example, at an inflation rate of 10 per cent *per month* this fraction was only 0.05.[12]

A careful distinction must be made between the use of money as a store of value and the use of money as a medium of exchange. It is quite clear that during these hyperinflations large quantities of foreign currencies (e.g. dollars and pounds) were illegally held as stores of values.[13] There is also some essentially anecdotal evidence cited by Graham that the foreign monies gradually began to be used as units of account in Germany. I suspect that such large amounts of foreign exchange were held not only because they were a hedge against inflation (any unregulated interest-bearing foreign or domestic asset could have served this function better), but because each of these countries also happened to be politically unstable. In this sort of climate, it is understandable that individuals would wish to be uncharacteristically liquid in a stable country's currency.

In any event, foreign monies were not held in these cases to satisfy a medium of exchange demand for money. The evidence appears to indicate that what is generally used as a medium of exchange is highly inelastic to the inflation rate. Perhaps this is because the decision to change what is used as the commonly accepted medium of exchange must involve a large subset of the population and hence implies very large transaction costs. Such social agreements and customs are therefore very costly to change rapidly, even if the immediate benefits to each individual separately appear large (cf. Tullock, 1975).

To sum up, we have seen that in order to make analytical sense of the argument that competitive substitution towards an alternative money is dependent upon the level of the inflation rate, we must concentrate solely on the currency or non-interest-bearing high-powered element of money. In that case, however, the substitution argument becomes empirically trivial. Once a dominant money is established, the medium of exchange demand appears to be essentially nonsubstitutable in a very wide number of circumstances. The empirical evidence therefore indicates that there does not appear to be a great deal of pressure, if any at all, towards substitutability of competing monies, either on the basis of price stability or price predictability. Hence the concern that a European parallel currency indexed against inflation will be accepted by the market at such a rapid rate that it will quickly drive out all non-indexed national monies and hence create political difficulties is completely unfounded.[14] What is much more likely is that the Europa will not be accepted at all. The existence of any significant amount of competitive switching between dominant monies has not, as yet, been empirically verified and, in fact, there is much evidence to the contrary within a wide band of non-crisis situations. The analysis of the potential attractiveness of a European parallel currency which largely considers differential yields of alternative monies to reach a conclusion of rapid and wide acceptance, completely ignores the overwhelming empirical evidence on the degree of rigidity that historically is present in these matters.

III. MONETARY CONFIDENCE AND SEIGNIORAGE

One reason for rigidity in accepting new monies is the importance of consumer confidence in a money, i.e. the credibility of the money issuer in fulfiling explicit or implicit promises regarding supply. And monetary confidence cannot be created overnight merely by an announcement of a promise regarding future behaviour. It must be built up gradually with successful performance over time.

Although the Europa Manifesto explicitly rejects the unrealistic assumption that a parallel currency and European monetary union can be created by official edict, it does appear to assert that such a goal can be accomplished in the market place fairly easily, by merely issuing a new money of stable purchasing power. Economists, often meeting in very pleasant places, have too frequently believed their textbook assertions that money merely is whatever 'society' (operationally defined as the relevant policy-maker) wishes it to be. Much of the discussion of international monetary reform, the creation of new monies, and the distribution of seigniorage suffers from this naïveté.

While the signers of the Manifesto claim not to rely on legalistic edicts, they make a similar error by assuming that a new fiat currency can evolve quite quickly in the market place as long as the issuer makes the right promise – in this case a promise to stabilize prices. As I have stated in detail elsewhere (Klein 1978), institutions are not perfectly malleable and a real effective market demand for a money cannot be produced by official proclamations. Demand depends upon the existence of consumer confidence on the money, which is costly to create. A low stated price of the money, either in the form of a low inflation rate or direct interest payments, is not sufficient to assure its acceptance. As the recent New York City experience vividly illustrates, official promises can always be withdrawn and market participants generally want more than governmental assurances at a particular moment.[15]

How monetary confidence is created is not a question we now have a precise answer to. It is crucial, however, to recognise in our analysis that the question is important and that reliable information about anticipated performance is costly to produce. Consumer confidence therefore is not a free good that can be created by mere assertion. Commodity money, for example, produces consumer confidence by placing a physical constraint on money production and hence on the possible unanticipated depreciation. 'Guaranteed' convertibility of a money into a commodity (or into another more predictable money) is another way to obtain consumer confidence. Any stocks of the commodity (or the high confidence money) held as reserves to increase that assurance should also be considered an investment (or what I have called a 'brand name' capital outlay) by the money supplier in building confidence in its 'brand name money'. And any institutional framework established to make these 'guarantees' more credible is also part of the investment in consumer confidence. This is the 'monetary constitution' question, largely ignored in the Europa Manifesto.

Most importantly, the major ways in which monetary confidence is produced is by successful past performance, i.e. a high confidence money evolves very gradually in the market place. Since the Europa has no history we would expect it initially to possess a very low level of consumer confidence, or a very high prior variance on the estimated anticipated rate of price change in terms of this money. Even after a short period of successful performance, with zero price inflation and zero price change variability, it is highly unlikely to expect long-term price change uncertainty for the Europa to be zero.

Once we assume a realistic world of positive information costs, money-supplying firms have a reputation of a finite value which I analytically identify as the firm's 'brand name capital'. And seigniorage is then just a normal rate of return on this brand name capital asset. It is this seigniorage return which makes it costly for a money supplier to 'mess up', i.e. to have an unanticipated inflation. In such a situation the brand name capital would depreciate, producing a downward shift in the demand schedule facing the firm and therefore implying a loss of future seigniorage. This is an operative competitive constraint or firm 'cost' on 'cheating' behaviour for all products where consumer pre-purchase quality determination information costs are positive.

The important theoretical point is that even under so-called fiduciary monetary arrangements, where money is costlessly produced on the margin, confidence-creating costs cannot arbitrarily be considered to be zero. To more fully understand the presence of brand name costs within the context of a fiduciary money system, it is necessary to think of these monetary confidence costs as the costs of 'selling' rather then 'producing' real cash balances. The fact that it is costless to 'add a zero', i.e. that the marginal cost of producing nominal money can reasonably be assumed to be zero, implies nothing about the marginal cost of creating real cash balances. Failure to distinguish between these two costs is a general problem present in the optimum quantity of money literature.[16]

Since *real* cash balances are not a control variable in a money-producing firm's production function, but rather are determined on the demand side, it is difficult to conceptualize 'the marginal cost of real cash balances'. A useful way to think of this theoretically is to start with the public's demand for 'monetary services' which implies a derived demand for 'monetary confidence' (similar to the derived demand for entrepreneurial services for any commodity). Given this demand for confidence, the marginal cost of producing confidence (for example, holding gold stocks, maintaining an army and police force, or expending resources on any other inputs, such as a marble edifice or an impressive vault, which create confidence capital) implies an equilibrium quantity of confidence and thus a demand for real cash balances function.

These confidence-creating selling costs are generally overhead or fixed costs with marginal production costs equal to zero. That is, it is generally costless for a fiduciary money supplier to increase the quantitiy of real cash balances by lowering the price of alternative cost of holding his money. The problems associated with this socially optimal policy are similar to those associated with all regulated natural monopolies – price equal to marginal cost implies that costs are not covered, i.e. price is less than average cost, and there is no profit incentive for the supplier to do a good job. In fact, there is a short-run profit incentive to do a poor job, in this case by overissuing.[17]

On the contrary, if the price of the money is set at a positive level so that seigniorage is earned, the money supplier now has something to lose (future seigniorage) if he 'messes up'. An unanticipated increase in the nominal quantity of a competitive firm's money now implies a cost to that money supplier of the loss of consumer confidence and resulting fall in his demand. This implies that consumers paying seigniorage are *necessarily* purchasing some quality assurance. Brand name capital is a form of collateral and seigniorage is equivalent to an insurance premium – paid not only to pool risks, but to decrease risks.[18]

Therefore, more generally, given information costs about future performance, monetary confidence or 'brand names' will have value independent of any explicit confidence-creating expenditures. Consumer demand for collateral or 'backing' would necessarily imply a positive price or alternative cost of holding money such that a normal rate of return is earned on the residually measured intangible brand name capital. This 'profit' stream or seigniorage can also be thought of as a cost to the money supplier of selling the real cash balances at the anticipated price rather than depreciating the monetary brand name. In a dynamic context the money supplier always has the alternative cost of 'selling' this real asset by intentional depreciation, i.e. by unanticipated money supply growth, thereby increasing short-run profit in exchange for lower long-run or steady state profit.[19]

Failure to explicitly consider these confidence costs results in misleading analysis and policy conclusions. This is especially the case in the international monetary area where monetary confidence remains a significant problem but where Utopian schemes for reform often ignore these costs. For example, Harry

Johnson (1969b) presents an obvious case of such an intellectual experiment which abstracts from these real world information costs and thereby produces misleading conclusions when analysing the social saving from substituting 'credit' for 'commodity' money.[20]

Johnson implicitly assumes that confidence capital has a zero cost of creation and maintenance. It would, of course, be nice if the world were different and scarcity were eliminated, but given the world in which we live a group of economists and policy-makers cannot merely get together and costlessly change informational constraints. These constraints are analytically similar to physical or technological constraints on the production process. In his analysis, for example, commodity money is considered to be merely a deadweight social cost and fiduciary money is merely a costless social invention which someone happens to think of. But if the confidence necessary to sell fiduciary money costs as much or more to produce as the commodity, then the social saving of substituting the credit money for the commodity money would be zero or negative. If, on the contrary, confidence is, as Johnson assumes, costless under a credit money arrangement, the obvious historical question is why credit money did not replace commodity before it did. A reasonable explanation cannot be that someone did not happen to think of the credit money idea. This is clearly untrue since many firms and countries tried unsuccessfully to introduce credit money quite early. Rather, reasonable explanation is that commodity money was, at the time, the cheapest way to produce confidence. For example, a forced movement from commodity to pure fiduciary money in the 19th century would have implied a negative social saving.

Grubel (1969) using an analysis very similar to Johnson in discussing the distribution of seigniorage from the creation of a fiat money 'acceptable to all countries in the settlement of debts' by a supranational agency, makes the crucial implicit assumption somewhat more transparent when he asserts that 'money is what society want it to be: precious metals, stones, coins, paper currency, demand deposits, saving accounts, negotiable paper, etc. Any of these instruments can serve the purposes of money as a medium of exchange and store of wealth *if the proper social and economic institutions and conventions exist.*' (p. 270, emphasis supplied.) The last phrase, of course, begs the important question of whether monetary confidence costs are positive or not. It is common for social reformers to make the assumption that institutions can essentially be altered or new ones developed costlessly, but seldom is it as explicitly stated as by Grubel.

The discussions of international monetary reform and the creation of SDRs (or 'paper gold') have also largely assumed that 'money is merely what society wants it to be' or, more formally, that the IMF has unlimited monetary confidence or brand name capital. The existence of SDRs is predicated on demand or acceptability, which is based on the real value of IMF brand name capital. That is, given flexible exchange rates, the IMF can make the *nominal* quantity of SDRs whatever it wishes. However, even if SDRs were a reserve currency, the *real* quantity outstanding is determined, like all monies, on the demand side. All this real demand is partially determined by the IMF's brand name or monetary confidence capital.

A stationary equilibrium market measure of the IMF's *limited* real brand name capital can be obtained by multiplying the difference between 'the' market interest rate and the rate that is paid on SDRs, by the real value of the SDRs 'in circulation'.[21] This finite value of the brand name of SDRs is largely based not on the confidence and coercion capital possessed by the IMF, but to a large extent on the brand name monetary confidence capital of the US and its willingness to accept SDRs.[22] In any event, it is this real, but intangible, brand name asset in the portfolio of the issuing institution that 'matches' the outstanding liabilities. Real SDRs cannot be merely 'created outright', i.e. net wealth cannot be created out of nothing.

It is this real IMF brand name asset, made visible by official international transactions, which also places a constraint on the real supply of SDRs outstanding. Given the real value of the brand name asset in steady state equilibrium and the market rate of interest, the real value of SDRs can only be increased if the IMF increases the interest it pays on SDRs, i.e. only if it increases real demand. Alternatively, if the real value of SDRs increases in the short run without an increase in the interest paid on SDRs, this implies that the brand name capital is depreciating. Current real profit has increased, but this is not sustainable. Future real profit must decrease to keep the present discounted value of real profit, or the given initial real brand name capital, unchanged. This short-run unsustained increase in real money which represents the depreciation (or 'sale') by a money supplier of some of its monetary brand name capital in international exchange, is the only theoretically meaningful definition of a balance-of-payments 'deficit' under fixed exchange rates. Operationally this can only be measured by pressure on the exchange rate and not by any essentially arbitrary measures of financial flows.

But more of this later. For now the major relevant point is both simple and obvious: we should not assume that a money, especially a newly proposed money, possesses unlimited monetary confidence and that its demand and market share will therefore depend solely on its current price or the inflation rate in terms of the money. The Europa proposal is therefore 'Utopian' and similar to other academic analyses that assume institutional and informational constraints can be altered costlessly.

IV. MONEY AS A NATURAL MONOPOLY AND "THE SNAKE"

The large fixed cost and small or zero marginal cost of creating money suggests that the money industry is essentially a natural monopoly or that it is economically efficient for there to be a single money within a trade area. I therefore agree completely with the Manifesto's presumption that European monetary union has large potential economic benefits. What is unfortunate, however, is that this proposition can only be supported by vague analogies to the gains of a monetary versus a barter economy. The simple fact is that although Mundell lucidly stated the theoretical problem of optimum currency areas more than fifteen years ago, definitive theoretical work has not been done to establish the costs that are present in a flexible multiple money arrangement.[23]

Basically the problem is that the theoretical microeconomic (information-transaction cost) foundation for the existence of money is still lacking. Instead of solely relying on the obvious increased computational and money conversion costs of a multiple money system, I think it is more persuasive to examine the historical evidence in this area. The evidence indicates that monetary arrangements have almost always consisted of a single money or of multiple monies convertible into a single dominant money.[24] The only important example I am aware of where distinct monies circulated side-by-side domestically at flexible exchange rates for any significant length of time is the flexible bimetallic (silver and copper) exchange standard that existed in China from about 1650 to 1850.[25] The only other multi-currency examples that can be cited are brief, atypical, wartime or postwar arrangements such as the simultaneous circulation of gold and greenbacks in the United States during the Civil War.[26]

This suggests that there are large economic gains from a common money and the growing interdependence among the countries of Western Europe and also the United States and Japan should only increase the economic pressure towards the establishment of a single dominant money. It is the very fact that cases of competing currencies or multiple monies circulating within the trade area are so rare, if at all existing, that is the strongest element in the economic case for a unified money. But it is also this fact which suggests that a new parallel currency such as the Europa is not likely to be successful.

It is also important to recognize that the benefits from a unified money cannot readily be achieved by a fixed exchange rate arrangement among multiple monies unless one of the monies is designated as the dominant money into which all the others are convertible. The 'snake', which did not specify such a dominant money in terms of which the other members would have had to maintain convertibility, was therefore destined to fail. Without such an asymetric relationship, it is necessary for the members of the arrangement to coordinate policies and establish explicit rules regarding whose responsibility it is to adjust.

If a community reserve fund, for example, is established to keep the snake within required bounds then this implies that low inflation or surplus countries would be partially financing the balance-of-payment deficits of the more inflationary countries. Once surplus countries even partially assume responsibility for adjustment, a competitive incentive is established for each country to inflate more rapidly than the other countries. This produces a deficit in the country's trade clearing accounts with the other countries, financed at least in part by the increased holdings by the other countries of its money – or a trade of its costlessly produced money for the real goods and services of the other countries. [27]

The European Monetary Co-operation Fund (FECOM) established for multilateral currency intervention to maintain the snake parities had much too small a reserve base to have any significant effect in this regard and surplus countries had to rather quickly temporarily float their currencies or readjust their exchange rates. The fact that Germany has accumulated the major portion of the European Community's international reserve holdings, however, indicates that this competitive force may have been present to some extent.[28] In addition, there have been discussions regarding the expansion of FECOM. Much of this discussion centres on the establishment of explicit bureaucratic rules governing adjustment responsibility. But all of these rules are essentially arbitrary guidelines based on objective but misleading financial flows and not as easily enforceable as a dominant money arrangement. In particular, the movement to a so-called gliding parities arrangement is likely to be less disruptive than the abrupt changes that have occurred in official exchange rates within the snake in the past, but are certainly not fixed exchange rates and represent a movement away from European monetary union.

The disruption that has occurred within the snake and its ultimate failure clearly indicates the difference between fixed exchange rates and rates that are 'convincingly' pegged as part of a currency area. Rates may be temporarily 'fixed' while the anticipated probability of an exchange rate change be significant, i.e. rates are merely 'fixed' between expected readjustments.[29] This essential continuum between fixed and flexible exchange rates is obvious, for example, when comparing the dollar exchange rates of the yen and mark to the dollar exchange rates of the pound and French franc over the 1951-71 'fixed' exchange rate period. At the extreme, a single money, by eliminating even the possibility of an exchange rate change, represents the most predictable 'fixed' rate arrangement along this more general continuum of fixed versus flexible systems.[30] In any event, the snake, with its many exchange rate changes due to lack of monetary coordination, was very far indeed from a European optimum currency area arrangement.

What remains of the snake is essentially a deutschmark currency area, with four currencies (the Netherlands guilder, the Belgian franc, the Danish krone and the Norwegian krone) now tied with varying degrees of predictability to a *de facto* dominant mark. The deutschmark is, of course, the obvious candidate for a European dominant money and as the centre point of an expanded workable snake arrangement. Perhaps if World War II had not occurred and its residual hostility were not present this could even be a distinct possibility for the future. Meanwhile, what remains of this experiment in European monetary coordination is this residual deutschmark area and increased European capital controls, put in place over the last six years in an unsuccessful attempt to maintain uneconomic fixed rates.[31]

V. THE INTERNATIONAL DOLLAR STANDARD AND EUROPEAN 'FREE-RIDING'

A dominant money is necessary if effective European monetary coordination is to exist. And if this money is not to be the mark, the obvious alternative is the dollar. European adoption of a dominant dollar standard is therefore a logical and practical way to effect European monetary union. The essential economic benefit of a monetary union could readily be obtained by fixing convertibility of each of the European national currencies at a given exchange rate into a dominant US dollar and permitting denomination of European bank deposits in dollars. In fact, much of the post-World War II period can be described as a movement towards such an international dollar standard. We would, I think, be continuing to move at a rapid rate in this direction if the US had not 'messed up' in the late 1960s and early 1970s by producing a large unanticipated increase in the dollar money supply. It was this unanticipated money supply increase and the corresponding large 'involuntary' holdings of dollar reserves by some European central banks (and Japan) to maintain dollar parity that effectively halted the move to an international dollar standard and produced the political and economic forces for the creation of a substitute, independent European monetary unit such as the Europa.

But it is more important to recognize that the dollar standard did, in a sense, give the Europeans the best of both worlds. They had some of the major benefits of a unified currency area without having to give up the seigniorage on the currency stock which the Europa proposal would largely require. The inflation tax on high-powered money, rather than necessarily being socially inefficient, is likely to be part of an optimal tax package. Given real transaction and distortion costs of levying and collecting all taxes, we would expect an excise tax on money holdings to be part of an efficient general equilibrium tax scheme, especially since the demand for high-powered money is price (interest) inelastic.[32]

What, then can we learn about the international dollar standard to help us explain US behaviour beginning in the late 1960s that destroyed the momentum towards effective world monetary union? Some obvious, but often neglected points, should be made at the outset. First, the dollar gained its dominant international position not by legalistic coercion, but voluntarily in the market place. No US governmental authority forces foreign individuals to hold dollar denominated deposits and to use the dollar as an international unit of account, medium of exchange, or store of value. The United States has its current international monetary position not because of artificially imposed governmental regulations, but primarily because of its past and prospective performance.[33]

Secondly, although competitive switching to a new dominant money is costly and will generally proceed very slowly, the US dollar's dominant position is not exogenous but can also be lost in the competitive market place. While formal international monetary models assume that the dominant money supplier can make its money supply whatever it wishes and is not subject to a balance of payments constraint, a reserve currency such as the United States is limited by the same competitive forces outlined above with regard to SDRs. These forces were analytically represented by a given finite value of real brand capital and the possibility of a short-run 'deficit' in the sense of depreciation of this capital. If the depreciation proceeds far enough, the country could, in the long run, lose its valuable reserve currency position. Although the dollar brand name has depreciated over the last decade due to unexpectedly poor inflation performance, the dollar does still remain as the primary international currency. However, as the fortunes of the pound over the last two centuries vividly illustrates, this position is certainly not a perpetual right.

The limited, depreciating value of the dollar brand name capital, evidenced by the recent movement out of dollars as a reserve currency and the implied foregone future profit or seigniorage, essentially is the balance-of-payments constraint under which the United States is currently operating. Seen in this context, concern by the US for its balance-of-payments position, correctly defined, is legitimate because it represents a loss of future seigniorage. This is analytically analogous to the concern of a business firm for its credit rating and therefore its future borrowing ability.

While there is no outside authority (e.g. a foreign central bank) willing to maintain the market price (exchange rate) of, for example, General Motors bonds, an unanticipated increase in the supply of these bonds produces a capital loss on previous bond holders similar to the capital loss imposed on dollar holders under flexible exchange rates. This policy will damage GM's future borrowing ability and at the extreme will lead to a complete destruction of the credit rating or bankruptcy, analytically similar to a policy of hyper-inflation by a money supplier. The existence of fixed exchange rates for a dominant money supplier merely creates the possibility of an added short-run wealth gain as foreigners temporarily 'involuntarily' accumulate reserves in an attempt to maintain the exchange rate commitment in the face of unanticipated dominant money increases. But under fixed or flexible exchange rates this 'deficit' or depreciation of monetary brand name confidence capital is costly. It implies the loss of future seigniorage represented by a greater rate of interest that must be paid on any given level of outstanding financial liabilities issued in the future.

The concern by the United States for its balance-of-payments position is, of course, contrary to most current economic thinking on the matter. It is commonly held that there is no reason why a reserve currency country such as the United States should, for example, create transitory unemployment to correct a balance-of-payments deficit. Such a deficit must be adjusted to by other countries in the form of their increased holdings of dollars, an increase in their money supply and a more rapid inflation rate, or by appreciation of their currency. This 'benign neglect' or passive international policy, originally stated by Haberler and Willett (1971) ignores the possibility of the loss of reserve currency position by the United States and the associated costs of the loss of future seigniorage. The United States should especially be concerned with its balance-of-payments position if international disequilibrium as existed in the late 1960s and early 1970s causes other countries to search for a new dominant money such as the proposed Europa and thereby leads to a substantial reduction in the international demand for dollars.

The United States has, in fact, followed the Haberler and Willett prescription since 1971 and appears to be slowly losing its dominant position, primarily to the Deutschmark and Swiss franc.[34] The empirical evidence indicates that the US balance-of-payments deficit significantly entered the US money supply reaction function negatively over the 1955-71 period when fixed exchange rates and a dollar reserve currency arrangement supposedly implied that the United States should have been unconcerned about its balance-of-payments position. Since 1971, however, the balance of payments has not entered the US money supply reaction function significantly.[35]

This period since 1971 can be thought of as one of disinvestment or consumption by the United States of its international monetary confidence capital. And, as we shall see, such a policy may, in fact, have been rational, i.e. wealth-maximising, for the United States. The seigniorage earned on foreign holdings of high-powered dollars should be thought of as payment by foreigners for the use of US monetary confidence and as a normal return on the dollar brand name capital. As already indicated, however, this seigniorage was extremely low under the *de facto* dollar standard because competitive foreign commercial banks and governments essentially obtained a 'free ride' on the dollar brand name by denominating bank deposits in dollars and by tying their currency to the dollar without being required to hold non-interest bearing dollar reserves against these liabilities. Foreign official and private holdings of 'dollars' consist primarily of US Treasury securities or of interest bearing Euro-dollar deposits which are essentially unbacked by high-powered dollar reserves.[36]

This 'free ride' is, of course, not complete because a foreign currency, even if tied quite convincingly to the dollar, is still distinct from the dollar and possesses a non-trivial probability of an exchange rate change.[37] And a Euro-dollar deposit is not identical to a US dollar deposit since, for one thing, neither the FDIC nor the US Federal Reserve has an obligation nor is likely to protect a foreign banking institution from failure.[38] Therefore Europeans did not get all the benefits of a currency area. But the free ride was rather close to being complete and, considering the differential cost of supplying these Euro-dollar substitutes, represented a major financial innovation – from the holders point of view.

From the point of view of the United States, however, this 'free ride' represented an attempt by foreigners to evade the seigniorage payment and may rationally explain why the United States may have intentionally depreciated the international brand name value of the dollar via the unexpectedly high inflation rate over the last decade. Because the growth in the 1960s of these competitive substitutes for the US dollar such as Euro-dollar deposits significantly reduced the per dollar seigniorage earned by the United States in supplying the dominant money, it also significantly reduced the incentive on the US to 'do a good job' (the fear of the loss of future seigniorage on this dollar base). In fact, these international institutional arrangements created a profit incentive for the United States to produce an unexpectedly rapid inflation and thereby make a large short-run profit. Wealth maximisation would dictate a short-run policy of deception and intentional depreciation of the dollar brand name since the longer-run reduced profit consequences would be minor. If the expected steady state seigniorage return is small, then little is being given up in the future with such a policy.

While the United States engages in short-run unexpected inflation, foreign (surplus country) governments accumulate dollar balances in an attempt to maintain the fixed exchange rate. This foreign sterilsation in the face of a balance-of-trade surplus implies a trade of foreign consumption and investment goods for dollar balances and an implicit transfer of wealth away from foreigners to US consumers. The purchase of US dollars by foreign central banks at incorrect (non-market) prices is a speculative activity that represents an implicit tax on foreign citizens, collected in part by US citizens.[39]

These are, of course, my conjectures. I am not claiming that this wealth transfer is necessarily conscious US policy, but merely that such a short-run policy is likely to be wealth-maximizing for the United States under current international seigniorage arrangements. Hence it is a policy that will be more likely to survive politically. If the insurance premium (seigniorage) is not paid by consumers then the money producer has nothing to lose if he 'messes up' and he should therefore sell his collateral (brand name capital) by international deception. The 'benign neglect' prescription makes some economic sense from a narrow US point of view, but certainly not from a larger world social welfare point of view. We may expect US monetary authorities to be relatively unconcerned about such 'free rides' in the dollar brand name on the part of domestic banking institutions such as non-member commercial banks and other domestic financial institutions not required to hold high powered dollar reserves. Since real cash balances are costless to produce on the margin, it is efficient to let the price of money fall by such domestic innovations. But in the international market there is a much smaller political incentive to forego such returns for the greater (global) social good.

VI. CONCLUDING COMMENTS

It is the recent unanticipated, and perhaps intentional, dollar inflation which is the primary economic motivation for the European break with the dollar (i.e. the explicit movement to flexible dollar exchange rates) and for the pressure to create a European substitute for the dollar standard.[40] If the dollar inflation rate did not fluctuate unpredictably there would have been little justification and therefore demand for the creation of the Europa. As noted above, the dollar seigniorage return was relatively small under the international dollar standard. In addition, although European countries (especially Germany) largely gave up the ability to engage in short-run independent macroeconomic stabilization policy, I agree with the Manifesto that such independent monetary policy cannot influence long-run unemployment and, as a practical matter, will only produce a political business cycle and increase the long-run inflation rate. If the Manifesto's arguments are correct that little will be given up by each of the European countries in adopting the Europa, then they are also correct with regard to adoption of the dollar as the dominant money.

What the Europeans would also give up with the adoption of a dollar standard is some 'national identity'. This may seem to be 'merely psychological', but such nationalistic forces are not necessarily irrational and represent perhaps the strongest argument against not the dollar but the Europa. The desire by countries to maintain their individual national currencies is so strong because control of a nation's money supply has important national defence implications. Such control carries with it the ability to quickly gain control of a significant quantity of the country's resources. It represents a very large potential tax that can be levied quickly and collected in a broad-based and efficient way, without short-run market or democratic tests.[41] Therefore it is unlikely that national currencies will be given up, as the Europa scheme ultimately requires, until national sovereignty is given up.

Once again the dollar standard potentially gives the Europeans the best of both worlds. By maintaining their individual national currencies they not only continue to collect the seigniorage tax which is likely to be an important element in an efficient national tax package, but also to maintain monetary sovereignty and the ability to inflate rapidly and float in times of national crises. All this is preserved while obtaining the major benefits of a unified currency area.

But the international dollar standard is now essentially moribund due to recent US inflationary behaviour. As we have seen, it is in the very nature of a dominant money for there to be an enormous profit incentive to inflate. Once the dominant money is established, demand is highly inelastic. For example, Cagan's (1950, p. 81) estimates of the constant (and therefore anticipated) rate of change in the qunatity of money and prices that would maximise the government's revenue in hyperinflation ranged from 12 to 54 per cent *per month.* This is, of course, the profit maximising rate determined where the elasticity of demand for real cash balances is -1 and not necessarily the wealth maximising rate. Over time we can expect increased substitution towards alternative monies and therefore a decrease in the demand for the money. But, more importantly, if we allow for unanticipated increases in the money supply, wealth maximisation could, in principle, imply short-run capture of the entire non-human wealth of the economy if there is a lag in the adjustment of prices and of consumer confidence to current unanticipated money supply increases.[42]

Political considerations, rather than purely economic (wealth maximising) considerations, are the effective constraints in this situation. Because of the extreme rigidity present with regard to social choice of a dominant money and the enormous wealth that can be gained by the dominant money supplier with a short-run policy of deception (i.e. unanticipated money supply increase), the private unregulated contractual solution would imply an extremely high 'premium' or seigniorage return. Only in this way would we guarantee by the loss of future demand and therefore future seigniorage that wealth maximisation would imply non-cheating behaviour by the private dominant money supplier. However, because the unregulated non-cheating price will necessarily be extremely high, i.e. the equilibrium seigniorage return will be extremely high, it is unlikely that the private contractual solution is the most efficient arrangement. In particular, some government intervention in the form of regulation or outright nationalisation is likely.[43] And under these circumstances some political – implicit or explicit constitutional – constraints must be placed on the government supply of the dominant money.

It was the absence of such international political constraints that led to the recent unanticipated dollar inflation and wealth transfer to the United States, and if the international dollar standard is ever to become firmly established some such credible political guarantee will have to exist. In retrospect, the dollar-gold convertibility arrangement may turn out to have been the cheapest method of creating this international credibility. Without such an institution a very long period of dollar price level predictability will now be necessary to undo the large loss in dollar confidence produced over the last decade.

Similarly, it is this important question of political or constitutional constraints on the money issuer, largely ignored in the All Saints' Day Manifesto, that is crucial. If a move towards European political unification occurs which will make the Europa feasible, it will be necessary to write a very explicit monetary constitution which does not give much room for discretionary policy except perhaps to fight (or deter) a war. It is important to recognize that once the European dominant money is established and demand becomes highly inelastic, there will be an enormous profit incentive to inflate and debase the currency like all sovereigns have done in the past, no doubt for a worthy cause. In fact, a single established money in Europe would eliminate whatever amount of competition between monies now exists and greatly increase the inflationary incentives. For the Europa proposal to be successful and actually represent a significant step towards a more predictable monetary framework, it will probably be necessary (as the Manifesto suggests) for the European monetary authorities to be relatively independent of the European Parliament and for the monetary rule to be imbedded quite rigidly in the European constitution. But on these essentially political issues economists now know very little. Hopefully in the near future our research will be able to catch up with our proposed policy reforms.

NOTES

1. The United States has recently passed legislation to repeal the 'gold clause' of 1933, which stated that no contract would be enforceable in US courts if it required payment in gold or a dollar equivalent to gold at a fixed gold price. Although it is therefore not legally permissable to index US contracts, both domestic and international, to gold, I would expect very little of such indexing to occur.
2. A very low high-powered dollar reserve ratio is maintained behind Euro-dollar deposits created by European banks in the form of a small desired US dollar deposit to Euro-dollar deposit ratio. These dollar deposits are held by the European banks at US commercial banks (primarily a few New York City institutions) which, in turn, must hold a fraction of this relatively small amount of deposits in non-interest bearing dollar reserves. European branches of US banks, on the other hand, have a 4 per cent reserve requirement set directly on their Euro-dollar deposits by Federal Reserve Regulation M and therefore generally pay less interest than European banks on these deposits. Bergston (1975) estimates that in 1972 only about 10 per cent of US short-term liabilities to foreigners were non-interest bearing.
3. While there appears to be no systematic time series pattern in *ex post* short-term dollar real rates, *ex post* long-term (10-20 year) dollar real rates have been consistently negative over the past 25 years. This is due to the largely unanticipated and very slowly recognised movement over the post-war period from a dollar-gold standard framework to a new fiduciary US monetary framework (see Klein (1975)). This evidence suggests that one cannot simply look at Box-Jenkins measures, i.e. at auto-correlations of errors, to determine if markets are efficient. The problem appears to be that we do not have enought independent observations of such similar fundamental changes in the underlying monetary framework to test if competitive market rates are unbiased estimates. Milton Friedman has convinced me, however, that the efficient markets theory can never, in principle, be tested in this way if one thinks of probability in the purely subjective (Savage) manner.
4. The dollar is still clearly the world's major reserve currency, while more new Euro-bond issues are now denominated in marks than in dollars (see Klein (1975) and (1978a) for operational measures of short-term and long-term dollar price uncertainty).
5. The two effects of an increase in price uncertainty (which lowers the 'quality' or monetary service stream from money) are (1) an increase in the demand for money necessary to produce any given monetary service flow (the substitution in production effect) and (2) a decrease in the demand for money due to an increase in the implicit price of monetary services (the competitive complementarity in consumption effect). See Klein (1977) for the complete theoretical framework.
6. See Klein (1977) and Klein and Teixeira (1977).
7. See Frenkel (1977). Frenkel's observations on price uncertainty are in a different range from my observations in Klein (1977). Since I do state that we should eventually expect the relationship to go from positive to zero and finally to negative as a function of interest elasticity, Frenkel's evidence is not inconsistent with my theory. If the money demand curve is linear we

would expect to be in a more elastic region during hyperinflations and therefore for the measured relationship to be reduced.

8. The existence of this competitive effect implies that a country increasing its money supply in an unanticipated manner will, under flexible exchange rates, export deflation. Such a policy will increase the demand for alternative monies. This is somewhat contrary to the common proposition that under fixed exchange rates such a country would be exporting inflation, while under flexible exchange rates other countries are fully insulated.
9. In the United States, for example, the results indicate that an unanticipated inflation, besides producing a once-and-for-all tax transfer to the government, will also increase future price uncertainty and thereby increase the demand fo money (see Klein (1977)). What places a limit on this possibility of increasing the tax base in the short-run by intentionally creating price uncertainty is the degree of competition, in the sense of the implied elasticity of demand for monetary services. The more important limits on this process are the domestic political constraints, rather than the competitive economic constraints, that are placed on money issuers.
10. This is an implicit assumption that is often made in international trade, often stated as the law of one price applied to assets and formulated as the equality of interest rates across assets adjusting for exchange rate risks. If, however, assets are less than perfect substitutes, this interest parity condition will not necessarily hold in portfolio (stock) equilibrium. For example, even two very similar domestic financial assets, say savings and loan shares and commercial bank time deposits, can exist side by side yielding unequal interest rates because of imperfect substitutability. Certainly the importance of differing non-pecuniary factors will be greater across countries. Equations estimating capital flows between countries therefore perform better when assumed to be related to changes in interest differentials rather than the interest differentials themselves.
11. The designation 'legal tender' means that creditors cannot legally refuse the money as payment for a claim, i.e. they cannot use the courts and police to force discharge of a contract in an alternative money. However, there is much evidence that relatively informal legally unenforceable contractual practices predominate in business and that reliance on explicit legal sanctions is extremely rare. See Klein (1974a, p. 448) and Hayek (1976) for further discussion and references to the historical evidence on the existence of non-legal tender circulating monies. Perhaps the most spectacular example is the Maria Theresa thaler which for more than a century circulated as the principal medium of exchange in the Red Sea area, particularly along the southern coast of the Arabian Peninsula and the Horn of Africa. The thaler was introduced in the Arabian Peninsula through commercial relations in the early 19th century, and remained the dominant unit of account and medium of exchange even though in 1858 it ceased to be legal tender in Austria.
12. On the contrary, the post-World War II German inflation, which was significantly milder than these hyperinflations, was unique in terms of the relative amount of domestic currency that apparently was replaced as a medium of exchange. For a period of time cognac and cigarettes were substituted for the dominant money in almost all transactions. This was, of course, due to the presence of extraordinary price controls that were very

rigidly enforced by the occupying armies, not because of a high inflation rate in terms of the money.

13. Graham (1930) and Bresciani-Turroni (1968) estimate the ratio of foreign to domestic real money holdings in October 1923 Germany to be between five and thirteen. Although reported estimates very a great deal from month to month and are rather unreliable, these figures should give us some general idea of the large magnitude of foreign currencies held. See Statistiches Reichsamt (1924, pp. 69-70) for an account of the German legislation attempting to regulate this large amount of foreign exchange.
14. See, for example, OPTICA Report 1976.
15. During the fixed rate exchange crises of the 1960s and early 1970s it was generally believed that the probability of a change in the official parity was positively related to the number of explicit assurances by the monetary officials that the exchange rate would be maintained.
16. See, for example, Friedman (1969).
17. If the demand for money function is linear we would expect the price elasticity to be highly inelastic in the range near the 'optimum' zero price and therefore for the money supplier to have an especially large short-run profit incentive to overissue his money because price uncertainty will increase real demand. The increase in the real monetary base and decrease in price elasticity increases the short-run profit from over-issuing. The 'optimum quantity of money' may therefore not necessarily be socially optimal if there are added real costs of creating institutions to prevent this short-run monetary deception from occurring. See section V below for further discussion of these issues.
18. See Klein (1978b) for a fuller discussion of these and related issues.
19. An obvious and possibly rational example of this type of intentional depreciation was involved in the decision by England after World War II to adopt a policy of inflation and devaluation, with a resulting loss of pound brand name capital, rather than a policy of a reduced rate of growth of money to 'repay' the borrowings it made against its monetary brand name capital during the war when it credited foreign accounts at the Bank of England in exchange for real resources.
20. See also Johnson (1969a).
21. Since SDRs cannot be freely used in transactions, even official international transactions, like dollars or gold, the quantity of SDRs effectively demanded, or voluntarily held, is difficult to measure. (In fact the IMF has explicit rules and penalties against 'excessive' use.) Aggregate IMF 'allocations' are clearly an overestimate of effective money demand. Even some SDRs voluntarily taken by a country after negotiation as payment for a balance of payments surplus may only be a new way to supply foreign aid credits and therefore also represent an upwardly biased measure of real money demand.
22. One possible explanation of US policy is that it is based on a failure to fully understand the international position of the dollar. To a large extent the post-World War II increase in foreign holdings of dollar assets has resulted from the relative rise of the dollar brand name. It represents the export of monetary services and therefore should be thought of as a surplus item in complete balance-of-trade accounts, rather than accumulating 'deficits', and hence does not imply the existence of a 'dollar overhang' problem which must be solved by the creation of a new international asset. See, for

example, McKinnon (1969).

An alternative explanation may be that it represents a strategic competitive move to discourage the development of gold or a European monetary unit as an international money substitute for the dollar.

23. See Mundell (1961) and McKinnon (1963) for the original statements of the problem. Mundell's assertion that if the number of currencies equalled the number of commodities trade might just as well be conducted in terms of pure barter because the usefulness of money as a unit of account and medium of exchange would disappear is incorrect. We would have the same number of prices, i.e. exchange rates, as in a pure barter economy, but transactions costs such as storage, valuation (weighting, etc.) may be saved. McKinnon's attempt to specify the exact nature of the monetary service flow from money and therefore make more than an intuitive argument in favour of an optimum currency area is also not successful. First, he incorrectly identifies the monetary service (or liquidity) flow from a money with price level stability, rather than price level predictability. He then claims that this will imply fixed exchange rates of a small country with a large country. But this will only be the case if the large country is also maintaining a stable price level. And, in any event, these arbitrary assumptions will only imply *constant* exchange rates and not necessarily a currency area – which is essentially a single money or perfect confidence that the monies are convertible into one another at *fixed* exchange rates. As noted below with regard to the European 'snake' arrangement the crucial analytical criterion for a currency area is a small probability of an *anticipated* exchange rate change. The theoretical work done in extending the original analysis (see, for example, Johnson and Swoboda (1973)) has not been very convincing. Hence the strong policy statements with weak analytical foundation present in the Manifesto.
24. Cipolla (1967, ch. 2) documents the fact that dominant monies existed over large areas and long time periods as early as the 5th century when the Byzantine gold solidus had a dominant position throughout the Mediterranean
25. Even this Chinese experiment may be an example of a market-induced optimum currency arrangement along industrial and hence regional groupings. See Chen (1975).
26. The classic US example of competitive domestic monies circulating at flexible exchange rates is often considered to be the pre-Civil War 'free banking' experience when many different bank-notes circulated side by side with one another and with gold at various market determined discounts. A closer examination of this period, however, indicates a monetary arrangement much closer to a single dominant money standard, with bank notes denominated in gold and generally circulating at par. See Klein (1974a, pp. 439-41).
27. US colonial experience in the first half of the 18th century is illustrative of this force. Separate paper money issues of each of the New England colonies were agreed to be acceptable at par in each of the other New England colonies in payment of taxes and in general exchange. This attempt to create a currency area led to rapid inflation via competitive issuance of increased money by each of the colonies and, finally, the abandonment of the arrangement.

28. Germany possessed about 47 per cent of the EEC's offical reserves in July, 1975 (See DeGrauwe, *et. al.* (1975), p. 31), while at that time it produced only about 30 per cent of the EEC's gross domestic product.
29. For example, forward exchange rates, which are highly significant for international trade, were frequently outside the 'guaranteed' band of the spot rate during the period of 'fixed' exchange rates in the late 1960s.
30. A single money reduces the monetary calculation costs by setting the fixed rate at one to one. All fixed exchange rate systems are not equivalent in terms of reducing transaction costs.
31. See, for example, DeGrauwe, *et. al.* (1975), Annex II.
32. Because of different transaction costs, the efficient inflation tax may vary across countries. (For example, a larger percentage of taxes may be more efficiently collected by inflation in Italy than in the US. In such a case, policy-makers must trade-off the economic gains of increased monetary union with the increased costs of collecting taxes by alternative means if inflation is limited to the US rate.
33. See McKinnon (1969) for a persuasive statement of the proposition that development of the dollar standard was largely a market solution to the problem of the need for an international money. It should be noted, however, that economists do not have a very good understanding of how and why a particular money becomes a dominant money. Research on the fundamental unanswered questions regarding the nature of the monetary service stream and the production function for monetary confidence is necessary to throw light on this issue.
34. Why the Germans and the Swiss have been resisting this movement towards use of their monies as international substitutes for the dollar, e.g. by imposing capital inflow controls, is somewhat of a mystery. Part of the answer is probably the short-run unemployment effects produced by the import surplus represented by this capital movement. In addition, these international movements potentially increase the short-run volatility of their domestic money supplies. And, finally, the long-run seigniorage returns are not all that great, as experience with the dollar indicates.
35. See Price (1978) for these empirical results. The balance-of-payments measure that enters significantly is the deflated (by the high-powered money stock) official reserve settlements measure, rather than the balance of trade or the liquidity concept. This is the result one would expect on theoretical grounds since private holdings of dollar liabilities are certainly not 'involuntary' holdings accumulated to maintain the dollar exchange rate. Therefore the official settlements measure is a more appropriate economic measure of pressure on the exchange rate.
36. The Federal Reserve has eliminated part of this private 'free ride' by requiring reserves be held against dollar deposits in foreign branches of US banks but, of course, are unable to regulate foreign dollar deposits in foreign banks. We should also note that some foreign holdings of dollars yielding less than a market rate may merely be an indirect payment for other services rendered. Germany, for example, may decide to 'voluntarily' hold additional dollar reserves as payment for the stationing of US troops in Germany. This political transaction was, in fact, made quite explicit at times during the 1960s. The increased foreign holdings of dollars in such a

situation should obviously not be considered as an official settlements deficit in the balance of payments, but rather merely as official payment to the United States for export of protection services.

37. An obvious example is the yen which did not fluctuate in value relative to the dollar for 25 years. With Japan maintaining a rigidly fixed exchange rate with the dollar until 1971, long-term Japanese monetary policy was essentially determined by the Federal Reserve Board in Washington, DC and a blurring of some of the distinction between the dollar and the yen in the minds of international transactors must have been produced. But, judging from the existence of a forward exchange market, the country was not considered as just another Federal Reserve District.
38. Since US and foreign dollar assets are not equivalent, we would not expect the interest rates on the different assets to be identical and, in particular, we would expect the Euro-dollar rate to be higher than the US rate in terms of financial crisis. More generally, assets possess many characteristics and are not necessarily perfect substitutes because they are denominated in the same units and are of the same maturity (see note 10 above).
39. To get some idea of the magnitude of losses involved, during the first quarter of 1973 the Bank of Japan purchased about $10 billion at about 300 yen/dollar in an unsuccessful attempt to keep the yen from appreciating. The yen market exchange rate rose to about 265 yen/dollar when the Bank of Japan finally gave up, implying a 'loss' of about $1.2 billion over a period of a couple of months.
40. McKinnon's (1969) assertion that flexibility would increase the private demand for dollars seems to be incorrect. Actually, a break in a convertibility arrangement, say of the mark with the dollar, has two contrary effects on the demand for dollars. It eliminates the 'free ride' by the mark on the dollar brand name, but it also creates a fully independent international competitor for the dollar. While the first effect clearly dominated in the case of the break in the gold-dollar tie, the second effect appears to have dominated in the case of the mark-dollar break. Part of the difficulty for the dollar is that flexible exchange rates were adopted in response to an extremely poor (i.e. unpredictable) dollar performance.
41. The mercantilistic doctrine of hoarding gold bullion similarly makes some sense because gold represented national defense security or advertising to potential enemies of the ability to quickly raise an army (e.g. hire mercenaries). Gold was an extremely liquid form in which to hold part of a nation's wealth similar to strategic reserves of soldiers or oil held by countries presently.
42. It is only the costs of increasing the money supply and buying up all the assets in the economy which places an economic limit on this process. See Klein (1974a), p. 437.
43. See Klein (1974a), p. 450 and Klein, Alchian and Crawford (1978) for a more complete discussion of these issues.

REFERENCES

Barro, Robert, 'Inflationary Finance and the Welfare Cost of Inflation', *Journal of Political Economy*, 80 (September/October 1972), 978-1001.

Basevi, Giorgio, *et. al.*, 'A Currency for Europe: All Saints Day Manifesto for European Monetary Union', *The Economist*, November 1 1975.
Bergsten, C. Fred, *The Dilemma of the Dollar* (New York: Council on Foreign Relations, 1975).
Bresciani-Turroni, Constantino, *The Economics of Inflation* (New York: Kelley, 1968).
Cagan, Philip, 'The Monetary Dynamics of Hyperinflation', in Milton Friedman (ed.), *Studies in the Quantity Theory of Money* (Chicago: University of Chicago Press, 1950), pp. 25-117.
Chen, Chau-Nan, 'Flexible Bimetallic Exchange Rates in China, 1650-1850: A Historical Example of Optimum Currency Areas', *Journal of Money, Credit and Banking*, vol. 7, no. 3 (August 1975), 359-76.
Cipolla, Carlo M, *Money, Prices and Civilization in the Mediterranean World: Fifth to Seventeenth Century* (New York: Gordian Press, 1967).
Commission of the European Communities, OPTICA Report 1975, 'Towards Economic Equilibrium and Monetary Unification in Europe', Brussels, January 1976.
Commission of the European Communities, OPTICA Report 1976, 'Inflation and Exchange Rates: Evidence and Policy Guidelines for the European Community', Brussels February 1977.
DeGrauwe, P., Heremans, D. and Van Rompuy, E., *Towards European Monetary Union*, Memo from Belgium, 'Views and Surveys', no. 17 (Brussels: Ministry of Foreign Affairs, External Trade and Cooperation in Development, 1975).
Friedman, Milton, 'The Optimum Quantity of Money' in *The Optimum Quantity of Money and Other Essays* (Chicago: Aldine, 1969), 1-50.
Frenkel, Jacob A. 'The Forward Exchange Rate, Expectations, and the Demand for Money: The German Hyperinflation', *American Economic Review*, vol. 67, no. 4 (September 1977), 653-70.
Graham, Frank K., *Exchange, Prices and Production in Hyperinflation: Germany, 1920-23* (Princeton: Princeton Univeristy Press, 1930).
Grubel, Herbert G., 'The Distribution of Seigniorage from International Liquidity Creation', in R.A. Mundell and A.K. Swoboda (eds.), *Monetary Problems of the International Economy* (Chicago: University of Chicago Press, 1969), 269-82.
Haberler, Gottfried and Thomas D. Willett, 'A Strategy for U.S. Balance of Payments Policy' (Washington, D.C.: American Enterprise Insitute Special Analysis, 1971).
Hayek, F.A., *Denationalisation of Money*, Hobart Paper no. 70 (London: Institute of Economic Affairs, 1976).
Johnson, Harry G., 'Inside Money, Outside Money, Income, Wealth, and Welfare in Monetary Theory', *Journal of Money, Credit and Banking*, 1 (February 1969(a)), 30-45.
Johnson, Harry G., 'A Note of Seigniorage and the Social Saving from Substitution Credit for Commodity Money', in R.A. Mundell and A.K. Swoboda (eds.), *Monetary Problems of the International Economy* (Chicago: University of Chicago Press, 1969(b)), 323-9.
Johnson, Harry G., and Swoboda, Alexander K., *The Economics of Common Currencies* (Cambridge, Mass.: Harvard Univ. Press, 1973).
Klein, Benjamin, 'The Competitive Supply of Money', *Journal of Money, Credit and Banking*, vol. 6, no. 4 (November 1974(a)), 243-53.

Klein, Benjamin, 'Competitive Interest Payments on Bank Deposits and the Long-Run Demand for Money', *American Economic Review*, vol. 64, no. 5 (December 1974(b)), 931-49.
Klein, Benjamin, 'Our New Monetary Standard: The Measurement and Effects of Price Uncertainty, 1880-1973', *Economic Inquiry*, vol. 13, no. 4 (December 1975) 461-84.
Klein, Benajmin, 'The Demand for Quality-Adjusted Cash Balances: Price Uncertainty in the U.S. Demand for Money Function', *Journal of Political Economy*, vol. 85, no. 4 (August 1977), 691-716.
Klein, Benjamin, 'The Measurement of Long- and Short-Term Price Uncertainty: A Moving Regression Time Series Analysis', *Economic Inquiry*, vol. 16, no. 3 (July 1978(a)), 438-52.
Klein, Benjamin, 'Money, Wealth and Seigniorage', in K. Boulding and T.F. Wilson (eds.), *Redistribution Through the Financial System: The Grants Economics of Money and Credit* (Praeger Publishers, Inc. forthcoming (1978(b)).
Klein, Benjamin, Alchian, Armen A. and Crawford, Robert G., 'Vertical Integration, Appropriable Rents and the Competitive Contracting Process', *Journal of Law and Economics*, vol. 21, no. 2 (October 1978).
Klein, Benjamin and Teixeira, Ernani, 'The Competitive Demand for Money: The Brazilian Evidence', unpublished manuscript, 1977.
McKinnon, Ronald I., 'Optimum Currency Areas', *American Economic Review*, vol. 53, no. 3 (September 1963), 716-25.
McKinnon, Ronald I., 'Private and Official International Money: The Case for The Dollar', *Princeton Essays in International Finance*, no. 74 (April 1969).
Mundell, Robert A., 'A Theory of Optimum Currency Areas', *American Economic Review*, vol. 51, no. 5 (September 1961), 657-65.
Price, John W., 'Time Series Analysis of Money Supply Reaction Functions: International Evidence', UCLA Ph.D. dissertation, 1978.
Statistisches Reichsamt, *Germany's Economy Currency and Finance*, Committees of Experts for the Reparation Commission, Berlin 1924.
Tullock, Gordon 'Competing Monies', *Journal of Money, Credit and Banking*, vol. 7, no. 4 (November 1975), 491-7.

COMMENT ON KLEIN

George Zis

Klein's study challenges the All Saints' Day Manifesto on two principal themes: firstly, it maintains that the potential superiority of the Europa over existing national currencies rests on arguments different than those advanced by the authors of the Manifesto. Secondly, it argues that historical experience as well as political considerations suggest that the Europa, if introduced, would not drive European national currencies out of circulation. Briefly, then, this study challenges the Europa proposal on both theoretical and empirical grounds. It merits, therefore, careful consideration not only because of its thoughtful nature but also, and perhaps primarily, because of the implications of its conclusions for the future of European unity and of international monetary relations.

A main feature of the Europa, according to the authors of the Manifesto, is that it will exhibit a constant value. Therefore, it is argued, national currencies, whose value is continuously depreciating, will be driven out of circulation. That is, competition is envisaged to occur on the basis of the respective inflation rates, with the Europa asserting its dominance because of the constancy of its value. Klein directly challenges this proposition and persuasively argues that it is the predictability of the value of a particular money that determines its competitiveness vis-a-vis other monies. In other words, a money that is depreciating at a rapid but *predictable* rate will not be rejected in favour of a money whose value fluctuates erratically even if on average it is maintained constant. The current position of gold is quoted in support of the proposition that 'competition between monies does not occur primarily on the basis of the average inflation rates of the different monies but on the basis of the variance or predictability of these inflation rates'.

Note that Klein does not deny that the average inflation rate is a determinant of the relative competitiveness of a money. What he does reject is that it is a quantitatively important determinant. This empirical proposition rests on the argument that a large fraction of the money supplied yields a competitive rate of interest. It is only high-powered money which does not yield interest and, therefore, it is only the demand for this fraction of the money supply that will be sensitive to varying inflation rates. Klein draws attention to empirical work consistent with the view that in the US 'bank deposits can usefully be assumed to be paying implicit competitive interest' and he expects 'this also to be the case for most European institutions'. It follows, therefore, that what is important is whether or not conclusions drawn from U.S. experience can be considered to apply to Europe. Some scepticism may be expressed on the ground that in a country, for example the UK, where there exist only a handful of banks, in contrast to the banking structure of the US empirical work would not yield conclusions similar to those reached with respect to bank deposits in the US. Given the sharp differences among national bank structures, this issue cannot be settled satisfactorily without further research.

Assume, however, that the entire money supply does *not* yield a competitive interest rate in any European country. This in no way would invalidate Klein's argument that competition between monies does occur on the basis of the predictability of inflation rates. All that it would affect is the relative quantitative importance of the two competitive forces, the average inflation rate and its predictability. Consequently, I do agree with Klein's criticism that the authors of the Manifesto were in error when placing exclusive emphasis on the inflation rate to be associated with the Europa as the main force that will ensure its rapid acceptance and force existing European currencies out of circulation.

It follows from the above that the theory of the competitive mechanism between alternative monies should reinforce the belief, expressed by the authors of the Manifesto, that the Europa would drive out of circulation exisiting European currencies. Confidence in the prediction that such substitution would occur rests not only on the zero inflation rate to be associated with the proposed Europa but also on the perfect predictability of its value. However, though such a prediction would follow logically from Klein's arguments, he, on the contrary, maintains that what is likely to happen 'is that the Europa will not be accepted at all'. He reaches this conclusion by examining the historical record which is interpreted to suggest that 'there does not appear to be a great deal of pressure, if any at all, towards substitutability of competing monies'. The absence of such substitutability is attributed to the large costs implied by the switching from one to another medium of exchange, to market imperfections and to domestic political constraints facing national money issuers. At the same time, Klein is less than impressed with the argument that competing monies did not develop because of legal restrictions imposed by governments.

Is there an alternative interpretation to the historical experience? If the answer to this question is positive, then it necessarily follows that the Europa's prospects to be accepted are not as poor as Klein suggests. Suppose, however, that the answer is negative. It can still be asked whether, given the Manifesto's proposals, Klein's conclusion regarding the Europa is unambiguously consistent with his interpretation of the historical experience.

I share Klein's scepticism about the effectiveness of legal restrictions to frustrate the market mechanism. However, with respect to the issuers under discussion, it may be argued that the experience with wage and price controls, trade barriers, rent controls, exchange controls, etc. is not, perhaps, particularly enlightening. Such an argument could rest on two propositions. First, legal restrictions may result in obscuring rather than in preventing the emergence of competing currencies. If that is the case, then it could be argued that our information regarding what happened in the past is rather incomplete and, therefore, cannot provide a basis for firm conclusions. Secondly, it may be argued that a currency backed by law cannot coexist with an 'illegal' currency for any length of time, however unpredictable the value of the former may be. These propositions could be illustrated by the experience of the use of British gold sovereigns in Greece and certain Middle Eastern countries during the 1950s. Gold sovereigns were used extensively both as a unit of account and as a means of exchange. Transactions in the housing market were predominantly conducted in gold sovereigns, though in official records declarations were made in terms of the domestic currencies. Thus our information on this relatively recent experience cannot be reliable, and as far as I know it has received no attention in empirical work. However, gold sovereigns were forced out of circulation when faked gold sovereigns produced in Italy appeared in the market. In reponse to that development an industry of 'experts', who could allegedly discriminate between the genuine and faked gold sovereigns, rapidly emerged. But it was soon recognised that these 'experts' were acting in collaboration with the producers of the faked gold sovereigns. The result was that confusion and uncertainty forced the rapid return to the use of domestic currencies. The combination, then, of law and the market mechanism ensured that the right of national governments to issue money remained essentially unchallenged. One can, therefore, conclude that legal restrictions are likely to be effective in preventing the emergence of competing currencies since the absence of legal penalties against forgeries of the 'illegal' currency would result in the value of the competing being highly unpredictable. If this line of argument were acceptable, then it would logically follow from the theory of the competitive mechanism between alternative monies that an illegal currency could not emerge as a substitute to a legal currency to any significant extent.

It may be objected that the above argument was based on the implications of transactions in a competing currency that had not the backing of the law, while competition could occur between existing legal currencies. Thus, for example, the dollar could compete with sterling in the UK, with British law providing for penalties against forged dollars. Given that transactions in dollars would not necessarily be legal we would still have the problem of information regarding their volume. But this, perhaps, could be rejected as a secondary issue. The question could still be asked as to why the dollar did not emerge as a substitute. This question cannot be answered without specifying the nature of the assumed exchange rate regime. Suppose that the dollar/sterling exchange rate was fixed. Fixity of exchange rates, then, would ensure that the value of both currencies would depreciate at the same rate and, consequently, the degree of predictability of the value of sterling and dollar would be the same. Thus, under fixed exchange rates one cannot expect a national currency to emerge as a substitute for another. This argument, of course, does not hold under a regime of flexible exchange rates. Under such international monetary arrangements national inflation rates can deviate and, therefore, the degree of predictability of the value of alternative currencies can differ. Now, up to the end of the 1960s under the Bretton Woods system the world was essentially on fixed exchange rates and, consequently, it is not particularly surprising that there is no evidence that at least the major currencies did not come under competitive pressures. Further, as Klein implies, since 1971 with exchange rates becoming more flexible the dollar's position has been weakened. A result of this weakening, reflecting the greater unpredictability of the value of the dollar, is that an increasing number of trade transactions are denominated in deutschmarks or Swiss francs rather than in dollars.

The above arguments may appear to lack validity if reference is made to the reported national inflation rates during the era of the Bretton Woods system. However, the counter-argument would be that observed differences in national inflation rates simply reflect differences in the weights attached to different categories of goods in the construction of national price indices and that in fact there existed a world rate of inflation common to all countries on fixed exchange rates.

Recognising, then, the implications of alternative exchange rates regimes and de-emphasizing observed differences in national rates of inflation because of the weights problem, there is some basis for regarding the absence of competition between alternative legal currencies as consistent with what one would predict on theoretical grounds. This, of course, cannot provide a complete explanation of the historical experience. However, an interpretation along these lines which, furthermore, allows for the implications of the competing money not being backed by law, is sufficiently plausible to suggest that conclusions based on Klein's interpretation may not be unambiguously well founded.

Klein considers that the loss of political autonomy that would ensue the introduction of the Europa is, ultimately, the main reason why the Maifesto proposal has hardly any chance to be adopted by national governments. This argument implies that they currently enjoy a degree of economic and political independence that would be jeopardised through the introduction of Europa. This I find difficult to accept. It cannot be argued that the UK is particularly independent when twice during the last decade it had to alter its policies at the insistence of the IMF. Nor is the 1968 Basle Agreement on Sterling consistent with the notion of the UK being free to determine its policies. Nor can Italy and Portugal be described as independent if one observes their negotiations with the IMF. Indeed, even with the current degree of exchange rate flexibility economic interdependence has forced the major countries to seek co-ordinated policies, each government being reluctant to act on its own. To argue that no country enjoys economic autonomy does not deny that European Monetary Union would involve greater limitations on the ability of an individual member government to determine its own policies. What it does imply is that European Monetary Union would lead to a quantitative and not to a qualitative change in the status of national governments. Of course, it may well be the case that EEC countries will not be willing to surrender further than currently their sovereignty. In this case the Manifesto proposal will not be adopted and, therefore, the issue of whether or not Europa will be rapidly and generally accepted does not arise. But the authors of the Manifesto are quite clear that their proposed scheme relies on the political willingness of member governments to provide, at least, the environment permitting its trial. In the absence of such political willingness there can be no doubt that the Europa scheme could not get off the ground and, therefore, have no chance and fail.

Assume that the political willingness to work towards European Monetary Union through the implementation of the Europa scheme exists. It could still be argued that Klein's interpretation of the historical evidence suggests that the existence of such political willingness, though necessary, is not sufficient to ensure the successful survival of the Europa. However, such an argument would be difficult to sustain. What Klein has shown, accepting his arguments in their entirety, is that competitive currencies failed to emerge *spontaneously* under market pressures. But this interpretation is not fully relevant in considering the prospects of the Europa. The Manifesto envisages the introduction of the Europa as a deliberate act of policy by EEC governments and, then, would leave its adoption or rejection to be decided by the market. That is, there is no historical precedent where a group of governments acted analogously to what is envisaged in the Manifesto to provide us with such information as to suspect that the Europa 'will not be accepted at all' even if the required political conditions prevail.

This raises questions relating to confidence in governments' pronouncements. Klein challenges the view that the declaration that the Europa will enjoy a stable purchasing power will be accepted at face value by the market. Distrust of governments would act as an obstacle to the acceptance of the Europa. That such distrust is justified, in most cases, cannot be denied. However, what is at issue is whether this distrust could prevent governments from actually introducing the Europa. As I understand the Manifesto proposal, the introduction of the Europa would be analogous to monetary reforms initiated by various governments at different times. On each occasion the new currency was accepted and inflation expectations were instantaneously revised. Thus at least for the short run governments in these cases were believed. If I understand the arguments correctly, then I can see no reason why the Europa should not drive out existing currencies though, of course, after a time interval confidence in the Europa could collapse either because governments opted out of the scheme or because its purchasing power was not maintained stable. No scheme could guarantee the long run survival of European Monetary Union but this cannot be interpreted as suggesting that a monetary reform along the lines of the Europa scheme cannot be implemented because governments are distrusted.

There is general agreement that 'European Monetary Union has large potential economic benefits'. But prompted by his doubts regarding the feasibility of the Europa scheme, Klein argues that 'the benefits from a unified money cannot readily be achieved by a fixed exchange rate arrangement among multiple monies unless one of the monies is designated as the dominant money into which all the others are convertible'. He attributes the failure of the 'snake' experiment to the fact that no currency was specified to be the dominant one. He goes on to argue that a logical alternative way of obtaining the economic benefits of European monetary union is, of course, European adoption of a dollar standard via fixed exchange rate convertibility of European deposits in dollars. In view of his own excellent analysis of the evolution of the international monetary system in the post-1945 period, it is difficult to see how opting for a dollar standard could either be more politically acceptable or result in a more viable set of international monetary relations than implied by the Europa scheme. Indeed, the very collapse of the Bretton Woods system reflects the rejection of the dollar standard. Furthermore, it could be argued that both the Bretton Woods system and the 'snake' experiment failed because of divergent national monetary policies. The implication of this diagnosis, which is consistent with Klein's analysis, is that a system of fixed exchange rates cannot be viable if any single national currency acts also as an international asset. The dominant reserve currency country will always have an incentive to impose an inflation tax on the rest of the world which may induce competitive and escalating rates of growth of national currencies.

As Klein himself notes, adoption of a dollar standard, abstracting from the economic consequences, would imply the perpetuation of the US political supremacy in the western world. Ultimately the effort to forge European unity is inspired by the desire of European countries to repossess the political autonomy which they lost in the late 1940's when the US coerced them to accept a dominant role for the dollar in international monetary relations. I do not share Klein's judgement that 'the dollar gained its dominant international position . . . voluntarily in the market place'. This judgement seems to dismiss as insignificant the impact on the subsequent evolution of the Bretton Woods system of the condition imposed by America that countries receiving US aid through the European Recovery Programme could not use the IMF facilities. Thus the volume of IMF transactions, which had totalled $606 million in the financial year 1947-8, fell in the three subsequent years to $119 million, $52 million and $28 million. It is, therefore, not surprising that the IMF did not evolve into a genuinely international organisation. In contrast the Europa scheme, if adopted, by increasing the monetary autonomy of Europa, since the Europa's stable purchasing power implies a flexible Europa to dollar exchange rate, would facilitate the emergence of a new structure of political relations between Europe and US that would be less biased in favour of the latter.

It is evident from the above argument that I do believe that a political case in favour of the Europa can be made. Indeed, I would argue that domestic political benefits could be reaped through the adoption of the Europa scheme. I do regret that the authors of the Manifesto confined themselves to presenting only the economic case for the Europa.

This comment has suggested that in evaluating the prospects of the Europa scheme, the interpretation of the historical evidence presented by Klein is not necessarily the only one consistent with the facts. But more importantly, perhaps, it has been argued that the past cannot provide us with such information as to enable an assessment of the feasibility of the Europa scheme. Thirdly, caution has been urged not to exaggerate the real political consequences of European Monetary Union. Therefore, contrary to Klein's conclusion, I do believe that if the Manifesto proposal were adopted then the Europa would rapidly and generally be accepted. However, it would be grossly unfair to end on a note of disagreement. Klein's thoughtful study poses a multiplicity of relevant questions which should concern both advocates and opponents of European Monetary Union.

COMMENT ON KLEIN

David O'Mahony

My first reaction to Klein's paper was to feel somewhat chastened and not a little guilty. I felt I had been reprimanded for meeting with my colleagues in a pleasant place and for believing the textbook assertions that money is whatever 'society (operationally defined as the relevant policymaker) makes it to be'. I also felt that I had been taken to task for misunderstanding the nature of the competitive process in the money supply market and for confusing the problem of inflation and the problem of monetary integration. Now seeing, as was mentioned yesterday, that we have come to be canonized I asked myself if Klein meant that, while we might be saints, we aren't scholars. Though I myself come from a country that was once renowned as the island of saints and scholars I cannot claim to be either a saint or a scholar. And while I cannot vouch for my colleagues' saintliness, I am in no doubt about their scholarship. That being so, I began to feel less chastened and less guilty. If I have been guilty of error, I thought, at least I'm in very good company. I must admit, though, that having listened to yesterday's discussion, I'm beginning to wonder if a mutual friend of Klein and of mine shouldn't have added another chapter to a book which he has recently published. The title of the book is *Defending the Undefendable!*[1]

There is a very wide spectrum of opinion as to the acceptability or otherwise of the Europa as proposed in the Manifesto. Some seem to think that it would displace the national currencies overnight, while at the other extreme Klein doubts if it would be accepted at all. Obviously the crucial question is the one Klein raises – would the Europa be accepted as money?

History affords many examples of bimetallism and of coins of the same metal but of different provenance circulating side by side – a fact, incidentally, that made money-changing a lucrative trade. But, and Klein accepts this, history affords virtually no example of the circulation of genuinely different monies in the same place at the same time. Such few examples as can be found relate to circumstances which are utterly different from ours. It is clear, then, that we have no direct evidence of what would be likely to happen under conditions of monetary competition or of an attempt to introduce monetary competition in conditions such as prevail in the Europe of today. All we have is evidence of what happens when there are national monopoly currencies. But such evidence cannot carry much weight one way or the other in regard to a new parallel currency. What happens in one set of circumstances can hardly provide conclusive evidence of what would happen in another quite different set of circumstances.

Moreover, some of the evidence Klein offers may be subject to a different interpretation from the one he puts on it. For example, as Zis has stressed, he dismisses the possibility that competing currencies do not develop, even in countries experiencing rapid inflation over long periods, because of governmental regulations prohibiting their existence, on the grounds that there is evidence in *other areas* that regulations, e.g. price controls and trade restraints, are generally evaded at least partially. But could it not be that the reason competing currencies did not develop in the *particular* context that we're discussing is precisely that there are no loopholes in the governmental regulations and that the regulations are so strictly enforced that they cannot be evaded? In other words, could the evidence on which Klein concludes that competing currencies fail to emerge under highly inflationary conditions not support the conclusion that the regulations prohibiting them are so effective that they could not emerge rather than there is an absence of a demand for them?

In fact, we find that under inflationary conditions people take several courses of action which indicate that there *is* a potential demand for a stable substitute currency. For example, there has been great interest in, and some practice of, inflationary accounting. This is surely due to the fact that accountants and businessmen recognize that inflation renders money, as a unit of account and calculation, highly inefficient. And remember that there is simply no way by which inflation can be predicted even for such a short period as five years hence. Besides, several artificial units of account (ACU) have emerged, some of them, as Ascheim and Park have noted, in the private sector.[2] Furthermore, indexing is widely practised – where it is allowed. What inflation accounting, ACUs, and indexing indicate is that people are seeking ways, in so far as governments allow them, to abandon depreciating money in regard to at least some of the functions of money.

There is no evidence that people resisted currency reform. When the new mark and the new franc were introduced people did not cling to the old ones. There was no 'black market pressure', to quote Klein, towards the old media of exchange. But if Klein is right, should people not have been reluctant to accept the new? That they so readily accepted the new mark and francs, etc., is presumably because they felt that the new ones couldn't be any *worse* than the old ones and that the probability they would be better was sufficiently high to justify not resisting their introduction.

Now, in the case of the Europa we cannot, of course, be absolutely *sure* that it would be adopted. But the Europa is no exception in that respect. No entrepreneur can ever be absolutely *sure* that if he launches a new product on the market it is going to be accepted. The only way to know if something is going to be competitive is to put it competing and find out. Does not the very process of the market arise because of uncertainty? We said we believed the Europa would be accepted. And we gave our reasons. People throughout Europe would be likely to accept a stable currency because it is a better unit of account, because of its superiority for purposes of long-term contracts, and because of its advantages in international transactions. It would be better than inflation accounting, than ACUs, than indexing. It would be better as a store of value than the existing currencies. In no respect would it be worse than them. Why then would people have no confidence in it? Can one seriously suggest that a money issued in accordance with a solemn treaty between the members of the European Community would lack monetary confidence? Rightly or wrongly, and mostly wrongly it seems to me, people do trust governments – if they didn't presumably the national currencies themselves wouldn't be accepted as money at all.

Thus it is not, I think, as Klein asserts, that we did not understand the nature of the competitive process in the money supply market. It is rather, I submit, that looking at the monetary scene through entrepreneurial, if not saintly, eyes we detected that people, businessmen, wage and salary earners, importers and exporters, etc., experience a need which they are trying to meet as best they can by the devices I've mentioned, but which we think could be met better if they were allowed to use a stable-valued parallel money. And, as we indicated, we think that this insight of ours should be put to the test of the market so that the public can decide whether they want a stable money and a monetary union or not.

Now, as regards our alleged confusion of these two matters – inflation and monetary integration – I don't think this charge can be sustained either. It is true that we are trying to kill two birds with one stone. But we're hardly confusing them. There are certainly tremendous political obstacles to the attainment of a monetary union, or even of a common market in currencies.

But the politicians can't have it both ways. If they want monetary union – and they *say* they do (though the bureaucrats and central bankers apparently don't) – they'll have to forgo the monopolization of currency in their respective territories. On the other hand if they want to retain national monopolization of currency they can't have monetary union. It's as simple as that.

One must agree with Klein that if the Europa is established it may eventually go the way of all currencies over which governments have had control. I don't think any consitution or statute or treaty can prevent that. What Hayek says in this connection is true, I think.[3] But what really makes monopoly in regard to money as in regard to anything else is not that there is only one supplier but that there isn't freedom of entry. The Manifesto proposals do not, as I understand them, envisage that governments would lose the *right* to issue their own money if they thought fit. The possibility that they *would* might well be the greatest deterrent to the abuse of the Europa in the long run. Paradoxically, therefore, political unfication might not be desirable if a tolerably stable European money is to be maintained. It's not desirable for a whole lot of other reasons too, of course!

In defending the Manifesto I do not mean to suggest that we left no loose ends in it. We did, and one of these is certainly the transitional phase. Another is the monetary rule that would continue to guarantee the purchasing power stability of the Europa. Whatever the details of that rule might be, and I don't want to anticipate Parkin here, it must, in a growing economy, involve an increase in the money supply. Seeing that this cannot be affected by means of a helicopter, I wonder if it is not going to produce problems of its own. In other words, I wonder if the attainment of a degree of stability in the purchasing power of the Europa by means of an increase in the supply of money really solves all the problems of inflation. Hayek, if I may refer to him again, seems to have changed his ground, as compared with his earlier analysis, on this issue.[4] In spite of what he says the suspicion remains that he may have been nearer the truth in 1933 than in 1976.

However, I must not get side-tracked on Hayek. I must come back to Klein and thank him for his very searching criticisms of our efforts. I'm sure you will agree, saints and non-saints alike, (I suppose I can't say sinner!) that he has greatly enlightened us and that we are all very much in his debt.

NOTES

1. Walter Block, *Defending the Undefendable* (Fleet Press, 1976).
2. Ascheim and Park, 'Artificial Currency Units: The Formation of Functional Currency Areas', *Essays in International Finance,* No. 114, April 1976 (Princeton University).
3. F.A. Hayek, *Denationalisation of Money* (London: Institute of Economic Affairs, 1976), p. 18.
4. Ibid, pp. 68-9.

PART III:

PARALLEL CURRENCIES AND EXCHANGE RATE ARRANGEMENTS

5 Minimising Imbalances in Monetary Union

ROLAND VAUBEL

There are so many advantages to the parallel-currency approach[1] – and so many of them are neglected – that it may seem quite arbitrary to concentrate on only two of them. On the other hand, there is so much to be said about each of them that it may even seem impossible in one paper to do justice to two of them. Nevertheless, this paper tries to establish the following two propositions:

i. the parallel-currency approach would minimise, and under certain conditions even avoid, stablilization-induced unemployment in the process of monetary unification; and
ii. even before full currency union[2], it would permit the formation of dynamic optimum currency domains on a regional (as well as industrial and functional) basis; indeed, it would not lead to full currency union unless the Community as a whole is an optimum currency area in the comparative static sense.

I. MONETARY UNIFICATION WITHOUT STABILIZATION CRISIS

The All Saints' Day Manifesto (1975) states that

> the transition to a European monetary union would not, of course, be without difficulties. The higher a country's rate of inflation is, the greater these difficulties would be. For a country with a rate of inflation as high as that in the United Kingdom the transition might involve a recession lasting for several years. . . . The introduction of a new stable money that is not subject to inflationary expectations will, however, minimise the transitional costs.

Michael Parkin, in a subsequent paper, notes some instances of monetary reform through currency substitution; he argues that

> although (these) cases do not constitute proof that a stabilization crisis is not a serious possibility, they do suggest that it is highly improbable,

and concludes that

> in sum, monetary union provides a rare opportunity to engineer an anti-inflationary monetary reform with the likelihood of minimum real disruptions.[3]

Max Corden, on the other hand, believes that

> the central problems would be the same (with the parallel-currency approach) – the unwillingness of national authorities to hand over their monetary power and the short-term costs in terms of unemployment in some countries that would possibly result from such a hand-over.[4]

In view of this lack of consensus, it may be useful to examine in some more detail why the stabilization of an inflating currency produces transitional unemployment and why the substitution of a stable currency for an inflating currency minimises such unemployment.[5] Since the problem of attaining disinflation without additional unemployment is probably the most pressing issue of our time, and since the traditional strategies for a return to price-level stability are incapable of solving it,[6] this aspect of the parallel-currency approach may indeed be more important than all its other advantages.

It is undisputed that the Werner approach to European monetary unification, aiming at fixed exchange rates between the existing member currencies, requires the assimilation of their inflation rates. Since the member countries with the lower rates of inflation are unlikely to accept an acceleration of inflation for the sake of exchange-rate unification, the more inflation-prone members would have to adopt a strongly disinflationary policy. Indeed, as has been shown,[7] consumer price inflation in these countries (Italy, the UK, Ireland) has to be several per cent below the rates prevailing in the other member countries if nominal exchange rates are to remain stable; for the historical evidence shows that Italy, the UK and Ireland have a considerable and persistent need for real exchange-rate depreciation. The downward harmonization of monetary rates of expansion and inflation is liable to produce temporary reductions in the level of employment because inflation expectations are slow to adapt. Since the current rather than the future inflation rate tends to be built into contracts concluded in nominal terms, reductions in the rate of inflation cause real wages, real interest payments and real debt principal to be higher than expected. They thus produce an unanticipated profit squeeze, stabilization-induced business failures, lay-offs, a slackening of investment activity and a slowdown in the creation of new jobs.

Traditional monetarism suggests three ways of reducing stabilization unemployment:

> monetary expansion and, hence, inflation should decelerate gradually so that the discrepancy between actual and anticipated inflation is kept

relatively small over the life of a contract and contracts can be renewed and adjusted during the stabilization process;

the decreasing rates of monetary expansion should be announced in advance so that inflation expectations can adjust in time;

indexation of contracts should be permitted and encouraged so that ignorance or disbelief of the pre-announced monetary target and the rate of inflation implied by it can be made irrelevant through contracting in real terms.

There is no doubt that these measures would 'reduce the cost of reducing inflation' (Parkin), but there is also no doubt that they would not eliminate it. This is because the 'spot market' prices of goods (and of some factors of production) cannot be indexed (upon themselves) by definition; some prices and price changes must remain flexible if relative price changes and changes in the rate of inflation are to remain possible. Indexation of term contracts, it is true, is also likely to raise the flexibility of non-indexed spot market prices,[8] but if some lag in the reaction of spot market prices to changes in monetary policy remains, the negative output and employment effects of a deceleration of monetary expansion cannot be avoided altogether. Given that most national member governments have to seek reelection every four or five years, it may be doubted whether even a gradualist and pre-announced stabilization policy that is backed up by timely incentives to contract in real terms can be maintained for long; and even those who regard a long-term trend of inflation deceleration as possible and probable have to ask themselves whether the implicit – even though transitory – unemployment is really inevitable. Could it be avoided through the introduction of a European Parallel Currency?

A currency that is newly introduced cannot by definition suffer from a record of inflation. Since inflation expectations depend primarily on inflation experience, a new currency cannot be subject to deeply engrained inflation expectations. Indeed, there are ways of ensuring that the expected rate of inflation is virtually nil. First of all, the bank that issues the new currency may be made constitutionally independent of the European governments.[9] Secondly, the issuing bank can be given a charter which obliges it to guarantee the EC purchasing power of its money, say, according to the indexed currency-basket formula.[10] In that case, the parallel currency would be expected to be as stable as a European index clause; however, unlike the latter, it would not only be a unit of account but also a means of payments and a store of value.

This has two important implications for the question of stabilization unemployment. In the first place, a full money offers functional economies of scale which a mere unit of account is bound to lack; from this it follows that an indexed money is more likely to be used to denominate term contracts than a mere index clause. Secondly, what is probably even more important, the introduction of a new indexed money permits the spot market for goods (and for factors of production) to deal in a money which, being stable, need not be stabilized. The inflating national member currencies, on the other hand, would not have to be stabilized because they would gradually be displaced as more and more contracts were denominated in the new money and provided for payment in it. The return to price-level stability would take the form of currency substitution instead of currency stabilization, of monetary reform instead of monetary deceleration. There would be no stabilization crisis due to lags in the adjustment of expectations and contracts because there would be no stabilization; and since one new currency would displace nine existing currencies, monetary reform would coincide with monetary unification.

Nevertheless, there are at least three arguments which purport to show that, even in the case of monetary reform, the return to price-level stability will require considerable unemployment.

In the first place, it may be argued that the introduction of the new stable currency would destroy pockets of money illusion that may have remained with some creditors (such as wage earners and small savers); for if it sharpened their awareness of the current rate of inflation, it would induce a rise in real wages and real rates of interest and hence reduce employment and investment. However, given that the experience of inflation in this decade has brought about an almost complete erosion of money illusion, this effect on employment seems to be negligible. The public does no longer err about the current rate of inflation but merely about the (changed) future rate of inflation.[11]

Second, there are those who seem to believe that, even in the absence of money illusion, most equilibrium real rates of interest are negative *ex ante* and that a stable money like the EPC, which in the form of notes and coins is bound to offer a zero real rate of interest, will exert an upward pressure on real interest rates in the whole of Europe and impede recovery. To argue that equilibrium real rates of interest are negative *ex ante* is to assume that *expected* rates of inflation (which are difficult to measure and may notably be lower than the current rate of inflation!) exceed the corresponding nominal rates of interest and that they would also exceed them in the absence of inflation. An alternative assumption which the present author considers more plausible is that the observed negative *ex post* real rates of interest are mainly due to unanticipated acceleration of inflation. In other words, we do not need inflation because some real rates of interest are negative *ex post*, but real rates of interest are negative *ex post* because there has been (accelerating) inflation.

Third and last, it is commonly assumed that, notably in the absence of indexed financial assets, high and variable rates of inflation induce savers to shift into real assets and to raise their relative prices. Thus, to the extent that these real assets (like 'concrete gold') are reproducible, inflation produces distortions in the pattern of production. Regardless of whether the return to price-level stability is brought about through stabilization or through currency substitution, the correction of these distortions tends to result in transitory structural or frictional unemployment. However, this type of disinflation-induced unemployment will mostly be confined to the building industry and can hardly give rise to a 'stabilization crisis'.

Clearly, currency unification through currency substitution does not require the creation of a new currency. It could, for instance, also be attained through free currency competition between the existing member currencies; for since there are large economies of scale in the use of money, the production of money must be considered a permanently declining cost industry and, hence, a 'natural monopoly': monetary competition destroys itself because the 'fittest money' tends to outcompete the others.[12] Alternatively, one member currency only (probably the most stable one) could be permitted to circulate in the other member countries and to replace their national currencies.[13] But quite apart from the political difficulties involved, neither strategy would avoid the need for the stabilization of the expanding national member currency, and the larger its domain at the time of the stabilization, the more widespread would be the stabilization unemployment. Of course, the same objection can be launched against the introduction of a new parallel currency whose value is linked to that of the stablest or strongest member currency.[14] There remains one obvious question to be answered. Why is it so easy to give an enforceable and, hence, credible value guarantee for a new parallel currency if it has proven so difficult to maintain the value of the national member currencies? After all, even the most stability-oriented monetarists do not recommend precise value (=price) guarantees but supply (=quantity) guarantees. Even they do not consider the demand for real money balances sufficiently predictable to allow the validation of precise value guarantees through *ex ante* supply adjustment. The utmost that seems to be attainable for monopolistic national monies is to keep the price level fluctuating around a constant mean.

The reason why a value guarantee for a parallel currency can be validated with certainty, i.e. instantaneously and with precision, is that it can take the form of an exchange-rate guarantee vis-à-vis a currency which circulates in the same area and/or industry. For example, if the parallel currency is defined as a basket of indexed amounts of the national member currencies, its value can be maintained by revaluing it vis-à-vis the weighted average of the member currencies by the weighted average rate at which these currencies lose their domestic purchasing power. The guaranteed exchange-rate adjustment can take place whenever and as soon as the change in the national price levels is measured; alternatively, it may be spread over, say, the following month. The guaranteed exchange rate would be the rate at which the public could convert national member currencies into parallel currency in unlimited quantities. Thus, supply would be free to adjust to demand so as to make the guaranteed exchange rate the equilibrium exchange rate.

This procedure can work only as long as the parallel currency remains a parallel currency. To the extent that it outcompetes the national member currencies, it can no longer use them as points of reference for the exchange-rate adjustment. When a member currency ceases to be issued, its weight in the currency basket can be taken up by the remaining member currencies at current proportions; however, when the last national member currency disappears, a precise domestic value guarantee becomes as unenforceable for the European currency as it is now for a national currency. Just as in the case of a national currency, it would still be possible to validate an external value guarantee, say, to maintain the European currency's US purchasing power; but to the extent that there are real exchange-rate changes between Europe and the US, such an external value guarantee does not imply stability of the currency's European purchasing power. It would also be possible to adjust the rate of the European currency's revaluation vis-à-vis the dollar by the real exchange-rate change between the US and Europe; however, this adjustment cannot be undertaken before the size of the real exchange-rate change and, hence, the implicit deviation from European price-level stability is known, and the correction of the deviation through the exchange-rate and the implicit money-supply adjustment must be expected to occur with a considerable lag. Since the result of such 'fine tuning' of exchange rates would be a stop-and-go monetary policy, the *unique* European currency, just like the present unique national member currencies, requires a supply guarantee instead of an exchange-rate guarantee. Thus, once the parallel currency accounted for a predetermined large proportion of the EC money supply (say, 60 per cent), the outstanding stock of national member currencies might conveniently be frozen (or withdrawn at a predetermined rate); monetary expansion in the Community would then be provided exclusively in the form of EPC issued by the EC Central Bank at a preannounced growth rate.

To sum up this section: it is characteristic of parallel currencies that their domestic purchasing power can be guaranteed with precision, and it is characteristic of new parallel currencies that their domestic purchasing power can be kept stable without causing a stabilization crisis. Indeed, guaranteed price-level stability seems to be the only attraction which can usefully be given to a European Parallel Currency but not to the existing national member currencies.[15]

II. CHOICE IN CURRENCY, REGIONAL BALANCE AND THE FORMATION OF OPTIMUM CURRENCY DOMAINS IN THE COMMUNITY

The parallel-currency approach to European currency unification offers economic agents a choice between their national currency and the European Parallel Currency (EPC). To the extent to which the (neo-) classical assumptions that

every user of money is the best judge of his own interest,

and that

the choice of money does not involve real-income externalities[16]

are met, the market's choice of currency must be expected to result in optimum currency domains. Indeed, this conclusion will also hold in a Keynesian framework if money illusion is confined to creditors (workers, savers); for inflation-conscious debtors would make sure that creditors' money illusion will not fail to be exploited.

In making their currency choice, economic agents weigh against each other the competing monies' usefulness as standards of value, stores of value and means of payment. The usefulness of a standard of value depends on the quality of information which it offers, and on the cost of information in contract denomination; high quality of information implies low risk. The attractiveness of a money as a store of value depends on risk and yield. As a means of payment, finally, a money is the more efficient, the lower are transaction cost.

Transaction cost and information cost are the lower, the larger the money's transaction domain. In sum, the users and choosers of money select that money which optimises their trade-off between monetary yield, risk, information cost and transaction cost, and the result will be optimum currency domains.[17]

The eclectic macroeconomic criteria of optimum currency areas which have been suggested by the so-called theory of optimum currency areas – such as factor mobility, fiscal integration, diversification of international transactions and mutual openness – can be shown to have (purchasing-power) information cost and (real exchange-rate) risk as their microeconomic counterparts; for the size and variability of real exchange-rate changes between regions and industries within the Community and hence of deviations from regional or industry price-level stability in a common currency domain tend to be the smaller, the larger factor mobility and the diversification and relative size of international transactions and the closer fiscal integration *between them.*[18]

However, since the present problem is not to find a pattern of optimum currency domains for a number of regionally or sectorally stable currencies, but to determine the domains which are in most urgent need of having inflating national currencies displaced by a stable Community currency, the theory of optimum currency areas has to be supplemented by a theory of optimum disinflation domains. To demonstrate the interaction of the two it is necessary to analyse in some detail the prospective process of EPC penetration.

It has frequently been observed that, in (hyper-) inflations, the depreciating national money at first loses its function as a standard of value, then its role of store of value and only in the last stage its function as a medium of exchange. The reasons for this sequence of functional displacement are that the benefit of stability of value as well as the cost of monetary innovation affect the various functions of money differently: it is relatively easy and highly important to denominate one's accounts and large term contracts in a stable standard of value, but it is cumbersome and not very rewarding to employ a new means of payments which, initially, is not readily accepted by many contract partners and which offers a higher yield only during the short intervals, and for the small amounts, in which it is held. The implication for the present analysis is that the EPC is likely to function at first mainly as a standard of value and, to a lesser extent, as a store of value, and that it will gain currency as a means of payment only at a later stage when holders of store-of-value EPC happen to enter into transactions with each other. Hence, the prospective usage of EPC in each of these functions will be discussed in this order.

A. The EPC's Expansion as a Standard of Value

The indexed-basket EPC reduces price risk: by guaranteeing purchasing-power constancy it eliminates price-level risk, and through diversification it minimizes the relative-price risk which intra-Community real exchange-rate changes involve for the partners to an international intra-Community contract. The EPC will therefore be used in particular by those economic agents who are most susceptible to price risk.

Price risk is the larger, *the longer the term of a contract* and, hence, the larger the variance of the prices expected by each individual. Thus, the EPC will mostly be used in long-term contracts such as forward supply contracts for investment goods, energy (oil, natural gas), shipbuilding and construction, long-term leases, leaseholding, insurances and long-term bonds. As a bond denomination, the EPC will tend to be used particularly frequently in member countries (like Germany and the Netherlands) where the average term of government debt is traditionally longest, and least frequently in member countries (like Italy and France) where it is traditionally shortest.[19] If the term of the contract is so long that it exceeds the period during which the EPC is expected to offer a direct value guarantee, the contract may be denominated in the indexed basket in which the EPC is defined initially rather than in the EPC itself.

Aversion to price risk, as any other risk, is stronger, *the larger the amounts at risk* (relative to the wealth of the risk taker). The relative amounts at risk are particularly large where the contract concerns not only a flow of income but also a stock of wealth, as is the case in capital markets. Thus, the prognosis that the EPC will preferably be used to denominate bonds, etc., is reinforced.

The EPC will spread faster, *the lower the quality, and the smaller the supply, of substitute instruments to reduce price risk.* For example, EPC bonds will be in less demand, the better equity and human capital serve as a hedge against price risk, and the more widespread are fixed-amount basket units of account and national price-index clauses.

Finally, the EPC is the more attractive as a standard of value, *the smaller the cost of introducing it.* Since information about the EPC's advantages involves mainly fixed costs, it is most likely to be used in large-scale contracts. But it will be adopted only slowly by those economic agents who face large long-term net claims or obligations denominated in the old standards, in particular by the various financial intermediaries for which balancing requirements imply relatively high costs of change.

While these determinants of EPC expansion concern both types of price risk, there are others which require a neat distinction between national inflation risk and international real exchange-rate risk.

1. Inflation Risk The indexed EPC will in the first place displace those member currencies which are subject to the most variable and, hence, least predictable rates of inflation. Variations in the rate of inflation and awareness of their unpredictability, in turn, tend to be the greater, the higher the rates of inflation.[20] The awareness of inflation risk will also depend on the extent to which index-linking has been permitted and practiced in the past. If economic agents are familiar with indexation on the national cost-of-living index, the step towards the indexed-basket standard of value would involve little information cost. At present indexation, notably of wages, is most widespread in Belgium, the Netherlands, Denmark and Italy. On the other hand, if national index clauses remained mostly prohibited in Germany and France, while the EPC were admitted, the lack of substitutes would render the EPC particularly attractive in these countries, too.

The question is of interest whether, from the point of view of inflation risk, the indexed-basket EPC is more likely to spread in the central or in the peripheral countries and regions of the Community. In the absence of money illusion and differences in risk aversion, demand for the EPC will mainly come from the peripheral member countries because these have experienced the highest inflation rates over the last few years (Italy, UK, Ireland). Only if the awareness of, and/or aversion to, inflation risk were more intense in the central regions, could the opposite currency pattern prevail and notably wage contracts in the peripheral and low-productivity regions continue to be concluded in the inflating national member currencies (as the Keynesian believers in the inflation trick would hope).

2. Real Exchange-Rate Risk The EPC will be used in the first place by those economic agents who suffer most from EC real exchange-rate risk. The reduction of EC real exchange-rate risk which the indexed-basket EPC brings about is the larger, the more closely the currency composition of the basket corresponds to the currency pattern of transactions of the economic agent concerned and the larger the variance of the expected real exchange-rate changes between his domestic currency and the other member currencies.

More generally, this means that the EPC will primarily be used by those companies and individuals who are most active in trade, travel and capital transactions between the member countries and that it will have least appeal with the local public of retailers, housewives, workers, etc., who normally do not enter into international transactions and who would face particularly high costs of information and of exchange or portfolio management if they employed a parallel currency. Moreover, interest in the EPC is likely to be stronger with internationally oriented national companies than with 'multinationals' whose assets and liabilities are already highly diversified by currency and which possess the necessary expertise to find hedges that are better tailored to their specific needs than the standard indexed-basket EPC.[21]

Since the central member countries and regions are most open vis-à-vis the rest of the Community and since they are at the same time most likely to be characterised by a pattern of transactions which corresponds to the currency composition of the indexed basket, there are reasons to expect that EPC expansion would exhibit a 'centralist bias'.

Real exchange-rate risk cannot be observed directly but it can be approximated. If it is assumed that the mean expected real exchange-rate change is zero for each pair of member currencies, the real exchange-rate changes which nevertheless occur are likely to determine the variance of expected real exchange rates and hence, real exchange-rate risk for the future. Real exchange-rate changes vis-à-vis the Community average are likely to be largest for the most peripheral and the most central member countries which tend to experience the lowest and the highest productivity increases, respectively. This hypothesis is supported by the evidence; for from 1959 to 1976, as well as from 1971 to 1976, the Netherlands benefited from the largest real exchange-rate appreciation, and the largest real exchange-rate depreciation was suffered by the UK (1959-76) and Italy (1971-6), respectively.[22]

If, alternatively, it is assumed that the trend of real exchange-rate change is anticipated, the precise nature of the trend affects only the purchasing-power information cost of using the EPC, and real exchange-rate risk must be measured in terms of deviations from the expected trend. In this case, (short-term) real exchange-rate risk is likely to be greatest with regard to the larger member countries which can best afford to conduct independent monetary policies. This hypothesis, too, is confirmed by the evidence: both in 1959-76 and in 1971-6, annual real exchange-rate changes vis-à-vis the Community average were least stable for France, the UK/Ireland, and Germany and most stable for Belgium/Luxembourg.[23]

However, it should be emphasised that large size or great instability of real exchange-rate changes vis-a-vis the Community average will only act as an incentive to use the EPC as a standard of value to the extent that the EPC is expected to be more stable in terms of the basket of goods and services relevant to the individual economic agent than the competing national currencies and standards of value. If his national currency is more stable in terms of his basket than the EPC, large and varying real exchange-rate changes between the EPC and his national currency will *deter* him from using the EPC. If allowance is made for the possibility that he may use more than one standard of value, this means that he will not prefer the EPC to the national money, if the latter keeps its domestic purchasing power, or to a national index clause, except to the extent that he has business with residents of other member countries, and his reluctance to make *more* use of the EPC will be the more pronounced, the larger and *less* stable real exchange-rate changes between his and the other member currencies. Thus, the direction of the effect which the size and instability of real exchange-rate changes between the national currencies will have on the demand for the EPC standard of value depends entirely on the baskets of goods and services relevant to economic agents in the Community. The only real exchange-rate changes which have effects of unambiguous sign are the real exchange-rate changes between the individual's basket on the one hand and the EPC and national index clauses on the other hand. The individual will choose his standard(s) of value in such a way as to minimise the real exchange-rate change between the monetary standard(s) and his personal basket.

B. The EPC's Expansion as a Store of Value

Just as in its standard-of-value function, the indexed-basket EPC should spread as a store of value primarily in those member countries in which the rate of inflation is high. But while, as a standard of value, the EPC will be in greatest demand in the high-inflation countries because higher rates of inflation tend to be less expected and less predictable, its attraction as a store of value in these countries does not derive from its ability to eliminate inflation risk but from the higher yield which it offers in comparison with non-interest-bearing forms of inflating national money. For analogous reasons, its expansion as a store of value will not depend on a country's absolute real exchange-rate changes vis-à-vis the other member countries or on the variance of these real exchange-rate changes but it will be the faster, the stronger the country's real exchange-rate depreciation. As has already been noted, both domestic inflation and real exchange-rate depreciation have been largest (say, since 1959 or 1971) for Italy, the UK and Ireland.

Just as in its standard-of-value function, the EPC will spread as a store of value mainly in those member countries in which high rates of inflation and depreciation and experience with indexation and basket units of account have left least money and exchange-rate illusion. But, unlike in its standard-of-value function, the EPC's expansion as a store of value will not be hampered by the simultaneous permission of national index clauses. For while national index clauses are substitutes for the indexed-basket standard of value, they are not a rival for the EPC store of value. National index clauses are not national index monies.

Since the loss of purchasing power to which national-currency deposits are subject may be offset through higher interest payments, the inroads which the EPC will make into a national member currency will tend to be greater, the larger the proportion of notes, coins and non-interest-bearing demand deposits in the national money supply. Table 5.1 indicates that, given the prohibition of interest payments on demand deposits in France, the proportion of the national money supply (M_2) that would offer less yield than the EPC seems to be largest in France and Belgium with the UK, Ireland and the Netherlands on the following places.

TABLE 5.1 The Composition of National Money Supplies (M_2) in the EC Member Countries (end of 1976)

	The share in M_2 of	
	Notes and Coins	Notes, Coins and Demand Deposits
Germany	8.6	25.0
France	13.3	53.1
UK	15.0	43.6
Italy	9.8	56.5
Netherlands	12.5	40.6
Belgium	24.0	52.6
Denmark	6.9	45.4
Ireland	14.9	38.2

Source: IMF International Financial Statistics.

Of course this, too, is merely a partial aspect which may be swamped by the fact that the EPC is less likely to be used by individual consumers and retailers than by producers and international traders whose demand for notes and coins is small.

C. The EPC's Expansion as a Means of Payment

A means of payment is more attractive, the higher its yield as a store of value and the greater its stability as a standard of value. However, the properties which render a money attractive as means of payment are low transaction and information costs.

In terms of transaction and information cost the EPC will initially be inferior to the national member currencies and its handicap will be largest in domestic transactions, for it is only in transactions with residents of other countries and currency domains that currency information cost and the cost of money changing arise in any case. Since information cost and, to some extent, conversion cost are fixed costs, the disincentive to use the EPC as a means of payments will be the smaller for an economic agent, the larger his volume of transactions across currency boundaries. Thus, as a means of payment, the EPC is most likely (or rather least unlikely) to be used in those areas which are most 'open' vis-à-vis the other member countries, i.e. notably in the smaller and central member countries and, in particular, in those regions which border on other member countries, and in those industries which are most actively engaged in international intra-Community transactions. The border of the EPC domain would then gradually move like a linguistic frontier: currency dualism, having started in the border regions, would spread into the homeland, and as the adjacent regions got acquainted with the parallel currency (language), the former border regions would give up the less useful currency (language) and return to a mono-currency (-language) standard.

To argue that the use of the EPC as a means of payment will be least disadvantageous for cross-border transactions is, of course, not to ignore that even in these transactions conversion via the EPC would cost far more than (initially about twice as much as) direct exchange of national currencies. At least this is true as long as the EPC has not yet developed the economies of scale which are a prerequisite for a vehicle currency. Only when the EPC exchange markets had gained a greater breadth, depth and resiliency than the dollar market could the EPC take over from the dollar as the vehicle currency which reduces the number of bilateral exchange markets from $\frac{n(n-1)}{2}$ to $n-1$.

However, although the EPC exchange markets will become increasingly competitive vis-à-vis the dollar exchange markets, their rate of growth may decelerate (and finally even become negative). For as more and more international payments are effected in EPC, it pays increasingly to possess EPC working balances instead of holding and converting national currencies via the EPC. And the fewer currencies need to be held in the portfolio, the cheaper its management and the smaller the required size becomes.[24] These effects will make themselves felt particularly strongly if the EPC is also increasingly used for domestic transactions.

D. The Pattern of EPC Penetration and Regional Balance

It has been shown that the indexed-basket EPC tends to expand so as to reduce real exchange-rate risk in all those regions and sectors of the member economies which are sufficiently open vis-à-vis other member countries. In this respect the pattern of EPC penetration will therefore conform to the real exchange-rate criterion which has been suggested as a comprehensive measuring-rod of the cost of currency union, or what is the same, of the benefit of currency diversity. Moreover, since, in terms of currency transaction and information costs, the EPC is most competitive (or, initially, least uncompetitive) in international intra-Community transactions, its pattern of penetration will also be consistent with the minimisation of the temporary costs of increasing currency diversity and with the maximisation of the permanent benefits of currency unification. Given that, both with respect to real exchange-rate risk and with regard to currency transaction and information cost, the EPC will spread primarily in the most open and central member countries and regions, and that these are also the countries and regions in which the diversification of international intra-Community transactions and the international intra-Community mobility of factors are most pronounced (and probably increase most as a result of EPC expansion), the pattern of EPC penetration will also conform to the partial criteria developed by the traditional theory of optimum currency areas. Thus, the creation of a basket parallel currency is a way of rendering the theory of optimum currency areas operational as well as dynamic.

Those reasons which indicate that the EPC might *not* prevail primarily in the most central and open member countries and regions belong into what I have called the theory of optimum disinflation domains. The optimality of a disinflation domain depends on domestic inflation risk and the opportunity cost of holding non-interest bearing national money, for the variance of the domestic inflation rate, the average rate of domestic inflation and the average rate of real exchange-rate depreciation are at present largest for the currencies of the peripheral member countries. Only Keynesians would argue that demand for an inflation-proof standard of value might be weaker in the backward regions (and industries) at the periphery where real wages may have to fall; for, if there were still a considerable degree of money illusion among workers and savers in the peripheral regions, debtors there would have an interest in exploiting it. For the EPC to have a 'central bias' it would then be necessary that the excess of the actual rate of regional inflation over the regionally optimal rate of inflation is larger at the centre than at the periphery. Whatever the outcome will be, with respect to disinflation the parallel currency will spread in the first place in those regions and industries where inflation is least effective in reducing unemployment and where protection against the damages of inflation is most desired.

Finally, the analysis implies that the parallel currency will not outcompete the national member currencies and thereby bring about full currency union, *unless* the European Community is an optimum stable currency area. Its success will prove that money and exchange-rate illusion is not as widespread as the opponents of currency unification tend to believe and that it is certainly not sufficient to justify expectations of sizeable international 'demonstration effects'[25] and talk about international 'differences in Phillips Curves'.

Currency competition will show whether it is correct to speak of 'national propensities to inflate' or whether these propensities must be ascribed to the money-producing state monopolists rather than to the economic agents who constitute a nation. It will show whether the lack of progress towards European monetary unification has been due to differences in money illusion on the part of money users or to differences in Phillips Curve illusion on the part of monetary-policy makers.

NOTES

1. For a fairly comprehensive statement of the case for the parallel-currency approach to European monetary unification see Vaubel (1977 a).
2. The term 'Currency union' is defined in this paper as a state of affairs in which a single currency is used in the whole union. 'Monetary union', on the other hand, will be employed as a general term comprising both

'currency union' and 'exchange-rate union' (i.e. fixed exchange rates between the national member currencies). This is also how the term 'monetary union' has been used by the Werner Committee and the EC Commission.

3. Parkin (1976), pp. 234, 239.
4. Corden (1976), p. 23.
5. For previous, less detailed expositions of this point by the present author see Vaubel (1975a, p. 40; 1975b, pp. 49 ff.; 1976b, pp. 8 ff.; 1977a, pp. 13 ff.).
6. 'When introduced into economies conditioned to high or moderate inflation, monetary policies better fitted to already lower inflation have tended to produce a slump in the process of reducing the inflation. Nor have the gradualist attempts at monetary counter-inflation generally escaped the problem of unemployment. This is the "crisis" of both Keynesian and Friedmanian policies . . . (In this respect) the contest between these two strategists would hardly be more starkly irrelevant' (Phelps, 1977, p. 2).
7. Vaubel (1976a), Section VI.
8. Cf. Giersch (1974), pp. 12 ff.
9. For an empirical analysis of the effect of central bank constitutions and independence on monetary policy see Parkin (1978).
10. Cf. Giersch (1973), Vaubel (1974), Riboud (1975), European Conservative Group (1975, p. 37) and the All Saints' Day Manifesto (1975).
11. Even if the remnants of money illusion were not negligible, they would – at least initially – be little affected by the introduction of the new stable currency. For, as will be shown in Section II, the indexed-basket EPC would spread primarily among those economic agents who are most accurately aware of current inflation (and of future inflation risk). Thus the inflating national currencies will be displaced in the first place in those regions (and industries) where (a constant rate of) inflation has little or no effect on employment anyway.
12. A detailed analysis of the implications of this strategy can be found in Vaubel (1977b, pp 456 ff.).
13. This strategy has been proposed by Cooper (1971).
14. Cf. the proposal by the Study Group on Optimum Currency Areas (1975, Ch. 4). See also Salin (1975), Claassen (1976) and Groupe Talent (1969).
15. A number of authors have suggested that the parallel currency's attractiveness should be enhanced through preferential discounting, special clearing services, official interventions to 'stabilize' its financial markets, subsidisation of banking charges and forward cover, and exemption from exchange controls and non-interest-bearing minimum reserve requirements. (Cf., e.g., Federal Trust for Education and Research (1972, pp. 10 ff.); Magnifico (1973, p. 126); Onida (1973, p. 60); Walter (1973, para, 24)). If these advantages were not offset by a depreciation of the parallel currency vis-a-vis its competitors, such measures would no doubt stimulate demand for it; but the problem is that, unlike a value guarantee, they are either not desirable in their own right or should be extended to the national currencies as well.
16. The proposition that the choice of currency does not involve Pareto-relevant 'real-income' (or 'technological') externalities but merely interdependence tnrough the market ('pecuniary externalities') and that these 'pecuniary externalities' are zero under perfect competition is developed in

some detail in my forthcoming book *Strategies for Currency Unification, the Case for a European Parallel Currency and the Economics of Currency Competition.*

17. Cf. Vaubel (1977b, Section III.2).
18. This point has been demonstrated in some detail in Vaubel (1976a, Section II)
19. For an international comparison of the term structure of government debt in the EC member countries see, e.g., P.K. Woolley and Coates (1974, Table III).
20. A strong positive correlation between the average inflation rate and variations in the inflation rate has been observed, e.g. by Okun (1971), Vogel (1974), Logue and Willett (1976), Heller (1976), Jaffee and Kleiman (1977) and Fischer and Modigliani (1977). However, as Gordon (1971), Klein (1975) and, again, Logue and Willett (op. cit.) have shown, this was not always and everywhere the case.
21. It may even be argued that exchange-rate risk is one of the reasons for the proliferation of multinational companies.
22. For the most up-to-date analysis of the evidence see Vaubel (1978, Section 5).
23. Ibid.
24. For a formula describing the economies in the total volume of working balances which result from a reduction of the number of currencies see Swoboda (1968, App. 2).
25. The 'demonstration effect' hypothesis has notably been advanced by Stahl (1974, pp. 99 ff.). It presupposes the existence of exchange-rate illusion, for it implies that, *owing to currency borders,* workers and trade unions do not know the wage level in neighbouring currency areas. To reject the 'demonstration effect' hypothesis is, of course, not to argue that at present trade unions and workers possess perfect information about wages in the other member countries (nor, of course, in their own country). It is merely suggested that the substitution of a common currency for the existing national member currencies will not have a noticeable effect on the quality of the information which they do possess.

    Moreover, even if there were 'demonstration effects', they might (as Corden, 1972, p. 14, has emphasised) just as well relate to wage *increases* and *reduce* regional imbalances.

REFERENCES

'All Saints' Day Manifesto for European Monetary Union' (G. Basevi, M. Fratianni, H. Giersch, P. Korteweg, D. O'Mahony, M. Parkin, T. Peeters, P. Salin, N. Thygesen), *The Economist,* London, November 1, 1975.

Claassen, Emil-Maria, 'Varianten einer europaischen Parallel-wahrung', *Neue Zürcher Zeitung,* November 13, 1976.

Cooper, Richard N., *Sterling, European Monetary Unification, and the International Monetary System,* The British-North American Committee, Palm Beach, December 1971.

Corden, W. Max, 'Monetary Integration', *Princeton Essays in International Finance,* No. 93, April 1972.

Corden, W. Max, 'European Monetary Integration. The Main Issues', Trade

Policy Research Centre, London, July 1976 (cf. also Chs. 10 and 11 in W.M. Corden, *Inflation, Exchange Rates and the World Economy* (Chicago and Oxford, 1977)).

European Conservative Group, *Community Policies for Economic Growth* (Luxembourg, 1975).

Federal Trust for Education and Research, *European Monetary Integration* (by Giovanni Magnifico and John Williamson) (London, January 1972).

Fischer, Stanley and Franco Modigliani, 'Aspects of the Costs of Inflation', paper presented at the Conference on the Economic Crisis of the 1970s: 'Lessons for Stabilization Policy', Baden/Austria, September 1977.

Giersch, Herbert, 'Final Remarks', in *European Economic Integration and Monetary Unification,* Study Group on Economic and Monetary Union, EC Commission, D.G.II, Brussels, October 1973.

Giersch, Herbert, 'Index Clauses and the Fight against Inflation', in *Essays on Inflation and Indexation,* Domestic Affairs Study No. 24, American Enterprise Institute, Washington, October 1974 (translated from: Indexklausen und Inflationsbekampfung', Kieler Diskussionsbeitrage, No. 32, October 1973).

Gordon, Robert J., 'Steady Anticipated Inflation: Mirage or Oasis', *Brookings Papers on Economic Activity,* 1971, No. 2.

Groupe Talent, 'La crise des paiments dans le marché commun', *Cahiers Economiques de Bruxelles,* 1969, No. 44.

Heller, H. Robert, 'International Reserves and World-Wide Inflation', International Monetary Fund, *Staff Papers,* March 1976.

Jaffee, Dwight and Ephraim Kleiman, 'The Welfare Implications of Uneven Inflation', in Erik Lundberg (ed.) *Inflation Theory and Anti-Inflation Policy* (Boulder, Col. 1977).

Klein, Benjamin, 'Our New Monetary Standard: The Measurement and Effects of Price Uncertainty, 1880-1973', *Economic Inquiry,* December 1975.

Logue, Dennis E. and Thomas D. Willett, 'A Note of the Relation between the Rate and Variability of Inflation', *Economica,* May 1976.

Magnifico, Giovanni, *European Monetary Unification* (London, 1973) (also published in French, German and Italian).

Okun, Arthur, 'The Mirage of Steady Inflation', *Brookings Papers on Economic Activity,* 1971, No. 2.

Onida, Fabrizio, 'Notes sur l'unification monétaire', in *European Economic Integration and Monetary Unification,* Study Group on Economic and Monetary Union, EC Commission, D.G.II, Brussels, October 1973.

Parkin, Michael, 'Monetary Union and Stabilization Policy in the European Community', *Banca Nazionale del Lavoro Quarterly Review,* September 1976.

Parkin, Michael, 'In Search of a New Monetary Constitution for the European Communities', this volume.

Phelps, Edmund S., 'Adaptive Guideposts for Disinflation without Recession', paper presented at the Conference on the Economic Crisis of the 1970s: 'Lessons for Stabilization Policy', Baden/Austria, September 1977.

Riboud, Jacques, *Une monnaie pour l'Europe – L'Eurostable* (Paris, 1975).

Salin, Pascal, 'Roads to Monetary Union', in Comments on 'Economic Policy for the European Community – The Way Forward', *Kiel Discussion Papers,* No. 38/9, June 1975.

Stahl, Heinz-Michael, *Regionalpolitische Implikationen einer EWG-Währungsunion* (Tubingen, 1974).
Study Group on Optimum Currency Areas, *Towards Economic Equilibrium and Monetary Unification in Europe* (1975 Report), EC Commission, D.G.II, Brussels, January 1976.
Swoboda, Alexander K., 'The Eurodollar Market: An Interpretation', *Princeton Essays in International Finance,* No. 64, February 1968.
Vaubel, Roland, 'Plans for a European Parrallel Currency and SDR Reform: The Choice of Value-Maintenance Provisions and "Gresham's Law" ', *Weltwirtschaftliches Archiv,* 1974, No. 2.
Vaubel, Roland (1975a), 'Roads to Monetary Union', in: Comments on 'Economic Policy for the European Community – The Way Forward', *Kiel Discussion Papers,* No. 38/9, June 1975.
Vaubel, Roland (1975b), 'Euro-Geld aus der Retorte', *Die Wirtschaftswoche,* December 18, 1975.
Vaubel, Roland (1976a), 'Real Exchange-Rate Changes in the European Community: The Empirical Evidence and its Implications for European Currency Unification', *Weltwirtschaftliches Archiv,* 1976, No. 3.
Vaubel, Roland (1976b), *The Parallel Currency Approach to European Monetary Unification and the Search for a New European Unit of Account,* report prepared for the EC Commission, Study Group 'Unité Monétaire Européenne' 81 pp., unpublished.
Vaubel, Roland (1977a), 'The Next Steps in European Monetary Integration: Optica 1975 and Optica 1976', paper presented at the Conference on US-European Monetary Relations, Washington, March 1977 (forthcoming).
Vaubel, Roland (1977b), 'Free Currency Competition', *Weltwirtschaftliches Archiv,* 1977, No. 3.
Vaubel, Roland, 'Real Exchange-Rate Changes in the European Community: A New Approach to the Determination of Optimum Currency Areas', *Journal of International Economics,* May 1978.
Vogel, Robert C., 'The Dynamics of Inflation in Latin America, 1950-1969', *The American Economic Review,* March 1974.
Walter, Norbert, 'Europäische Währungsunion und die Reform des Weltwahrungssystems', in Zur Neuordnung des Internationalen Währungssystems, *Beihefte der Konjunkturpolitik,* Heft 20, 1973.
Woolley, Paul K. and Jeffrey B. Coates, 'Debt Management in the EEC', *National Westminster Bank Quartely Review,* February 1974.

COMMENT ON VAUBEL

Rainer S. Masera

It is Vaubel's contention that the introduction (à la All Saints' Day Manifesto) of an inflation-proofed European parallel currency (IPEPC) would minimise the costs to employment of disinflation and lead to the formation of an optimum currency domain in Europe. His paper is purported to justify these contentions, by providing an economic rationale for them.

These comments are likely to be vitiated by an incomplete understanding of the arguments developed by Vaubel, possibly owing to the limitations of the present commentator and/or to an inadequate explanation of the underlying theory (which may perhaps be more satisfactorily set out in the forthcoming book on this subject by Vaubel).

Be that as it may, I fail to be convinced by the analysis developed by Vaubel, and therefore by his policy recommendations.

Even if one were to accept a 'monetarist' explanation of the process of price-wage formation, doubts arise as to the desiderability of an approach based on the introduction of an IPEPC. In the exchange of letters published by *The Economist* following the presentation of the Manifesto I remarked that

> The assured maintenance of a constant purchasing power of the Europa will make the new money the dominant monetary asset in European portfolios, at a time when deflation in terms of domestic currencies is neither present nor foreseeable. This will imply an excess demand for Europas at the official crawling-peg-exchange rates between the national currencies and the new money, which, in turn, will very shortly lead either to a market demand-determined total substitution of the latter for the former, or to the abandonment of full convertibility and hence to 'free market' quotations for Europas. In the first case, it will be necessary to resort immediately to *domestic* money creation rules guaranteeing absolute price constancy (with all the attendant real costs), in the latter case, the significance of the Europa will be lost.

There is no easy way round the fact that a necessary condition for sustainable price stability is the ability to maintain an appropriate balance between growth of the demand for money and money supply creation, since the price of the quantity of money is none other than the reciprocal of the general price level. Indeed, as Professor Davidson observed (also in a letter to *The Economist*)

> The Manifesto's signatories' myopia involves the failure to recognize the crucial role of contracts for forward delivery of goods and services, and especially long duration money wage contracts, in endowing any money with purchasing power and liquidity.
>
> If a Europa was to circulate alongside national monies and if workers expected the Europa to be more inflation proof than the national currency, then rational workers would insist on setting their wage contracts in terms of the Europa. Once the institution of wage contracts in Europa units became widespread, then if, over time, money wages in Europa units rose more rapidly than productivity, the Europa could not maintain a stable purchasing power over producible goods and services. What would be required is an incomes policy which stabilizes unit labour costs and profit margins in Europa units.[1]

Along the same lines, one can state that, when the necessary distinction is drawn between money and credit, the availability of an asset guaranteeing a zero real rate of return and offering the pecuniary and non-pecuniary advantages of money would necessarily force real ex-ante rates of interest to substantially positive levels. This of course need not pose problems in a steady-state dynamic growth model where, presumably, the real rate would coincide with the marginal productivity of capital, but would certainly cause a host of difficulties in the real world, especially when account is taken of the actual experience in terms of ex-post real yields throughout the Community. These points have been recently elaborated by the Villa Pamphili group, and I do not wish to dwell on them here.[2]

The crucial point in assessing the 'real' short and long term costs of stabilization and disinflation policies resides of course in the interpretation of the process of price and wage formation.

Here, however, Vaubel would appear to hold inconsistent views. On the one hand he seems to adhere to the standard monetarist view, whereby downward harmonisation of rates of expansion of monetary aggregates[3] is liable to produce frictional costs because of the slow adaptation of inflationary expectations.[4] His acceptance of this model of interpretation is also evident when he asks the rhetoric question 'whether it is correct to speak of "national propensities to inflate" or whether these propensities must be ascribed to the money-producing state monopolists rather than to the economic agents who constitute a nation'.

However, as regards the regions which would be likely first to accept the IPEPC, Vaubel adheres to the view that 'in the absence of money illusion and differences in risk aversion, demand for the EPC will mainly come from the peripheral member countries because these have experienced the highest inflation rates over the last few years (Italy, UK, Ireland)'. Inflation would be least unwelcome in regions which, partly owing to their less favourable location, suffer from slow growth of physical productivity and real exchange rate depreciation, but which do not content themselves with correspondingly smaller wage increases.

This theoretical framework is of the wage-standard type.[5] Indeed the views come close to the extreme argument put forward by those who reject the validity of the European integration approach. The spatial counterpart of trade diversion effects implies unfavourable dynamic repercussions on peripheral regions: the attempt to maintain real wages must lower employment possibilities in those regions. Workers migrate to central poles of the area, which – owing to an imperfect assessment by market forces and by the price mechanism of externalities – involves generalized dynamic welfare losses.

Ambiguity on this point cannot be accepted. As has been shown, notably by Magnifico, if national propensities to inflate (NPI) differ, the costs of monetary unification unaccompanied by a comprehensive set of regional, fiscal and structural interventions cannot be neglected.

It must be observed in this respect that the NPI concept need not be identified with simplistic wage-pushfulness approaches. Indeed, if we abandon the 'old universally flex-price system',[6] sophisticated models of price-wage determination can yield results of the NPI type.[7]

It is relevant to quote in this respect Giersch, who had already suggested that 'a Europa that is floated in competition with national currencies will probably be used first in wage contracts in the industrial core of Europe. Wage contracts in peripheral areas are likely to be fixed in national currencies for quite a while–just as it takes some time for national languages to replace dialects in areas farther away from the centres of communication'.[8] Giersch, however, set these remarks in terms of a specific set of measures dealing with regional problems, and aimed at supplementing the operation of market mechanisms, to deal with externalities. More specifically, he clearly stated that the beneficial effects stemming from the floating of the Europa connected with the likelihood of its penetration in central areas would be of a transitory nature. 'When all wage contracts are concluded in "Europa", the distorting effects of the principle of "equal pay for equal work" will make themselves felt. This then would be the time for large scale regional policy measures to support peripheral areas.'

It must be stressed in this respect that critics of the EMU approach – and indeed of the idea of floating an EPC – have pointed out that, as a result, a tendency might develop towards nominal wage equalisation throughout the community, which would have disastrous effects for 'backward' regions.

All this is completely neglected by Vaubel, who does not distinguish between transitory and permanent effects, and does not admit the need for explicit regional policies (inconsistently with his 'spatial' theory). Many of Vaubel's arguments on the advantages of the IPEPC rest on his belief that the parallel currency would exhibit a 'centralist bias'. The validity of this conclusion is, however, open to question.

Even the incomplete analysis developed by Vaubel yields, at best, mixed results.[9] Indeed, I have some difficulties in reconciling Vaubel's statements on this point. Thus, while he argues that the IPEPC will tend to displace first EC currencies with high and variable rates of inflation, and that it should also spread first in countries characterized by stronger rates of real exchange depreciation, he still concludes that 'both with respect to real exchange rate risk and with regard to currency transaction cost, the EPC will spread primarily in the most open and central countries'.

Perhaps Vaubel himself is not too clear in his own mind as to the final outcome, but (as an act of faith(?)) he still claims that 'Whatever the outcome will be, with respect to disinflation the parallel currency will spread in the first place in those regions and industries where inflation is least effective in reducing unemployment and where protection against the damages of inflation is most desired.'

As will be clear from the considerations developed so far I remain unconvinced by an approach to EMU essentially based on the launching of an IPEPC.[10] Quite apart from the consideration that this approach would hardly be realistic, I believe it would increase total real (welfare) costs of the unification process.

Let it be added in this respect that it is by no means true that these costs are simply to be identified with the assumption of money and exchange-rate illusion, as Vaubel seems to believe. More fundamentally they are, however, associated with the rejection of a generalized acritical application of flex-price models and the recognition of static and dynamic externalities in the process of European unification.

NOTES

1. Attention must be drawn to the fact that arguments of this type had already been developed by Magnifico (1973, pp. 163-4), well before the publication of the Manifesto, to show why a constant purchasing power parallel money was not desirable.
2. See Balassa (1976, pp. 303 ff.), the Preface to the Italian edition of Magnifico's book (1976), and his forthcoming paper.
3. Also in this respect I must express some doubts about Vaubel's arguments. He claims that 'since the member countries with the lower rates of inflation are unlikely to accept an acceleration of inflation for the sake of exchange-rate unification, the more inflation-prone members would have to adopt a strongly disinflationary policy. Indeed, as has been shown, consumer price inflation in these countries (Italy, the UK, Ireland) has to be several per cent below the rates prevailing in the other member countries if nominal exchange rates are to remain stable.' In the first place – unless the argument is made that the lower the rate of inflation, the better – the asymmetry in adjustment policies must be questionable. Secondly, his contention would imply that 'peripheral and backward' regions should, under present

4. However, in the rational, competitive world which is assumed in these analyses, rational rather than adaptive models of price expectations ought to be used.
5. See Magnifico (1973, p. 63), Hicks (1959, p. 88) and Hicks (1977, p. xii).
6. Hicks (1977).
7. On these issues, with respect to the peripheral countries mentioned by Vaubel, see the interesting paper by Henry, Sawyer and Smith (1977, pp. 60-71). Evidence of the relevance of (national) trade union pressure for money wage increases is offered by applying the Sargan (1964) approach, whereby the net real-earnings bargaining target of trade unions is obtained via money wage demands which allow for expected price changes.
   An important study on the mechanism of wage formation in Italy which is not consistent with the pure monetarist approach is that by Modigliani and Tarantelli (1977).
8. Cf. Giersch (1973, p. 115).
9. The main sources of incompleteness are the lack of proper treatment for (i) portfolio analysis on the asset demand side; (ii) borrower cost considerations on the supply side (private operators); (iii) IPEPC – base creation mechanisms and guarantee clauses in the short and the long run.
10. A recent exposition of what I consider more promising approaches to EMU – allowing for the launching of a non-inflation-proof EPC – can be found in Magnifico (forthcoming) and Massera (1977).

REFERENCES

Giersch, H., 'The Case for a European Regional Policy', in *European Economic and Monetary Unification,* Brussels, European Communities, 1973.

Henry, S., Sawyer, M. and Smith, P., 'Models of Inflation in the United Kingdom: an Evaluation', *National Institute Economic Review,* 1977.

Hicks, J.R., *Essays in World Economics* (Oxford: Oxford University Press, 1959).

Hicks, J.R., *Economic Perspectives* (Oxford: Clarendon Press, 1977).

Magnifico, G., *European Monetary Unification* (London: Macmillan, 1973).

Magnifico, G., *Una moneta per l'Europa* (Laterza, 1976).

Magnifico, G., 'European Monetary Unification: Problems and Perspectives' (forthcoming).

Masera, R., 'La moneta europea nell'attuale contesto dei pagamenti internazionali', *Studium,* November-December 1977, pp. 757-70.

Modigliani, F. and E. Tarantelli, 'Market Forces, Trade Union Action and the Phillips Curve in Italy', *Banca Nazionale del Lavoro Quarterly Review,* March 1977.

Sargan, J., 'Wages and Prices in the United Kingdom: a Study in Ecometric Methodology', in P.E. Hart, G. Mills and J.K. Whitaker (eds.), *Econometric Analysis for National Economic Planning* (London: Butterworth, 1964).

COMMENT ON VAUBEL

Theo Peeters

Both questions raised by R. Vaubel can be answered affirmatively. First, Vaubel argues that with an inflation-proofed European parallel currency (IPEPC), the goal of attaining disinflation without transitional unemployment can be achieved. Second, Vaubel asserts that the IPEPC will tend to alleviate rather than aggravate the problem of regional imbalances in the Community.

If both points were valid they would represent strong arguments for the IPEPC approach towards EMU. Indeed, they address two of the strongest arguments traditionally put forward by the opponents of EMU, namely that (i) the transition to a European monetary union, and therefore a Community inflation rate, would impose upon the high-inflation countries a recession lasting for several years, and (ii) the surrender of the exchange rate instrument will imply an 'excessive' level of unemployment in the structurally weaker areas of the Community, even to the extent that they may become permanently depressed areas. More specifically, opponents of EMU argue, rather loosely, that membership of a European monetary union would condemn countries like Britain or Italy to a status comparable to the current situation of Northern Ireland as a region of the UK, and like the Mezzogiorno as a region of Italy.

My remaining comments indicate that I largely agree with Vaubel on the first problem; that I have some doubts about his conclusion for the second; and, perhaps most important, that I feel that there may be a contradiction between both claims being right simultaneously.

The key element in the argument that the inflation-proofed Europa would avoid the stabilization-induced transitional unemployment is that with this new unit, the expected inflation rate is virtually brought down to zero. Consequently, economic agents are able, as in a non-inflationary period, to calculate in real terms. Thus when, as the result of successful disinflationary policies, the actual inflation rate turns out to be lower than the anticipated inflation rate, they can avoid building excessive real wages, real interest payments and real debt principal into contracts concluded in nominal terms and based upon their erroneous expectations.

Two problems nevertheless remain. First, the Europa will eliminate inflationary expectations because it has an absolute and credible value guarantee. The value guarantee takes the form of an exchange rate guarantee vis-à-vis the currencies which circulate in the same area. As Vaubel mentions, 'this procedure can work only as long as the parallel currency remains a parallel currency'. Therefore, for the inflation-proofed Europa to make sense its introduction has to be gradual. If the existing currencies were to be quickly driven out of the market, the advantages of launching a parallel currency over a once-and-for-all currency reform, in which the existing currencies are replaced by a single European currency, would be rather illusory. As the paper by Vaubel indicates, the penetration of the Europa can be expected to take time. Klein even argues that there are reasons to believe that the Europa will not be accepted at all.

A second problem, to which I have no clear answer, arises from the differential speed by which the Europa will spread over the Community, for the reasons spelled out by Vaubel in the second part of his paper. Does this affect differently the adjustment of inflationary expectations throughout the Community? And if that is the case, does this mean that the extent to which stabilization-induced unemployment will be avoided will differ throughout the Community? What will guarantee that the stabilization crisis will be avoided where it is needed most, in the countries with the highest and most unpredictable inflation rates? The most commonly given answer is that the Europa is needed most where the threat of a stabilization crisis is greatest.

This brings me to the second advantage put forward by Vaubel, the problem of regional balance. The regional unemployment problem can be stated as a situation where nominal factor payments tend to be equalised throughout a monetary union under conditions of regional productivity differentials. The result is higher real wages in the weaker, peripheral areas and lower real wages in the stronger, central areas. The result is out-migration of capital from the peripheral to the central areas. Combined with a lack of labour mobility this results in underemployment in the periphery and over-employment in the centre. To the extent that a minimal degree of money- and exchange-rate illusion does still exist in the peripheral areas, it is possible to alleviate the regional unemployment problem through exchange rate adjustment that results in some real wage flexibility.

A rapid spread of the inflation-proofed Europa in the peripheral areas would swamp the just-mentioned adjustment possibility and increase the structural problems in the weaker areas. It is, therefore, important to notice that, according to Vaubel's analysis, the Europa will penetrate in the first place in those regions where inflation is most ineffective in reducing unemployment, i.e. in the central areas, whereas the peripheral and structural weaker areas would be less affected.

The argument hinges crucially on the rate of penetration of the Europa being highest in the central areas with the strongest currencies. However, from the point of view of avoiding the stabilization crisis, I understand that the need for the Europa is greatest in the weaker areas with the inflation-prone currencies.

The possible conflict is hardly resolved in the last section of Vaubel's paper, where it is apparently left to the reader to make up his mind. First, he writes that 'both with respect to real exchange-rate risk and with regard to currency transaction and information cost, the EPC will spread primarily in the most open and central member countries and regions'. But in the next paragraph one is led to believe that the 'reasons which indicate that the EPC might *not* prevail primarily in the most central and open member countries and regions' (*my italics*) have to be taken rather seriously too, unless one accepts Keynesian type arguments to justify a weaker demand for an inflation-proofed standard of value in the backward regions at the periphery.

6 Units of Account and Parallel Currencies in Transnational Transactions

ROBERT TRIFFIN

I. INTRODUCTION

Three recent developments should revive interest in the launching of a relatively stable unit of account as a parallel currency. This currency would be an alternative to national currencies and Euro-currencies (overwhelmingly the US dollar and German mark) for the denomination and even settlement, of transnational contracts which cannot – by definition – be *simultaneously* expressed in the national currency of each contracting party.

1. The first is the aggravation of exchange risks resulting from recurrent exchange crises and the present and prospective instability of major currencies, particularly the US dollar. This is pointed out in the concluding section of two articles of the *IMF Survey* (November 7 and 21, 1977) on 'Recent Development of Units of Account Designed to Serve Borrowers and Lenders' and 'Increase in Exchange Rate Flexibility Spurs Use of Official Units of Account' (see particularly p. 363 of the second of these articles).

2. The IBLC (Institut Belgo-Luxembourgeois de Change) has indicated its readiness to extend to any bank, without restriction, the authorisation granted by it to a Belgian commercial bank, on September 26, 1977, to open and remunerate time and even sight deposits in the official European Unit of Account (EUA) of the Community, in the name not only of European organisations and their foreign employees, but also of foreigners, and of Belgian 'regnicoles' and residents. Such accounts are subject to the same regulations as foreign currency accounts, thus assimilating the EUA to other foreign currencies now widely used in bank contracts.

The EEC Commission has such accounts with nine banks, in all member countries except Germany, and it hopes that such accounts will become increasingly common.

3. The President of the EEC Commission, Roy Jenkins, has recently

developed in various speeches[1] powerful arguments for the resumption of the drive toward European Monetary Union, on the eve of the enlargement of the Community and of the first direct election of the European Parliament. The European Council of December 5 and 6, 1977, has reaffirmed its attachment to the objective of European Monetary Union, and noted the intention of the Commission to evoke this problem before the European Parliament, the Economic and Social Committee, and in the framework of future Tripartite Conferences. It has retained among immediate objectives the strengthening of monetary and financial solidarity and the adjustment ['aménagement'] of the short and medium term credit mechanisms, has approved the principle of a new instrument of Community borrowing and loans to be managed by the European Investment Bank, and introduced the EUA in the budget of the European Communities, beginning on January 1, 1978.

This should create a far more promising climate than could have been hoped previously for the initiatives that commercial banks and financial intermediaries could take in order to meet the needs of their customers – borrowers and lenders – in the face of the formidable exchange rate risks and uncertainties confronting them today, and probably – alas – for many months and even several years to come.

II. A LIMITED BUT REALISTIC OBJECTIVE

I shall allude only briefly and incidentally in my remarks to 'ideal' long-term reforms – such as full monetary and economic union – on which opinion is still deeply divided in academic as well as in business and official sectors. I shall concentrate instead on what could possibly – and should urgently – be concretely attempted in the very near future, in the light of the general consensus now existing, rightly or regrettably, on the following points:

1. There exists no early prospect for the restoration of presumptive *exchange rate stability* among major countries – including particularly the United States – or even among the countries of the Community.

2. There exists no early prospect for the general acceptance of *freely floating* exchange rates, abandoned to the tender mercy of supply and demand on the market. Indeed, official interventions in the exchange markets have developed, since the generalization of floating rates in March 1973, to new heights, without precedent in world history. Gross interventions are reported to have averaged about $30 billion from March 1973 through January 1975, $40 billion and $73 billion in the following two years, and to have been running at an annual rate of $120 billion from August through October 1977.

3. Finally, there is no early prospect for meaningful, generally accepted

and implemented guidelines for such official interventions in the exchange market and for concerted management of exchange rate policies.

It is worth nothing that the Second Amendment to the IMF Article of Agreement is largely confined to the legalization of this cahotic 'non-system', leaving each country free to adopt whatever exchange arrangement it wishes, and not even providing a 'common denominator' for the definition and readjustment of exchange rates.

Given this somber background, the best that can realistically be hoped for in the immediate future is an attempt by the private economic sectors to adjust to this new environment by reducing, to the extent possible, the exchange risks inevitably entailed in their transnational borrowing and lending contracts. They used to do so in the past by using as a unit of account settlement and working funds denominated in so-called 'key currencies' expected to remain stabler than other national currencies. The pound sterling, and later the dollar, have long been the major currencies used in that manner, and the German mark is now competing increasingly in this respect with the US dollar. Their huge fluctuations, however, in terms of one another and of other major currencies, make them a less and less satisfactory instrument in this respect.

As pointed out in the article of the *IMF Survey* quoted above, the generalization of floating rates makes any *national* currency less and less satisfactory as an effective shelter against exchange risks.

The most ambitious solution of the problem would be, as suggested and powerfully argued by a number of economists,[2] the creation of a new unit of account and parallel currency, defined in terms of constant purchasing power as measured by a weighted average of national cost-of-living indices. Such a radical proposal might conceivably emerge some day as a last resort against generalized hyperinflation and flight from national currencies. It raises, however, formidable objections and is not likely to gain broad acceptance in the immediate future with which I am concerned here.

1. The least of them is the difficulty to explain and make credible to the public the complex and inevitably controversial calculations of national indices and of their European average.

2. The greatest would be to bridge – presumably through low, or even negative, interest rates – the enormous gap between its attraction to prospective lenders and its frightening risks for prospective borrowers.

3. Last but not least, would be the likely opposition of the monetary and political authorities to the introduction of a currency unit presented by its proponents as a rival to national currencies, threatening them with rapid and total extinction for domestic as well as for international transactions.

The first and admittedly modest step which I wish to explore here would be to provide an alternative, not to national currencies, but only to foreign currencies and Euro-currencies already and increasingly used today as parallel currencies for international transactions. It would be initiated by commercial banks and financial intermediaries for the denomination of Euro-bonds, bank deposits and lending operations in which foreign currencies and Euro-currencies are already legally authorized in all member countries. No other decision need be expected at the start from the official authorities of either the European Community or of national governments within or outside the Community. It should be hoped – and expected – however, that some of them might also find it an attractive instrument for their own lending, and particularly borrowing, operations and those of local authorities and parastatal organizations.

The hoped for resumption of progress toward European Monetary Union would of course, call at a later stage for major political decisions to which I shall briefly allude in the concluding section of this paper. The early introduction of a parallel currency as an alternative to Euro-dollars and Euro-marks for transnational transactions could only be a first, but 'seminal' step in this direction. It should also be equally welcome, however, even to those who reject this ultimate goal, but recognize the urgent need to shelter the Community countries against the devastating external shocks repeatedly and unnecessarily imparted to their economy today by an excessive reliance on *national* currencies – particularly the dollar – in *international* contracts and settlements within as well as outside the Community.

III. ALTERNATIVE DEFINITIONS OF THE EUROPA

Various names have been suggested to distinguish the proposed parallel currency from the multiple 'units of account' now in use, and to give it a less abstract and esoteric denomination, easier to popularize with the public. The term 'Europa' would seem particularly attractive as a symbol of European unity and, in any case, as avoiding the need for translation in different national languages, both within and outside the Community.[3]

1. The first possibility that comes to mind is obviously the definition of the Unit of Account officially agreed upon among all the countries of the Community – and the other OEEC (Organization for European Economic Cooperation) countries – in 1950, and which was used most satisfactorily and successfully for more than eight years (1950-8) as the anchor of the *European Payments Union* (EPU) operations. It also served as a model for the unit of account adopted in the early 1960s, at the initiative of Fernand Collin, for multiple Euro-bond issues syndicated by the Kredietbank of Luxembourg, totalling today the equivalent of more than \$1½ billion, i.e. considerably more than all other units of account taken together.

The EPU Agreement of 1950 defined, at my own suggestion, this unit of account as equivalent at all times to whichever member currency would have retained in fact the greatest exchange rate stability. But stability in terms of what? The *legal* definition took as benchmark a given weight of gold which might, however, be changed by unanimous decision of the OEEC Council in which no country would veto an appreciation, or depreciation, no greater than that of its own currency since the inception of the Union. The Kredietbank wisely foresaw the possible demise of the EPU and of the role of the OEEC Council in such decisions, and defined its unit *directly* as invariable in terms of gold, unless *all* member currencies changed their par value and or majority in the same direction, in which case the unit of account would remain equal to the currency that had remained the stablest, i.e. appreciated, or depreciated, the least within the majority.

The gradual disintegration of the Bretton Woods system has unfortunately imposed a number of successive switches from gold at first to the official par values of the IMF, and when these disappeared to the 'central rates' of the Smithsonian Agreement. When these were also abandoned with the generalization of floating rates in March 1973, the currencies of reference remained those which effectively maintained agreed limits of fluctuation vis-à-vis one another, i.e. the currencies of the 'snake'. If the snake itself were to disappear, the unit of account would remain equivalent to the last currency to leave it. If different currencies were to leave the snake at the same time, it would become identical to the most stable currency, i.e. 'that chosen from among those currencies by the Fiscal Agent in the interest of holders of bonds and coupons and without liability on its part'.

2. A second obvious alternative definition would be that officially adopted by the Community in 1974 and progressively extended to more and more of its operations. This European Unit of Account (EUA in English, or UCE in French) is a weighted basket of the nine currencies of the Community, whose effective market exchange value in terms of the dollar, the yen, the Swiss franc and seven other major currencies is calculated and published daily by the Commission.

This definition is highly appropriate for the purposes in which it is now used, for example many of the operations of the European Development Fund, the Coal and Steel Community, and the budget of the Economic Community.

It remains questionable, however, whether the EUA would be acceptable to the market, and even to central banks, as long as sharp exchange rate fluctuations between the currencies of the Community may continue to impart to it excessive depreciation risks in terms of the strongest currencies. As of the end of September 1977, for instance, it would have depreciated in terms of six of the nine currencies (the mark, the guilder, the Belgian and Luxembourg francs, the Danish Krone and the French franc) by percentages ranging from 1 per cent to 30 per cent since the end of 1969, and by 3 per cent to 15 per cent even since the introduction of the EUA in June 1974. The German mark rose vis-à-vis the EUA by as much as 6.85 per cent in three months, from December 1975 to March 1976, and 3.71 per cent in March 1976 alone, that is at yearly rates of more than 27 per cent to 44 per cent.

The EUA appreciated sharply and systematically in relation to the other three currencies (the British and Irish pounds, and the Italian Lira) and would have been an attractive investment for residents of these countries. What matters, however, is its ability to attract investments from the stronger currencies of countries in surplus, particularly the German mark.

3. These considerations would lead me to suggest as the most promising definition for the Europa a reinforced EUA basket, excluding – temporarily – from its calculation whichever currency depreciates by, let us say, 5 per cent or more in terms of the official EUA, but reintegrating it in the basket whenever it regains stability and does not depreciate again by 5 per cent for a period of, let us say, one year.[4]

Past experience shows that such a Europa would have appreciated, by September 1977, by about 14 per cent in terms of the EUA, and 29 per cent in terms of the US dollar since the end of 1969, and by about 8 per cent and 5 per cent respectively since the end of June 1974. The strongest currencies would, of course, have risen in terms of all alternative units, but substantially less toward the Europa than toward either the dollar or the EUA. The accompanying table shows the cumulative and average yearly exchange rate variations between each Community currency, on the one hand, and the dollar, the EUA and the Europa, on the other, over such an 8 year period of violent exchange rate turbulence.

TABLE 6.1

	Exchange rate fluctuations over 8 years, vis-a-vis			Average yearly fluctuations vis-a-vis		
	US dollar	EUA	Europa	US dollar	EUA	Europa
Mark	+ 63.2	+ 43.4	+ 26.1	+ 6.3	+ 4.6	+ 2.9
Guilder	+ 49.6	+ 31.4	+ 15.6	+ 5.2	+ 3.5	+ 1.8
B-L franc	+ 41.4	+ 24.3	+ 9.3	+ 4.4	+ 2.8	+ 1.1
Danish krone	+ 21.9	+ 7.1	– 5.8	+ 2.5	+ 0.9	– 0.7
French franc	+ 13.6	– 0.2	– 12.2	+ 1.6	–	– 1.6
Pound	– 24.9	– 33.9	– 41.9	– 3.5	– 5.0	– 6.6
Lira	– 29.0	– 37.6	– 45.1	– 4.2	– 5.7	– 7.3
EUA	+ 13.8	x	– 12.0	+ 1.6	x	– 1.6
US dollar	x	– 12.1	– 22.7	x	– 1.6	– 3.2
Europa	+ 29.4	+ 13.7	x	+ 3.3	+ 1.6	x

Assuming that such exchange rate fluctuations could be correctly forecast, the German mark would obviously have been the most attractive currency throughout for the lenders, but also the least acceptable to the borrower. In order to be acceptable to prospective lenders from the stronger currency countries, interest rates on any parallel currency obligation would have had to be higher than on obligations denominated in appreciating national currencies, but the required interest rate differentials would have been considerably less on Europa obligations (1.1 per cent above the Belgian franc, 1.8 per cent above the guilder, and 2.9 per cent above the mark) than on EUA or US dollar obligations. The latter, particularly, would have required interest rate differentials 2 to 4 times higher than Europa obligations.

Conversely, the interest rate differential on Europa obligations would have had to be higher than on EUA or dollar obligations in order to attract borrowers from the weak currency countries. This means, however, that interest rates on Europa obligations would have carried interest rates about 7 per cent lower than on pound or lira obligations, rather than 5 – 6 per cent lower on EUA obligations, and only 3 to 4 per cent lower on obligations expressed in dollars. Indeed, Europa obligations should carry interest rates approximately equal to a weighted average of the interest rates prevailing on similar obligations expressed in the currencies entering the calculation of the Europa basket.

This average would be higher than on obligations expressed in the currencies currently deemed strongest, but lower than on dollar, EUA, and particularly weaker currency obligations.

Investors having a clear judgment different from that of the market would of course prefer obligations in a national currency, but the Europa should be more attractive to all those who wish to minimize their losses rather than maximize profits. The Europa would be attractive to prudent investors, but not to speculators preferring to gamble on their own judgment and intuition.

Exchange gains, or losses, on national currency obligations would, of course, be the largest of all, and could not conceivably be offset by feasible interest-rate differentials even if correctly predicted by speculation. The pound, for instance, depreciated by 24.75 per cent vis-a-vis the German mark from September 1975 to September 1976 and by 8.36 in three months (at a yearly rate of 33.44 per cent) from December 1975 to March 1976. Interest rate differentials in December 1975 on comparable money market or 12-year government obligations were below 6 per cent, and the three months forward rate was about 5.21 marks per pound, while the spot rate declined to 4.86 in March 1976.

IV. FROM A PARALLEL EUROPA CURRENCY TO FULL MONETARY UNION?

If and when the drive toward Monetary Union can be resumed, the Europa would provide a far more relastic path toward it than the *sudden* and *simultaneous* switch from all national currencies to a common currency envisaged in the Werner Plan.

Long before that, the development of a private market in short, medium and long term Europa obligations would help, and be helped by, official transactions in the Europa. This market, first of all, would provide the Community, national governments, and other official organizations–within and even outside the Community – with a currency unit alternative to those now in use (primarily the US dollar) for the denomination of their borrowing and lending operations and investments. It would provide, in particular, a most logical form of exchange-rate guarantee for the 'new instrument of Community borrowings and loans' envisaged in the decisions of the European Council of December 5 and 6, 1977.

Secondly, it could become a far more appropriate instrument than a widely fluctuating dollar for central banks' interventions in the foreign exchange market.

A parallel Europa currency, properly defined and guaranteed, should become in time the main – or, at least, an alternative – means of foreign exchange intervention and settlements between the countries of the Community, and even play an increasing role in transactions and settlements with other countries, including the OPEC countries.

It should also provide a more logical *common denominator* for member countries' exchange rates and a *bench mark* for the exchange rate readjustments that will still prove necessary in the medium term as well as for their eventual, hoped for, stabilization in the longer term. Trade, services and capital transactions among member countries are probably today more than ten times larger than their transactions with the United States, and several times larger also than their transactions with other countries whose currency is precariously pegged to the dollar. A European foreign exchange unit would provide a far more logical 'centre of gravity' than the dollar for the definition and occasional readjustments of member countries' exchange rates. Yet, in the absence of such a unit, the dollar remains in fact the only common denominator in which their currencies are quoted by the market to the man in the street.

Admittedly, a Europa parallel currency and exchange area would leave unsolved the major obstacles to full monetary union and the actual merger of the national currencies into a single common currency for the Community.

I shall not dwell here on the multiple and difficult policy *and institutional* reforms that will be necessary to make such a goal realistic and possible. I am confining myself now to what seems most urgent and feasible, rather than on the policy and institutional problems that still divide deeply academic and business circles as well as responsible policy makers and their advisers.

The proposals outlined above would be valuable for their own sake, and constitute in any case a prerequisite step toward more ambitious objectives. If and when sufficient progress has been achieved to make monetary union conceivable as a practical policy goal, the proposed Europa would provide a far more realistic transition than the Werner Plan for the eventual switch from national currencies to a single European currency.

Rather than the *abrupt* and *simultaneous* jump envisaged in the Werner Plan, it would *permit each country to move at its own pace,* enlarging gradually the use of the Europa from the external transactions legally admitted at the start—for operations now conducted already in Euro-dollar and other Euro-currencies – to more and more internal transactions as well.

Even the most sceptical or jingoist opponents of monetary union should be enthusiastic supporters of the Europa as an urgently needed shelter against foreign shocks repeatedly unleashed by past, present, and foreseeable exchange crises in the disorderly monetary system inherited from the collapse of Bretton Woods.

NOTES

1. See particularly his Jean Monnet Lecture in Florence of October 27, 1977, and his Bonn address to the Deutsche Gesellschaft für Auswärtige Politik of December 8, 1977.
2. See Chapter 2 of this volume and the carefully articulated proposals of Jacques Riboud, notably in *Une Monnaie pour l'Europe: l'Eurostable,* Paris, 1975.
3. Throughout this paper the definitions of the Europa will differ from that employed in the Manifesto proposal (cf. Ch. 2.).
4. The 5 per cent benchmark and 12 months period were retained after extensive calculations of the comparative impact of a number of alternative depreciation limits and periods of stability upon the value of the Europa, if the system had been introduced at various past starting dates, beginning with the end of 1969.

7 Vicious and Virtuous Circles and the Optica Proposal: A Two-Country Analysis

GIORGIO BASEVI and PAUL DE GRAUWE

I. INTRODUCTION

In a recent article we have tried to present the theory on which a proposal for managing exchange rates among countries of the European Community – the so-called OPTICA proposal – is based.[1] Important limitations of our study resulted from the fact that the analysis was conducted in a one-country model and it was not explicitly made dynamic. Thus, at least two weak spots were left in the paper. First, we could only suggest the hypothesis, but not analyse it, that vicious and virtuous circles could reinforce or dampen each other when two countries were confronted. Secondly, we were – wrongly, as we shall show in this paper – induced to 'prove' that the OPTICA intervention guidelines could impede real adjustment when a country needed to let its terms of trade fall (its 'real exchange rate' rise). We were, therefore, admitting that the OPTICA proposal might be open, on this side, to criticism.[2]

The purpose of this paper is to set up an explicit two-country model so as to come to grips with the second difficulty just mentioned. On the other hand, since we shall continue to use a model whose dynamics are not fully spelt out, we cannot deal thoroughly with the first problem.[3]

In Section II the OPTICA proposal is restated. Section III briefly summarizes the model already presented in our previous paper, adapting it to a two-country world. Section IV deals with the interaction between developments in 'vicious' and 'virtuous' countries. In Section V we show that the asymmetrical nature of the OPTICA proposal for intervening in exchange markets does not impede real adjustment, neither when an increase nor a decrease of the terms of trade is required.

This paper has benefited in a substantial way from comments by Jürg Niehans presented at the Conference. In particular, those comments enabled us to eliminate several errors and shortcomings.

II. THE OPTICA RULE FOR EXCHANGE RATE MANAGEMENT

The proposal contained in the OPTICA 1976 Report was much influenced by the events of 1976 in the countries of the European Community, particularly the United Kingdom and Italy on the one hand, and Germany (but also Switzerland) on the other. It was the opinion of the authors of that Report that '. . . progress towards European monetary and economic integration has been blocked and, indeed, set back by the persistence of large discrepancies in rates of inflation among European Community member countries, high levels of unemployment and a succession of crises in the exchange markets. The reaction to these crises has been a reintroduction of foreign exchange controls and of trade restrictions of more or less disguised kinds. These, if maintained, threaten to destroy the chance of further progress towards European economic union.' In order to stop this process the authors of the Report proposed, in addition to the launching of a European parallel currency, a plan for managing exchange rates based essentially on a purchasing power parity rule. According to this rule, during every intervention period (e.g. a month) the currencies of countries whose price level had been rising in the recent past relative to the foreign price level would not be allowed to depreciate (in effective terms) by more than the amount implied by their relatively higher inflation rate; however, they could freely appreciate if market forces would indicate so. Conversely, the currencies of countries whose price level had been falling in the recent past relative to the foreign price level would not be allowed to appreciate (in effective terms) by more than the amount implied by their relatively lower inflation rate; however, they could freely depreciate if market forces would so indicate. In other words, the proposal is a sort of crawling reference rate proposal, where reference rates change on the basis of purchasing power parity, and they are defended by monetary authorities in only one direction during every period, namely against excessive depreciation for relatively inflationary countries, and against excessive appreciation for relatively deflationary countries.

III. THE MODEL

The economies of both countries – which we shall call the home and the foreign country – are synthetically described by a financial block and a price block of equations. The financial block in each country consists of a money market plus the assumption that home interest rates are at parity with foreign interest rates, except for the forward premium or discount on the home currency. In symbols and denoting with asterisks the variables of the foreign country, we have:

$$\frac{M_d}{P} = L(y,r) \qquad (1)$$

$$\frac{M^*_d}{P^*} = L^*(y^*,r^*) \quad (2)$$

$$M_d = M_s \quad (3)$$

$$M^*_d = M^*_s \quad (4)$$

where M_d and M_s are the nominal stocks of money demanded and supplied, P is the price level, y stands for real income, and r for the rate of interest;

$$r - r^* = \frac{F-S}{S} \quad (5)$$

where F and S are the forward and spot exchange rates respectively, both defined in terms of the amount of the home country's currency necessary to buy one unit of the foreign country's currency, so that

$$S = 1/S^* \quad (6)$$

$$F = 1/F^* \quad (7)$$

It will be assumed that the speculator's schedule is infinitely elastic so that the forward rate is always equal to the expected future spot rate,[4] i.e.

$$F = E(S) \quad (8)$$

where E(S) is the expected future spot rate

The price submodel consists of a short-run reduced form equation:[5]

$$P = P(U, P^*S, E(P), P_{-1}) \quad (9)$$

$$P^* = P^*(U^*, PS^*, E(P^*), P^*_{-1}) \quad (10)$$

where U and U* are unemployment rates. The equations capture the short run 'mechanical' relation between the exchange rate and the general price level. When the spot rate increases the general price level increases in proportion to the share of imports in the general price index.

In the long run the condition of purchasing power parity should hold, i.e.

$$P = P^*S \quad (11)$$

Whenever the exchange rate deviates from this long-run equilibrium relationship an adjustment mechanism is set in motion: if the domestic currency is undervalued ($S > \frac{P}{P^*}$) an expansionary process in the goods market will tend to reduce unemployment and to increase the domestic price level. Similarly, if the domestic currency is overvalued ($S < \frac{P}{P*}$) a deflationary process in the goods market is set in motion.

IV. GRAPHICAL REPRESENTATION OF THE MODEL

In this section the model consisting of equations (1) to (11) is represented graphically using a four-quadrant diagram (see Figure 7.1). In the *north-east* and *south-west* quadrants the asset market equilibrium is represented by the lines mm and m*m* for the home country and the foreign country respectively. These lines represent the combinations of exchange rates and price levels for which the asset markets are in equilibrium. The mm-line is derived from equations (1), (3), (5) and (8). Assuming that the initial spot and forward exchange rates are equal to one the slope of mm is given by the expression:

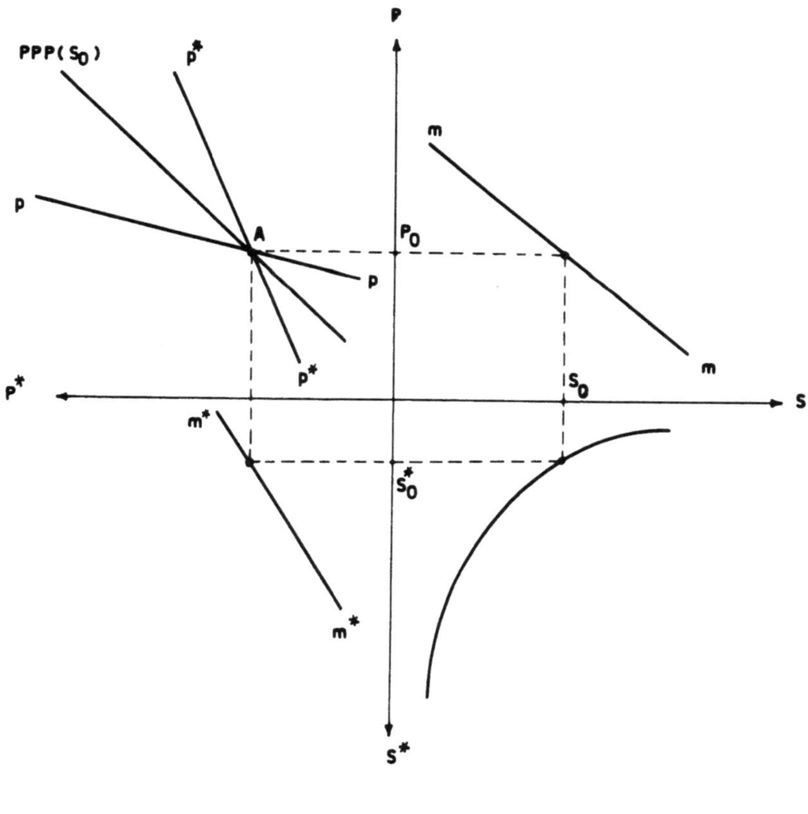

Figure 7.1

$$\frac{dP}{dS} = \frac{PL_r}{L} < 0$$

From this it follows that the slope of mm is influenced by the interest sensitivity of the demand for money (L_r). The larger is this sensitivity, the steeper is the mm-curve. An increase in the domestic money supply shifts the mm-curve upwards. This is so because a monetary expansion reduces the domestic interest rate. In order to maintain interest parity the spot rate then has to increase assuming a given price level. The effect of an increase in the foreign interest rate is similar. It also displaces the mm-curve upwards. In other words with an unchanged domestic price level and unchanged expectations the spot exchange rate has to increase in order to maintain interest parity.

In a similar way the slope of the m*m* curve can be derived

$$\frac{dP^*}{dS^*} = \frac{P^*L^*_{r^*}}{L^*} < 0$$

In the *south-east* quadrant the definitional equation (6) is represented. An increase in S means by definition a decline in S*.

In the *north-west* quadrant the short-run and long-run relations between the price levels of the two countries is represented. The short-run price equations (9) and (10) are represented by the lines pp and p*p* respectively. Their slope, relative to the axis on which the own price level is measured, is higher (lower) the larger (smaller) is the importance of imports in determining the general price level. This can be seen from rewriting (9) and (10) in differential forms:

$$dP = udU + \mu dP^* + \mu dS + \ldots \tag{9'}$$

$$dP^* = u^*dU^* + \mu^*dP + \mu^*dS^* + \ldots \tag{10'}$$

where $0 \leqslant \mu \leqslant 1$.

With increasing import shares μ increases and the slope of the pp-line increases.

The long-run condition of purchasing power parity is represented by the PPP-line. The slope of the PPP-line is unity. The three lines PPP, pp and p*p* in Figure 7.1 are defined for a given exchange rate S. From equation (9') it follows that when the currency of the home country depreciates (S rises) the pp-line shifts upwards by an amount equal to μdS. From equation (10') it follows that a depreciation of the home currency (S* declines) leads to a rightward shift of the p*p*-line. Finally, the depreciation of the home currency shifts the PPP-line upwards by the same rate as the increase in S, and therefore by more than the shift of pp (since $\mu < 1$).

The long-run equilibrium of the system is obtained when the different price lines intersect. This equilibrium is depicted in Figure 7.1 by point A. At the same time this point determines the spot rates and the interest rates which will produce asset market equilibrium in the two countries.

V. VICIOUS OUTCOMES

The effects of a monetary expansion in the home country are shown in Figure 7.2 by an upward shift of the mm line. Through the ensuing depreciation of the home currency (appreciation of the foreign currency) the pp and p*p* lines shift until they intersect at point B, while the PPP line shifts further upwards. Short-run equilibrium is attained at the points numbered 2 in the various quadrants of Figure 7.2. Note that the outward shift of the mm line corresponds, in the south-west quadrant, to an inward shift of the m*m* line, because with a lower interest rate in the home country the demand for the foreign currency increases: asset market equilibrium in the foreign country can only be maintained by an appreciation of its currency and/or a decline in its general price level.

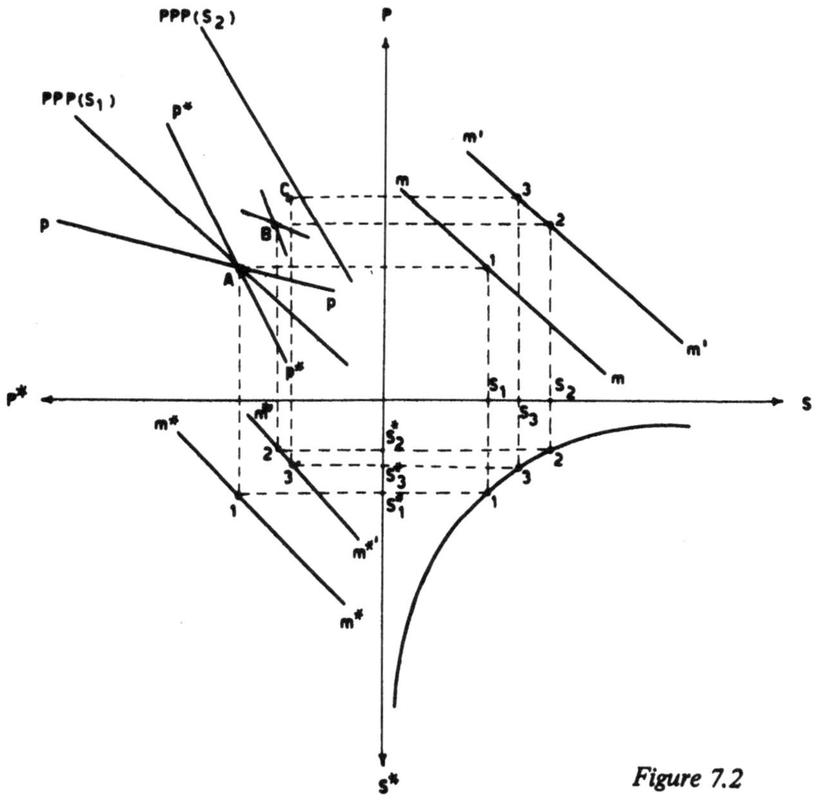

Figure 7.2

In the short-run position of equilibrium (point B) the home country's currency is undervalued, so that its current account tends to improve; the opposite is true for the foreign country. This disequilibrium is measured by the distance of point B from the new PPP line. As a result, a mechanism of long-run adjustment is set in motion: excess demand in the products market of the home country leads to further price increases, whereas excess supply in the foreign country leads to further price declines. The pp and p*p* lines keep shifting northward, while, due to partial recovery of the home currency, the PPP line moves southward to meet them at a point such as C. Note that the exchange rate overshoots, in the sense that the home country's currency, in the short run, depreciates (at S_2) by more than in the long run (at S_3).

Let us now assume that prices are inflexible downwards. As a reflection of this the pp and p*p* lines have a flat segment to the east and to the south, respectively, of the initial equilibrium point at A, in Figure 7.3. A rightward shift of the p*p* line following the depreciation of the home currency – induced as before by an expansionary monetary policy in the home country which shifts outward the mm line and inward the m*m* line – is only defined for

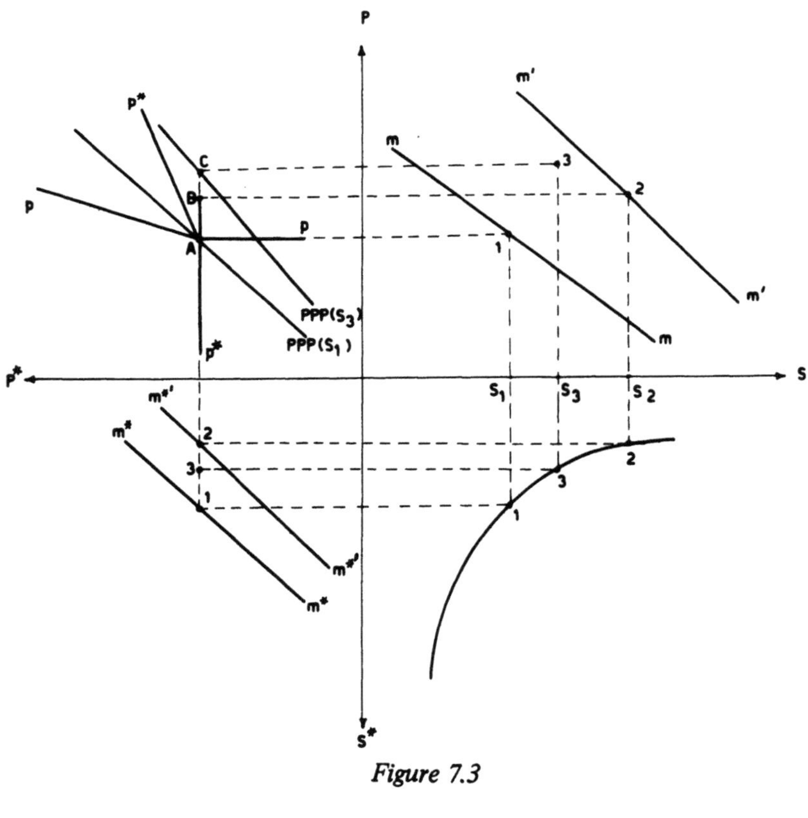

Figure 7.3

those points implying a higher price level in the foreign country. In the short run we move to point B and the points numbered 2. This implies a lower depreciation but a higher price increase in the home country, relative to the flexible price case. The reason why the home country now has a lower depreciation and a higher price increase than in the flexible price case, can be explained, *a contrario,* by the fact that in order to have a lower price increase and a higher depreciation in the home country, prices would have to fall in the foreign country, which is excluded by assumption.

Since B is below the PPP line (not drawn) that corresponds to the short-run exchange rate S_2, long-run adjustment is set into motion through the expansion of net exports by the home country. This shifts upward the pp and p*p* lines in Figure 7.3, because of larger unemployment in the foreign country and lower unemployment in the home country, while the PPP line shifts downward because of the reappreciation of the home country's currency. Long-run equilibrium will settle at a point such as C and points numbered 3 in Figure 7.3, which correspond to a certain inward shift of the final position mm curve (not drawn) because of higher real income in the home country, and to a certain outward shift in the final position of the m*m* curve (not drawn) because of lower real income in the foreign country. Again, as already in the short run, the amount of depreciation is lower and the increase of prices higher in the home country, relative to what they would have been in the case of downward flexible prices.

Thus, we have reached a first interesting conclusion; namely that when prices are rigid downwards in the foreign country monetary expansion in the home country is more inflationary there than if prices were downward flexible in the foreign country.

Let us now suppose, that, besides downward price rigidity, countries are also characterised by an inability to control the money supply in the short run because the authorities keep fixed the level of their interest rate. In this case the asset market equilibrium line mm becomes a vertical line. This is so because with a pegged domestic interest rate, and a given foreign interest rate and expected future spot rate, there is only one spot rate for which the interest parity relationship holds.

We now analyse the effects of an exogenously determined decline in the demand for money in the home country (e.g. due to a political scare). The effect of this shock is to displace the vertical $\overline{m}'\overline{m}'$-line to the right, as shown in Figure 7.4. Short-run equilibrium moves to point B and points 2, which necessarily imply a higher depreciation and a higher price increase than the corresponding situation depicted in Figure 7.3, and represented in Figure 7.4 by points (B) and (2).

Suppose now that the monetary authorities of the home country reinstate in the medium run their control of the money supply; this implies, in Figure 7.4, that $\overline{m}'\overline{m}'$ takes over as the medium-run asset equilibrium curve, and that the home currency appreciates. The final equilibrium point 4 in the north-east quadrant of Figure 4 can now be either to the right or to the left of the

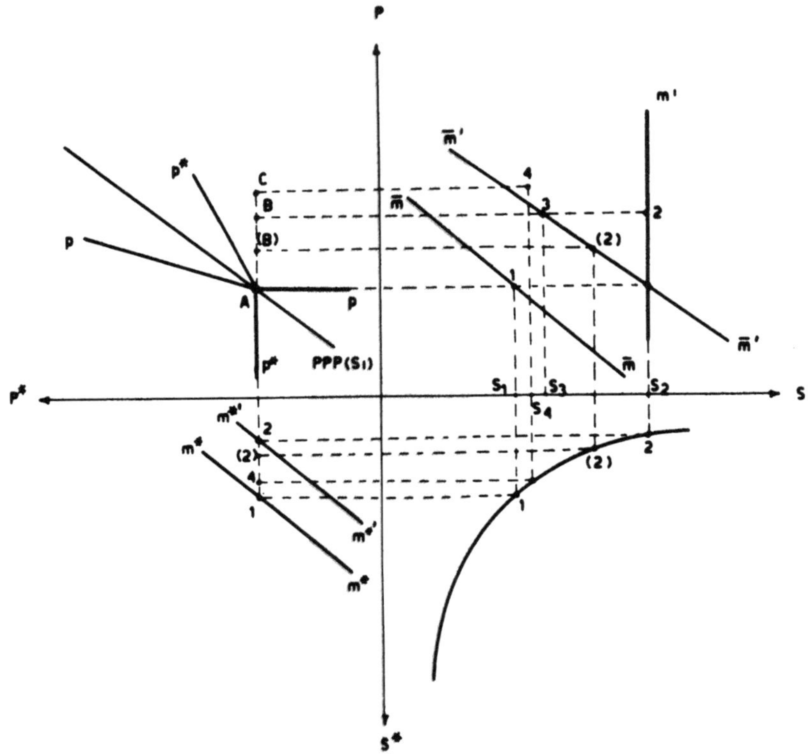

Figure 7.4

medium-run-curve $\bar{m}'\bar{m}'$. It will be to the left of it when the appreciation of the home currency following the reinstatement of the initial money supply (from S_2 to S_3) does not shift the PPP line below the short-run point B, so that the home country, through the demand pressure coming from an undervalued currency, experiences larger employment and real income. On the other hand point 4 will be to the right of the medium-run $\bar{m}'\bar{m}'$ curve, as shown in Figure 7.4, if the reinstatement of the initial money supply shifts the PPP line below the B point, so that the home country experiences the deflationary consequences of an overvalued currency, and can only find a final position of equilibrium in C with a lower level of employment and real income. The latter case is particularly interesting, because it implies for the home country an even higher price increase than if the authorities had continuously controlled the money supply, and it implies, also for this country now, the larger unemployment that is necessary to eliminate overvaluation of its currency when prices are downward-rigid.

The previous analysis shows that particular policy scenarios can lead to an amplified effect of a currency depreciation on the price level together with a deflationary impact on the goods market. This situation is often referred to as a 'vicious' circle. The present analysis does not reveal the existence of such vicious circles. Nevertheless the framework establishes a 'vicious' characteristic of the final position of equilibrium to which the system may converge.

VI. THE OPTICA RULE

In this section we analyse the effects of the OPTICA rule. According to this rule monetary authorities are assumed to maintain the exchange rate such that it continuously reflects PPP. In this section we assume that the rule is applied in a symmetrical way. In the next section we shall analyse the asymmetrical rule. The implications of such an intervention rule in our model is that the equilibrium points in the price and exchange rate space must always lie on a 45° line, e.g. the $\bar{m}'\bar{m}'$ line in Figure 7.5 There exists such an $\bar{m}'\bar{m}'$

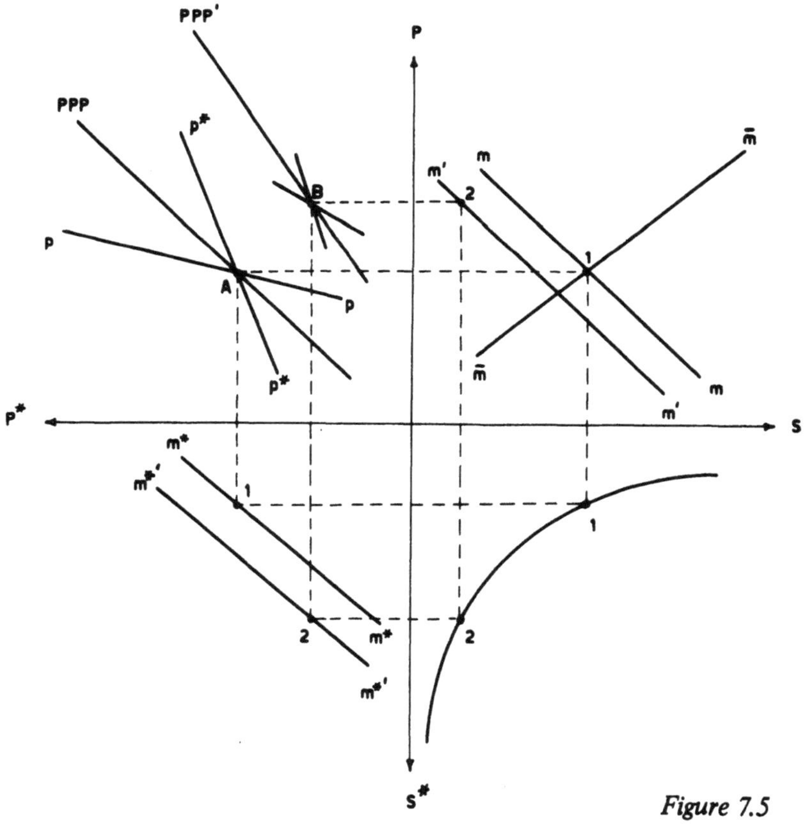

Figure 7.5

line for every different level of the foreign price level. For example, if the foreign price level P* increases then the $\bar{m}\bar{m}$ line will shift upwards. This means that if the domestic price level is unchanged the authorities must intervene to reduce the spot exchange rate (to appreciate the domestic currency).

It can easily be shown that when the rule is applied continuously the characteristic of the system is close to a fixed exchange rate system.[6] Suppose, for example, an exogenous decline in the demand for domestic money. This will tend to shift the mm curve upwards, tending to increase the exchange rate more than the price level. As, however, the authorities have to maintain proportionality between P and S they will have to intervene in the foreign exchange market. This means that they will have to buy the domestic currency (sell foreign exchange) in the exchange market. In order to maintain proportionnality between P and S they will have to absorb the whole amount of domestic currency sold by private agents as a result of the exogenous decline in the demand for money. The result is that the mm-line does not move, and that the price level and the exchange rate remains unchanged. The overshooting problem is eliminated. However, the system is essentially equivalent to a fixed exchange rate system, as far as the effects of monetary disturbances is concerned. The OPTICA intervention rule, therefore, avoids the kind of 'vicious' outcomes described in the previous section. In a sense, the OPTICA-rule automatically avoids the policy errors that the authorities commit when they first peg the domestic interest rate and later on try to peg the domestic money supply.

VII. REAL EXCHANGE RATES

In this section we take up the issue of how the real exchange rate can be made to change when the authorities use an OPTICA intervention rule. The occurrence of 'real' shocks makes it necessary that the exchange rate be allowed to deviate permanently from its purchasing power parity. The question then is whether the use of an OPTICA rule may not be an obstacle to the need to accommodate changes in the real exchange rate.

Let us assume that the real exchange rate of the foreign country increases.[7] This situation is shown in Figure 7.5 by an upward shift of the PPP line. Note that, by definition, this implies that the real exchange rate of the home country decreases.

The OPTICA intervention rule requires the monetary authorities of a country to buy their own currency so as not to allow a depreciation larger than the excess of the country price increase over the foreign price increase, and conversely for an appreciating currency. The rule is asymmetrical, in the sense that it does not require a country's authorities to slow down appreciation if this occurs when that country's price performance is more inflationary than the foreign one, and conversely it does not require a country's authorities to slow down depreciation if this occurs when that country's price performance is less inflationary than the foreign one.

The OPTICA intervention line of the home country – the positively sloped $\bar{m}\,\bar{m}$ line in Figure 7.5 – is defined for a given price level in the foreign country.[8] If the price level of the foreign country increases, then, for a given P, S will have to decline. Hence, when P* increases, the $\bar{m}\,\bar{m}$ line shifts to the left.

As a result of the upward movement of the PPP line, point A implies a relative undervaluation of the home currency. The accompanying current account surpluses exert an expansionary effect in the home country's goods market. As a result the pp line shifts upwards and the mm line downwards. In the foreign country the overvaluation shifts the p*p* line to the right and m*m* away from the origin. The long-run equilibrium point B will be attained because the asymmetrical nature of the OPTICA rule does not require

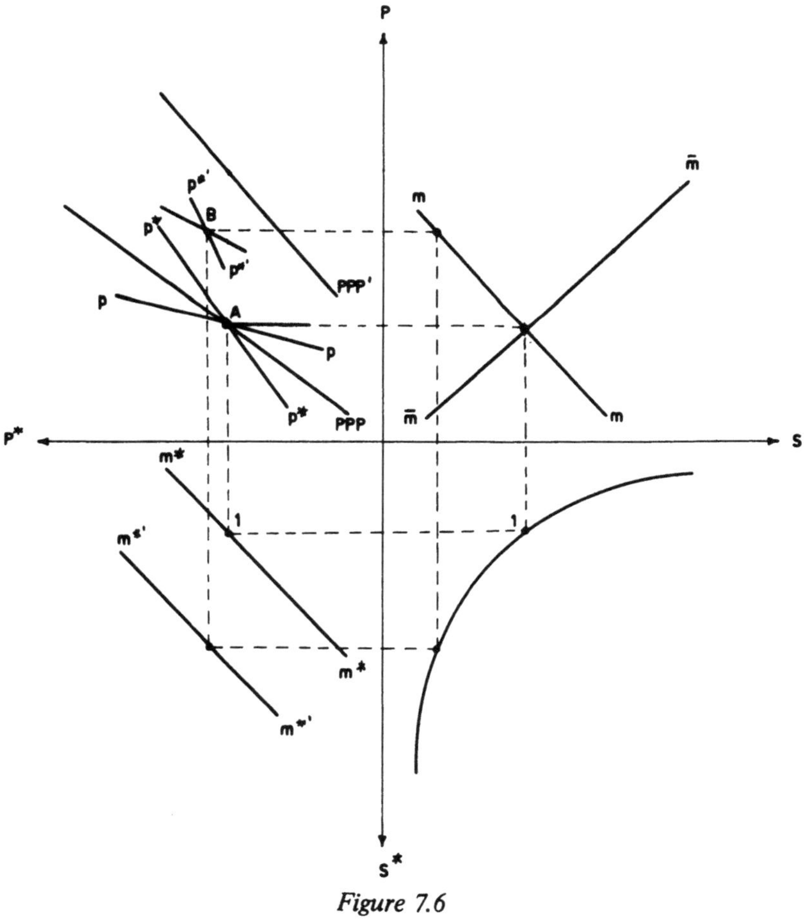

Figure 7.6

intervention in this case. The reason is that the price level in the home country increases while its currency appreciates. The OPTICA rule will not prevent the necessary adjustment in the real exchange rate.

However, in the one-country version of our model, it was shown that problems may arise with the application of the OPTICA rule when prices are inflexible downwards in the country which experiences an increase in its real exchange rate. In Figure 7.6 we develop this case within our present two-country version of the model. Following the upward shift in the PPP line the short-term equilibrium point should move upwards. We have assumed that the movements of the different lines are such that in B the price level of the foreign country and its exchange rate increase. However, in B the price level of the home country increases even more. As a result the $\bar{m}\,\bar{m}$ line shifts upwards. Since the price level increases more in the home country than in the foreign country, the home currency will be allowed to appreciate in the market and the system will move towards its long-run equilibrium level.

CONCLUSION

In this article a simple two-country model was developed. The purpose of the model was to describe how, due to policy errors, 'vicious' developments of prices and exchange rate changes may develop. In addition, it was shown how the use of an intervention rule based on purchasing power parities may prevent the occurrence of such a 'vicious' outcome.

In a last section we showed how an asymmetrical PPP-rule (the OPTICA rule) does allow real exchange rate changes to occur. In other words the use of the OPTICA rule would not prevent deviations from PPP when these are necessitated by disturbances in the real sector.

NOTES

1. See Basevi and De Grauwe (1978). The OPTICA proposal is contained in Commission of the European Communities (1977).
2. See Vaubel (1977) and Balassa (1977).
3. An explicit dynamic analysis, albeit in a one-country model, is presented in Steinherr, De Grauwe, and Basevi (1978).
4. This assumption, together with interest parity, imply that the speculator's and arbitrageur's schedules, both horizontal, coincide. The amount of commercial hedging then determines the net purchases of foreign exchange.
5. The lagged values of the dependent variable in equations (9) and (10) are meant to capture the Phillips curve relationship between rate of unemployment and rates of wage and price changes.
6. In Basevi and De Grauwe (1978) the effects of the operation of the OPTICA-rule are analysed in more detail in the framework of a one-country model.
7. This means that to maintain external equilibruim the currency of the

foreign country has to depreciate more (or appreciate less) than implied by PPP. This may be due, for example, to a relative decline in productivity.

8. In this two-country framework, only one country needs intervening, if at all. In any case, the rule prevents the countries from intervening at cross purposes.

REFERENCES

B. Balassa, 'European monetary arrangements: problem areas and policy options', *European Economic Review*, vol. 9, no. 3, August 1977.

G. Basevi and P. De Grauwe, 'Vicious and virtuous circles: a theoretical analysis and a policy proposal for managing exchange rates', *European Economic Review*, vol. 10, 1978 (forthcoming).

Commission of the European Communities, Optica Report 1976; Inflation and Exchange Rates – Evidence and Policy Guidelines for the European Community, Brussels, February 10, 1977.

A. Steinherr, P. De Grauwe and G. Basevi, 'The dynamics of intervention rules in foreign exchange markets', paper presented at the Conference on The Economics of Flexible Exchange Rates, Vienna, March 29-31, 1978.

R. Vaubel, 'The next steps in European Monetary Integration: OPTICA 1975 and 1976', paper presented for the Conference on US-European Monetary Relations, sponsored by the American Enterprise Institute and Georgetown University, March 17-18, 1977, Washington, DC.

COMMENT ON BASEVI AND DE GRAUWE

Jürg Niehans

The numerous groups and committees that issue statements on international monetary arrangements (usually after a meeting in some pleasant spot) are rarely willing to do the analytical homework their proposals would require. It is, therefore, a great pleasure for me to discuss a paper that represents one of the few serious attempts to provide an economic analysis of some of these proposals. While some of my comments will be critical, this criticism should be seen on the background of this introductory remark. I believe that the analysis of this paper does not quite achieve its purpose, but it still represents a big step forward from discussion without analysis.

I. THE MAIN POLICY CONCLUSIONS

The paper presents two main conclusions:

a. The exchange market produces no vicious spirals of progressive inflation or deflation. This constitutes a major criticism of OPTICA 1976, and one with which I would tend to agree.

b. The primary monetary expansion may result in a secondary expansion through exchange rate overshooting, which could be avoided through purchasing-power-oriented exchange management. This conclusion however, is weakened by the fact that it is based on the assumption of a ratchet effect from wages, for which, despite numerous dogmatic assertions, there is no convincing evidence.

II. THE NEED FOR A DYNAMIC MODEL

The subject of this paper is the adjustment path of an economy after a change of its monetary policy, including the stability and the monotonic or oscillatory character of this path. These are problems of economic dynamics. They are handled in this paper by static techniques. It is always nice if a seemingly difficult dynamic problem can be shown to be amenable to static analysis. In the present case I am not sure that the authors succeeded. In particular, I am not convinced that a PPP intervention rule could be relied upon to reduce fluctuations.

In principle, changes in the price level may be regarded as a function of past money supplies:

$$P_t = a_1 M_{t-1} + a_2 M_{t-2} + \ldots + a_n M_{t-n}.$$

Exchange rate fluctuations, reacting more quickly, may be regarded as a function of past and present money supplies:

$$e_t = b_o M_t + b_1 M_{t-1} + \ldots + b_n M_{t-n}.$$

By the OPTICA rule the current exchange rate change is made equal to the rate of price change; i.e. $e_t = P_t$.

This provides an automatic rule for M_t, by which the present money supply becomes dependent on past money supplies,

$$M_t = c_1 M_{t-1} + c_2 M_{t-2} + \ldots + c_n M_{t-n},$$

where the c's depend on the a's and b's. The decisive question is whether the c's are certain to be such that the process is stable and, if it is, that it does not involve serious oscillations. So far, the proponents of the OPTICA rule have, to my knowledge, not addressed this question. I do not see how the OPTICA rule can be seriously advocated before it is resolved, and I do not see how it can be resolved without a dynamic analysis.

III. NON-MONETARY ASSETS

The Basevi-De Grauwe model is extremely monetarist: what matters is only the quantity of money and not the way it is created. In particular, there is no difference between money created by open market operations and money created by foreign exchange purchases. As a consequence, the model can be shown to work in exactly the same way if central banks never intervene in the foreign exchange market, provided exchange rates are taken into account in open market operations.

It seems to me a meaningful model of foreign exchange intervention should account for the difference between the effects of open market purchases and foreign exchange purchases. In fact, it is this difference which makes the question of exchange market intervention interesting. It is clear that the analysis of this difference requires at least one additional asset besides money.

IV. CONSIDERATION OF NET CAPITAL FLOWS

Basevi and De Grauwe assume that exchange rates are at the interest parity at every moment. There is never any net inflow or outflow of private capital. Correspondingly, the trade deficit is rigidly tied to the foreign exchange purchases of the central bank day by day. As a consequence, the discussion of export or import surpluses seems to be up in the air analytically. In reality, private capital flows and their counterpart, the trade balance, play a very important part in the dynamic process of adjustment to monetary change.

A satisfactory analysis of this process should thus incorporate those elements which were traditionally used to explain the adjustments of export and imports in disequilibrium. In particular, these elements include the price elasticities of demand and supply. What is needed is an integration of the monetarist approach and the elasticity approach.

COMMENT ON BASEVI AND DE GRAUWE

Jaques van Ypersele

I would basically agree with the realistic interpretation given in the paper concerning the vicious-virtuous circle hypothesis, and I found the model also interesting.

However, being more in the policy-making area, I would like to focus on the policy conclusions of the paper: namely the OPTICA proposal for managing exchange rates on the basis of the evolution of their relative purchasing power. The rule is summarized as follows in the paper

> during every intervention period (e.g. a month) the currencies of countries whose price level has been rising in the recent past relative to the foreign price level would not be allowed to depreciate (in effective terms) by more than the amount implied by their relatively higher inflation rate; however, they could freely appreciate if market forces would indicate so. Conversely, the currencies of countries whose price level had been falling in the recent past relative to the foreign price level would not be allowed to appreciate (in effective terms) by more than the amount implied by their relatively lower inflation rate; however, they could freely depreciate if market forces would so indicate.

The main purpose of the rule is that it would be, and I quote, 'a powerful built-in stabilizer both for avoiding excessive inflation and depreciation in "vicious" countries, and for preventing monetary authorities from causing unnecessary unemployment on the basis of their rigidly set monetary targets'.

I must confess that, although ingenious, I do not believe that the application of the rule would lead to the desired results. I might even go further and suggest it might lead to the opposite results. Why would that be? If following the suggestion of OPTICA, one were to establish for countries with a relatively high inflation rate a downward limit to the exchange rate depreciation, one can and should expect the exchange rate to move to that downward limit even if that is not desirable for the economy as a whole.

I know that the authors of the paper will answer me that what they have set in this case is a downward limit which should not be transgressed, but that they would allow this exchange rate to 'freely appreciate if market forces would indicate so'. What I am saying is that the mere fact of setting this downward limit might induce a move towards this limit. In many cases it will probably lead the market to move to that downward limit, even if that is not desirable from an economic point of view. That is a very clear danger of this formula.

I will go further and say that in some cases authorities are right in resisting a downward movement of the exchange rate, even if they are induced by market forces, according to purchasing power parity. To make my point clear, I will take the example of my country: Belgium. Partly as a result of the external shock of the oil price increase on a very open and indexed economy, Belgian prices increased substantially in 1974, 1975 and 1976. The rate of price increase has been higher in Belgium than in Germany. If the PPP rule had applied, we would have experienced a larger depreciation of the currency rate than turned out to be. Several times market forces tried to push the Belgian franc in a downward direction. According to the rule exposed here, we should have accepted a lesser appreciation of our effective exchange rate or a downward movement of our parity vis-a-vis the DM. We should have accepted it until the limit set by the PPP, and should have intervened only then.

As most of those here know, we have not followed this policy and on the contrary have stayed close to the DM, and have let our effective rate appreciate more than would have been the case if we had followed the simplistic PPP rule. I strongly believe we have been right in following this policy. This has enabled us to follow a much more effective anti-inflationary policy than if we had followed the PPP rule. On the other hand, I do not believe that our unemployment would have been much different in an economy as open as ours. The competitive benefits we would have gained by depreciation would have been quickly lost. Also, we might have started in the beginning of this period (1973) with a somewhat overvalued currency.

I could go on with more details but I believe I have said enough to show that application of the mechanism proposed by the authors of the paper would have done more harm than good.

Let me now take an opposite case which will also cast doubts on the validity of this rule. The authors have recognized the value of this objection but they dismiss its actual importance. This is the notion that the PPP rule might prohibit the occurrence of real exchange rate changes. The United Kingdom and Italy have managed in the recent past to effect some real exchange rate changes. These were necessary to allow them to get back to equilibrium. Some of us would perhaps dispute the extent of the real exchange rate movement which was necessary and say that in addition to a necessary real exchange rate change there also occurred some unnecessary overshooting in the exchange rate. This might be quite true. But the point is that some real exchange rate movement was warranted. The authors point out that the asymmetrical nature of the proposal accommodates real exchange rate changes. However, it is not altogether clear from their discussion at the end of the paper that under the rather realistic assumption of downward wage and price inflexibility, the rule would still allow a smooth accommodation of needed real exchange rate adjustment. If this proposal had been submitted for consideration by the

EEC Monetary Committee, we would have rejected it. I would add that even if the proposal were a good one, I would have doubts about its practical application. This is due, among other things, to the delay between the actual PPP limits available and the actual expectation of price movements. Let me give an example. Suppose at time *t* wage bargaining in a given country results in an excessive wage increase, from which one can expect inflationary tendencies to develop in the next few months. According to the rule the authorities cannot intervene so long as the PPP relationship has not changed. The market, on the other hand, can safely forecast that as a result of the excessive wage settlement and its effect on prices, the PPP limit will have to be lowered in the next few months. The market will thus be induced to speculate heavily towards this devaluation and the authorities, bound by the PPP rule, will have to defend it by losing reserves; a behaviour which they know will have to change in a few months.

PART IV:

THE INSTITUTIONAL PROBLEM

8 In Search of a Monetary Constitution for the European Communities

MICHAEL PARKIN

I. INTRODUCTION

The current monetary constitution of the European Communities (EC) is extremely complex. It consists of a set of national laws establishing and delimiting the behaviour of nine Central Banks as well as the relationships between those Banks and their respective national governments. It also consists of a set of laws and regulations concerning the role which may be played in EC member countries by xeno-currencies (most notably the United States dollar). The Community-wide content of the current monetary constitution covers three areas. First, there is a statement of intent in the Rome Treaty to move towards European Monetary Union (EMU) at an unspecified speed and by an unspecified date. Secondly, there already exists a European Unit of Account (EUA) which is used for the purpose of defining Community regulations. Thirdly, there are a series of committees at various levels, including Central Bank Governors, which facilitate the exchange of information on monetary policy and related matters, but which do not make monetary policy.

In the period since 1970, the nine European currencies (seven independent currencies) have moved against each other and against the US dollar in a dramatic manner. The three weakest currencies, the Italian lira, the UK-Irish pound and the French franc, have depreciated against the two strongest currencies, the deutschmark and the Dutch guilder, by almost 70 per cent while the US dollar has kept almost exactly halfway between these two diverging groups.[1] Through this period, the US dollar has been gaining ground dramatically, Euro-dollar deposits having increased from $38 billions in 1968 to $258 billions by 1975.[2]

Thus, at the present time, the EC effectively has eight different kinds of money (the seven independent national currencies plus the US dollar) and

In revising this paper I have benefitted from helpful comments by André Fourcans, Jacques Melitz, and Manfred Neumann, and the discussions at Leuven.

one additional unit of account. It is to bring some order to this chaos and to reap the economies of a stable monetary environment that many are now advocating some form of EMU. This paper does not go over the ground again on the arguments for and against such a move. Rather it assumes that the pro-EMU case dominates.[3] Further, it deals not with transitional arrangements[4] but with the constitutional requirements of a unified monetary system for the EC. Specifically it asks the question: assuming we are to have EMU and a new European monetary system, what should the monetary constitution which governs that monetary system contain? Should there be a European Central Bank and, if so, how should it be constituted and what rules should delimit its behavior? It may appear that questions of this type are excessively premature and only need be addressed at a much later stage, if and when EMU becomes a serious likelihood. However, EMU is again a live issue in the EEC Commission, and is therefore once more on the agenda at least for political discussion if not for political action. Further, one of the chief arguments in favour of EMU is that monetary policy is currently in a less than satisfactory state in many of the member states of the EC, and therefore monetary union may provide an opportunity to achieve a much needed monetary overhaul – not to say monetary reform – in these countries. It must be possible, therefore, for those who advocate EMU also to specify a detailed set of institutional arrangements for the conduct of monetary policy at the broader level of the EC which delivers a better outcome than the monetary policies currently being pursued.

There appear to be three sets of issues which may usefully be kept distinct in thinking about monetary union and monetary reform, which are most sharply delineated by considering the following three questions: first, what is monetary policy capable of doing? Secondly, what ought monetary policy to be used for? Thirdly, how does the design of monetary institutions affect the achievement of the desired characteristics of monetary policy? Each of these issues has been addressed in an important (and yet apparently little known) volume, the title of which inspired the title of the present paper (*In Search of a Monetary Constitution*, Leland B. Yeager (ed.) (1962)). Further, the first two of the above questions have received voluminous attention in the literature on monetary history and monetary economics which has developed over the past two hundred years. This paper has nothing new to say on those first two questions. It is simply noted that, on the first, concerning the effects of monetary policy, there has emerged a broad consensus that, in the short run, monetary policy can have effects on real output, employment and on resource allocation as well as on income and wealth redistribution. In the long run, however, monetary policy affects only the rate of inflation, the scale of the inflation tax, and has some (presumed) second-order effects on resource allocation. Specifically, monetary policy cannot, in the long run, affect the overall level of employment and economic activity. Further, the more it is used to achieve short-run real effects on employment and output, the more uncertainty is thereby engendered concerning the long-term rate of inflation. This in turn leads to potentially serious inter-temporal and other allocation inefficiencies.

On the second issue – how ought monetary policy to be used – there is no professional agreement. Indeed, it is not going too far to say that this is one of the issues on which the profession is most sharply divided. This paper in no way addresses or attempts to resolve that dispute. On the one side there are those who believe that monetary policy should be used to achieve maximum predictability of inflation rates and who couple that (although there is no logical but rather an empirical connection between the two) with the prescription that monetary policy should be used to achieve steady inflation at a rate close to zero. On the other side, there are those who argue that because monetary policy has the power to achieve a temporary increase in the level of output, to refuse to use it for that purpose when there is a clear and identifiable excess of unused capacity in the economy is at best wasteful and at worst both foolish and unjust. In the present state of knowledge, and if monetary policy were the only available policy for returning a depressed economy to full employment, it would be impossible to come out definitively on one side or the other of this debate. However, with the possibility of using tax incentives and other fiscal policies to achieve a recovery from a recession, there need be no conflict. Monetary policy can be assigned the task of achieving a steady and predictable rate of inflation with real instability minimized by appropriate fiscal adjustments. It is true that in some countries (notably the United States of America) existing institutions make fiscal policy an inflexible weapon and thereby strengthen the view that monetary policy should be used to achieve macroeconomic stability. However, when considering in the abstract the design of a hypothetical monetary system for a group of countries which do have a great degree of fiscal flexibility, such constraints are of no immediate concern.

Further questions concerning how monetary policy ought to be used are those concerning the choice of indicator and intermediate policy targets. This paper has nothing to contribute to that debate. The evidence seems to point fairly strongly in favour of monitoring and attempting to achieve target growth rates for monetary aggregates and the abandonment of the more conventional concern for orderliness in interest rate movements, and apparently this view is increasingly being accepted even by policy-makers.

Important though the above questions are, they are not explored further in this paper. Rather, the central concern here is to explore the relationship between the way in which the type of monetary policy pursued depends on the way in which the institutions which conduct monetary policy are constituted. There is very little previous literature on this topic. However, several of the essays in Yeager (1962) address this issue and these are reviewed in Section II. There is also a recent paper (Parkin and Bade (1977)) which examines the relationships between Central Bank laws and monetary policies in the modern industrial world. The findings of that work are reviewed and summarized in Section III. In Section IV, a monetary constitution for the European Communities is set out based on the lessons drawn from the existing literature and the current state of knowledge.

II. REVIEW OF THE LITERATURE ON MONETARY CONSTITUTIONS

Any analysis of ideal monetary constitutions must begin by clarifying the basic objective of monetary policy. With the exception of a 35-year aberration following the adoption of Keynesian macroeconomic stabilization policies, the consensus view on the objective of monetary policy has been to achieve '*predictability* in the value of the monetary unit or reciprocally in the absolute level of prices' (James M. Buchanan (1962), p. 156). Given predictability as the objective of monetary policy there are three broad alternative monetary constitutions which, it has from time to time been argued, would best achieve that objective. These are first a commodity standard, secondly, an independent Central Bank and thirdly, the legislation of a simple single rule for the conduct of policy.

Many alternative commodity standards have been advocated and some of them indeed have been used. The most obvious examples of commodity standards are those based on gold and silver. There are also some more fanciful commodity standards such as that based on the common brick (apparently suggested by a Dr Hardy in the 1930s) (see Buchanan (1962), pp. 164-6) and the even more fanciful labour standard (apparently first suggested by Armen Alchian) (Buchanan (1962), p. 166) in which money machines are installed on each street corner, the machines being capable of delivering dollar bills in return for a certain amount of manpower cranking of a foot pedal. Friedman ((1962), p. 227) strongly and convincingly argues against commodity standard solutions on two grounds. First, the real resource cost of acquiring and maintaining the commodity stock is too great and, secondly, where commodity standards have been employed in the past, they have been supplemented by the issue of fiduciary money, thereby degenerating from a pure commodity standard to a fiduciary standard and thereby forcing us to address the question of how the fiduciary standard itself should be constituted and managed.

This naturally leads to a comparison of the other two alternatives – an independent Central Bank and a monetary rule. Pursuing this question, Viner (1962)

> 'explores the extent to which it is possible and desirable to limit the discretionary activity of a monetary authority by subjecting it, by statute or otherwise, to conform in its operations to a precise rule (p. 244). [He] takes for granted that some limitations of consequence in the monetary field can be effectively imposed on a monetary authority in the form of an obligation to follow an explicit code of general "principles", and more explicitly in the negative form of prohibition, from pursuing some

specified goals and from engaging in some specified types of activity. Beyond this it does not seem possible to limit the discretion of a monetary authority unless one can impose on it adherence to a single rule which is fairly simple, objective, and operationally workable' (p. 244).

Viner points out that, unless a 'single rule which is fairly simple, objective and operationally workable' can be devised, conflicts and ambiguity will arise leading to the necessity for discretionary action on the part of the monetary policymakers. Viner suggests that in practice, the 'rules' versus 'authorities' dichotomy is not a sharp one, it being possible for an 'authority' to follow very stable principles and for 'rules' to be changed so frequently as to lead to 'rules' being less predictable than the discretionary actions of 'authorities'.

Implicitly agreeing with Viner concerning the necessity for a single simple rule, Friedman (1962) argues strongly in favour of such an arrangement. He suggests that there are both political and technical economic objections to an independent Central Bank – what Viner calls an 'authority'. The political objection is stated in the form of a rhetorical question, 'Is it really tolerable in a democracy to have so much power concentrated in a body free from any kind of direct effect of political control?' (p. 227). The technical objections raised are first that with an independent Central Bank, responsibility for macroeconomic stability is dispersed, the Central Bank shirking its responsibility in times of uncertainty and difficulty; and secondly that too much dependence is placed on personalities 'which fosters instability arising from accidental shifts in the particular people and the character of the people who are in charge of the system' (p. 227). Thirdly, Friedman suggests that an independent Central Bank will almost 'inevitably give undue weight and emphasis to the point of view of bankers since, in modern societies, although analytically distinct, credit and interest rate policies and monetary policies are closely related to each other'. Friedman develops a detailed historical – anecdotal – account of the way in which the vagaries of personality, in particular in the interwar years, gave rise to monetary instability. For Friedman, the legislation of a monetary rule overcomes the problems to which independent Central Banks give rise. 'The enactment of rules would enable the public to exercise control over monetary policy through its political authorities, while at the same time preventing monetary policy from being subject to the day to day whims of political authorities' (p. 239).

Standing in sharp contrast to the literature which has sought to find a monetary policy constitution ensuring maximum predictability is the practice and legal establishment of new and reconstituted Central Banks in the postwar world. It has become a common pattern for Central Banks to be placed under detailed day-to-day instructions from elected politicians in the formation and conduct of monetary policy. This arises from the widespread acceptance of the view that governments, armed with the theories of the post-Keynesian macroeconomics synthesis, should bear the responsibility for maintaining high and stable employment levels. In the post-Keynesian postwar climate, the traditional question concerning how monetary predictability might best be achieved was, with few exceptions, largely forgotten. However, by the late 1960s and early 1970s, unemployment seemed to be conquered and, as inflation returned to the centre of the stage, so there was a return to an emphasis on predictability as a desirable attribute of monetary policy and to placing the reduction of inflation ahead of full employment in the policy priority list. Country after country found itself tolerating unemployment rates which would have been politically unthinkable earlier. A consensus appears to be emerging that, after all, it is predictability of the price level that matters most for monetary policy and, if necessary, even the achievement of high and stable employment levels must take second place to (and perhaps even depend on) this.

The question remains: what monetary constitution can best deliver predictability and stability of the price level? The literature which has been briefly and selectively reviewed above is, in large measure, *a prioristic* and therefore clarifies the questions, but does not provide the answers. What is needed to supplement that *a priori* literature is an empirical enquiry into the nature of the policies pursued by monetary authorities with different constitutions. Of course this limits a comparison to those alternatives which have been experienced and excludes hypothetical constitutions. However, it may permit some tentative conclusions concerning the appropriate degree of independence. It does not, unfortunately, permit an empirically based evaluation of the performance of a monetary rule since such a rule has been adopted only very recently and in a limited number of countries, so that experience with it has been brief. It does, however, permit a comparison of the monetary policies of Central Banks whose constitutions places monetary policy under the day-to-day control of government and those which have varying degrees of independence from government control. Such an empirical investigation is the subject of the next section.

III. CENTRAL BANK TYPES AND MONETARY POLICIES IN THE MODERN INDUSTRIAL WORLD

The study on which this section is closely based[5] examined twelve countries, Australia, Belgium, Canada, France, Germany, Italy, Japan, the Netherlands, Sweden, Switzerland, the United Kingdom and the United States. It first characterized, in a somewhat qualitative and abstract fashion, the Central Bank constitutions of these countries; secondly, it characterized their monetary policies; and thirdly, it searched for 'correlations' between constitutions and policies. This briefer account of that paper follows the same basic order.

1. Central Bank Laws[6]

Central Bank Laws and related legislation differ in a large number of important respects and a much more detailed classification and analysis could be undertaken than that presented here. However, those limited aspects of Central Bank Laws are focused on which, based on existing economic analyses, have some *a priori* interest and importance. The small but growing 'political economy' literature on monetary policy[7] suggests that policy will depend in large measure on whether the policymaking agent is a short-lived democratically elected government or longer-lived autonomous Central Bank. One feature of potential importance therefore concerns the relationship between the Central Bank and its major policymaking organs on the one hand and Central Government on the other. There are two areas which need to be examined; first, the role of government in the day-to-day supervision and control of monetary policy; and, secondly, the role of government in the appointment of members of the Central Banks' policymaking organs. In addition to examining this aspect of Central Bank Law, it was also felt interesting to examine the declared objectives (if any) embodied in the appropriate legislation governing the establishment and operation of the Central Bank.

The broad characteristics of the twelve Central Bank Laws are summarized in Table 8.1. The first column deals with the legislated objective of the Banks, the second with a characterization of the final authority for the making of day-to-day monetary policy and the remaining colums deal with the composition of the Bank Board and the responsibility for appointing (and removing) Directors as well as their terms of office.

Looking first at legislated objectives, six of the Central Banks in the group studied have no explicitly declared general policy objectives. These are the Central Banks of Belgium, France, Italy, Sweden, the United Kingdom and the United States. Three of the remaining six Central Banks, whilst having an explicit clause on objectives in their statutes, are too imprecise to be distinguished from the above cases. These are the Central Banks of Germany,[8] Japan and Switzerland. In contrast to these nine banks, those of Australia, Canada and the Netherlands do have explicit objectives. Those for Australia and Canada are virtually identical and embrace the pursuit of both price and foreign exchange rate stability as well as high and stable employment and real economic activity. The objective of the Netherlands' bank is much narrower and more precise and is 'to regulate the value of the Netherlands' currency in such a manner as shall be most conducive to the country's welfare and in that connection *to stabilize the said value so far as possible*' (my italics) (Article 9(1) of the Netherlands Bank Act of 1948, Aufricht (1967), p. 477).

The final authority for monetary policymaking is summarized in the second column of Table 8.1. Here there are two categories: government (g) and Bank Board (b). The classification of a bank in this regard is based purely on the legal statute and in no way based on 'custom and practice'. It may well be that 'custom and practice' deviates from the legal statute. However, this study has made no attempt to identify separately such characteristics of the way policy is made. In all cases where the government

TABLE 8.1 *Central Bank Laws: Summary*

Country	Legislated Objective	Final Authority	Government Officials on Board	Proportion of Directorate Appointed by Government	Number of Directors	Term of Directors	Term of Governor/ Chairman
(See note below)	(a)	(b)	(c)	(d)		(e)	(f)
The Netherlands	p	g	0	1	5-7 -	7	7
Australia	p-u	g	1	1	10	5	7
Belgium	–	g	0	1	14-17	6	5
Canada	p-u	b(1967-) g(1967+)	1	1	15	3	7
France	–	g	2	14/15	15	4	4
Italy	–	g	0	1	14	3	3
Japan	–	g	2	1	7	4	4
Sweden	–	g	0	1	7	3	3
United Kingdom	–	g	0	1	18	4	5
United States	–	b	0	1	7	14 (N)	4
Germany	–	b	0	10/21	21	–	8
Switzerland	–	b	0	5/8 (indirect)	–	4 (N)	4 (N)

Notes: (a) p-u = price level & general macroeconomic stability
p = price stability
– = non-specified
(b) b = Bank; g = government
(c) number of government officials who sit on Bank Directorate
(d) number represents proportion of directors appointed directly or indirectly by the government
(e), (f) years (N = not eligible for re-election)

(typically the Ministry of Finance) is the final monetary policymaking authority, the Central Bank Law is explicit on the nature of the relationship between the relevant government department and the Central Bank.

The fourth column indicates the proportion of the bank directorate appointed directly by the central government. It is immediately clear that in all cases except two the appointment of the Bank Governor and Board is a state appointment. However, in the two cases, Germany and Switzerland, there is some element of indirect election to the Bank Board. In the German case, ten of the 21 man directorate are appointed by the Federal Government and the other 11 members are the presidents of the 11 Länder Central Banks who are appointed on the nomination of the Bundesrat (the second chamber of the parliament, and on the recommendation of the Länder concerned). In the case of Switzerland, the bank policymaking board is elected indirectly by the bank council. The latter body consists of 40 people, 25 of whom are appointed by the Bundesrat (the Cabinet), and 15 of whom are elected by the shareholders of the Swiss National Bank at a general meeting of shareholders. That 40 man body then elects a smaller (unspecified size) board to make and manage monetary policy. The terms of Directors and Governors are indicated in the final column of Table 8.1.

Considering the summary statement of Central Bank constitutions in Table 8.1, it is apparent that there are a large number of alternative combinations of the various attributes of Central Banks. There are three alternative possibilities under 'legislated objectives' – the pursuit of price stability, the more generalized pursuit of both price stability and other macro objectives, and finally cases in which there is no specified objective. There are two possibilities concerning final authority – either the government or the bank board. Then there are cases where the government has a representative directly sitting on the bank board, and those where the government has no direct representation on the board. Next there are cases where the government is responsible for appointing all the bank directors and those where the government appoints some fraction of them. Finally the terms of office of the directors and Governor or Chairman vary considerably. Ignoring this last matter, there are 24 alternative combinations of the first four attributes. With only 12 banks being examined, it is clear not all 24 possible combinations are represented. In fact, on the basis of these classifications, there are 12 entirely different Central Banks. No two banks fit into the same category even at this fairly coarse level of aggregation of attributes. It is desirable therefore to perform some further aggregation. One possibility which has much to commend it is the reduction of the 'legislated objectives' category from three to two cases. There is a good case for regarding those Central Banks that have as their objective the pursuit both of price stability *and other general macroeconomic objectives* as being in the same category as those Central Banks which have no explicitly legislated objective. As Viner (1962) has noted, unless a Central Bank is charged with pursuing a well-defined single objective, conflicts and ambiguities arise enhancing the scope for discretion. Next it seems desirable to perform an aggregation in the area of the ultimate authority for the conduct of monetary policy. What is required, is a simple division into those banks which are responsible through their own board for the conduct of monetary policy and those which are distinctly subservient to government. A Central Bank is treated as having final authority for its monetary policy actions if and only if the following characteristics are satisfied: first, the bank board is the final authority for monetary policy-making; secondly, no government ministerial representative sits on the bank board. In other words, columns (b) and (c) of Table 8.1 are being combined and, in so doing, Canada, even pre-1967, becomes classified as a non-independent bank because of the official government representation on the bank board. This alternative aggregation yields an eightfold classification of Central Banks based on two objectives; two ultimate authorities for monetary policy; and finally, two procedures for appointing the Bank Directorate. Of these potential eight classes, four are empty. Thus in practical terms there is a fourfold classification of Central Banks. The first class is that in which the bank is charged with the pursuit of price stability to the exclusion of all other macroeconomic objectives and where the bank is subservient to the government in the formulation of monetary policy and in which the bank directors are directly government appointed. There is just one bank in this category, that of the Netherlands. All the other cases are those where there is a multiple or unspecified general objective for the Central Bank. The largest class is where the government is in command of

TABLE 8.2. *A Fourfold Classification of Central Banks*

Final Authority/ Appointment of Directors	Legislated Objective	
	Price Stability	Multiple or None
Government/ Government	The Netherlands	Australia Belgium Canada France Italy Japan Sweden United Kingdom
Bank/ Government		United States
Bank/ Government and Others		Germany Switzerland

monetary policy and in the appointment of the bank directorate – Australia, Belgium, Canada, France, Italy, Japan, Sweden and the United Kingdom. The next class has the bank board responsible for the making of monetary policy but that board is directly appointed by government – the United States. Finally, there is the case where the bank board is responsible for the making of monetary policy and the board itself is appointed by a diffuse process in which the government is not the sole dictator – the cases of Germany and Switzerland.

This fourfold classification will be employed in searching for any differences between policy and in attempting to identify the effects (if any) of Central Bank legislation on the nature and conduct of monetary policy.

2. Monetary Policies

Just as a ruthless simplification process was employed in dealing with the constitutions of Central Banks, so also in the analysis of monetary policy it is necessary to abstract and simplify. Specifically, three aspects or features of monetary policy are focussed on. First, the relative inflationary/deflationary stance of monetary policy; secondly, the variability of policy and thirdly, the proximate variables to which policy reacts or responds. Since cross-country rather than time-series data are being used, there is no concern with the detailed temporal evolution of policy in the various countries considered. Rather, summary statistics are examined which provide a basis for a comparison across countries for the whole postwar period. A key feature of much of the postwar history of most of the countries studied is that it was characterized by fixed exchange rates. From the beginning of the postwar era through to the early 1970s rates were fixed. Thereafter exchange rates have been flexible. It may be felt therefore that aggregation over time and over a period of exchange rate fixity on the one hand and flexibility on the other hand is inappropriate. However, in the interests both of simplicity and sharpening the focus on issues of central concern, such an aggregation is performed.

First, consider the average inflationary/deflationary quantity of each country's monetary policy. The major question which must be addressed initially is: how may the inflationary stance of policy by measured? The most obvious measure that suggests itself is the national rate of inflation averaged over the postwar years. However, such a measure has problems, the primary one being that such a measure compounds both absolute price level and relative price level phenomena. The rate of change of a national price index under fixed exchange rates is, by definition, a weighted average of the rate at which prices in the world as a whole are increasing and the rate at which prices of the individual country's non-traded goods are rising. A country that is experiencing rapid productivity growth in its tradeables' sector will thereby be experiencing rapid real wage growth which will in turn be reflected in prices of (typically labour-intensive) non-traded services. Thus such a country's measured price index will inflate at a faster rate than a country experiencing low productivity and real wage growth. This consideration is extremely important empirically, there being a strong positive correlation between growth rates and measured inflation rates of the twelve countries analyzed. (See Parkin (1977) on the years to 1970.) Thus, if measured inflation rates were used to rank the average inflationary stance of monetary policy, that ranking would be dominated by the ranking of real growth rates.

A second way of comparing inflation across countries is to compare the average rates of growth of some monetary aggregate. However this is likely to be misleading for a variety of reasons. First, the particular monetary aggregate would have to be comparable across countries at least in terms of the income elasticity of demand for that aggregate. If it were not thus comparable, we would have to estimate the appropriate income elasticity of demand and real growth rate in order to compute the excess of money supply growth over the non-inflationary rate of growth. In principle, such calculations could be performed and then used to calculate an adjusted excess money supply variable to compare the degree of inflation embodied in each country's monetary policy. However, such an exercise has not been undertaken and, in the absence of such calculations it may be suspected that a straight comparison of money supply growth rates would be highly misleading as an indicator of relative degrees of inflation.

A third possibility, and that which is used, is to examine the behavior of a country's exchange rate over the postwar period. Specifically, the degree of inflation embodied in a country's monetary policy is ranked by the average rate of change of the country's foreign exchange rate treating the United States and the US dollar as the numeraire. This procedure is not without problems but, seems to be one of the cleanest available ways of performing a ranking of countries' average inflationary tendencies.

Next consider the variability of monetary policy. What is of ultimate interest of course is the variability of inflation and real output and employment. However these are not variables which are even potentially under the direct control of the monetary authorities and therefore in no way could be used to characterize the variability of policy. Most Central Banks (see Hodgman (1974)) use interest rates as their proximate instruments of policy. It may be felt, therefore, that these should be looked at in order to judge the variability of monetary policy, variable interest rates being identified with variable policy. This would however produce a misleading view. First, nominal interest rates ought to vary in order to reflect variations in the anticipated rate of inflation. Therefore any unwillingness of the Central Bank to allow interest rates to move in line with variations in the inflation rate would have to be interpreted as a source of variability rather than a source of constancy in policy. This suggests that perhaps real rates of interest and their variability should be examined. However, even this is an exercise which would be of limited value since there are many factors which lead to variations in equilibrium real rates of interest, all of which would have to be

TABLE 8.3 *Average Inflation and Variability of Monetary Policy (1951-1975) Grouped According to Central Bank Type*

Final Authority/ Appointment of Directors	Country	Percent Exchange Rate Change		*Annual Money Supply Growth* Standard Deviation		*Annual Money Base Growth* Standard Deviation	
Government/ Government	The Netherlands	33.44	(3) *	4.62	(7)	3.99	(3)
	Australia	16.96	(7)	6.22	(11)	10.78	(11)
	Belgium	26.43	(4)	1.75	(1)	3.67	(2)
	Canada	3.39	(8)	5.49	(10)	5.26	(5)
	France	− 22.47	(11)	4.02	(4)	8.69	(10)
	Italy	− 4.45	(10)	4.17	(5)	12.40	(12)
	Japan	17.81	(6)	7.43	(12)	7.78	(9)
	Sweden	19.74	(5)	4.27	(6)	6.89	(7)
	United Kingdom	− 26.05	(12)	4.82	(9)	7.60	(8)
Bank/ Government	United States	0.00 (numeraire)	(9)	2.25	(2)	3.23	(1)
Bank/ Government and Others	Germany	41.35	(1)	3.20	(3)	6.79	(6)
	Switzerland	40.97	(2)	4.65	(8)	4.80	(4)

* Rank is given in brackets.
Source: International Financial Statistics, vol. XXIX, no. 5, May 1976.

controlled for before one could use the observed variability of the real rate of interest as an indicator of the variability of monetary policy. Even though interest rates are the proximate instruments of monetary policy, they are typically manipulated with a view to achieving a particular behavior for the growth rate of various monetary aggregates such as the money supply (somehow defined), the monetary base or more broadly defined concepts of 'liquidity'. It is variations in aggregates such as these that are regarded as providing some indication of the variability of monetary policy. Ideally a variety of measures of policy variability based on various definitions of money should be computed. In the present study however, only two such measures, based on the money supply and monetary base data published in *International Financial Statistics,*[9] are used.

Additionally, an attempt was made to assess the main macroeconomic targets to which monetary policy responds by examining the policy reaction function literature. Studies are available covering ten of the twelve countries, the two missing being the Netherlands and Switzerland.[10] Details of the policy reaction function studies are summarized in tabular form in Appendix 2 and are summarized in more compact form in Table 8.4. The way to read Table 8.4 is as follows: an algebraic sign (+, –) indicates the sign of the response of monetary policy (+) for expansion and (–) for contraction to a positive change in the variable at the head of each column. A zero indicates that at least one of the studies reviewed did search for the effect of the variable in question but found no significant response. The sign (· ·) indicates that the effect of that variable has not been searched for in any of the studies reviewed. Individual reaction function studies differ in the monetary policy variables which they have sought to explain, the list of explanatory variables employed, the dynamic structure of the responses searched for, as well of course as the time periods studied. Further they differ in the precise definitions of the various explanatory variables used. In general, if any one study has found a significant effect, it has been recorded as indicating a significant response in Table 8.4. There were no conflicts of findings but some studies have found insignificance where others have found significance. The only matter which could give rise to confusion and to which attention is drawn, is that some of the signs recorded in Appendix 2 are opposite to those recorded in Table 8.4. The reason for this is that the signs as recorded in the Appendix relate to the dependent variable used in the relevant regression whilst those recorded in Table 8.4 refer to the effects of the various macroeconomic targets on the direction of monetary policy change. Thus, for example, if a study has used an interest rate as a dependent variable, a policy response which leads to a lowering (–) of the interest rate is the equivalent of one which leads to a rising (+) of the money supply growth rate.

With the above remarks in mind, Table 8.4 can be examined to reveal the following major patterns. Only in the case of Japan and the United States does there appear to be a systematic monetary expansion in response to an increase in the fiscal deficit. In Germany, there is even a tendency for the

TABLE 8.4 *Policy Reactions Grouped According to Central Bank Law*

Final Authority/ Appointment of Directors	Country	Expansionary Monetary Policy (+)/Contractionary Monetary Policy (–) in Response to:			
		Fiscal Deficit	Real Output fall/ Unemployment rise	Inflation Rise	External Deficit
Government/ Government	Australia	. .	+	–	–
	Belgium	. .	+	–	–
	Canada	+	+	+	–
	France	0	0	0	0
	Italy	0	+	0	0
	Japan	+	–	0	–
	Sweden	0	–	0	0
	United Kingdom	0	+	–	–
Bank/ Government	United States	+	+	–	0
Bank/ Government and Others	Germany	–	0	0	–

Code:
. . indicates that the variable was not included in study
\+ indicates a positive significant coefficient
– indicates a negative significant coefficient
0 indicates an insignificant coefficient
Significance is at the 10 per cent level or better.

Source: Tables in Appendix.

Bundesbank to offset a rise in the fiscal deficit. Six of the ten countries (Australia, Belgium, Canada, Italy, the United Kingdom, the United States) operate a standard counter-cyclical monetary policy engaging in monetary contraction as the economy moves into a real boom. Japan and Sweden behave in a perverse manner in this regard, accentuating the real cycle. France and Germany seem to ignore the movements of real economic activity in adjusting the stance of monetary policy instruments. Four countries (Australia, Belgium, the United Kingdom and the United States) respond to a rise in the inflation rate with a tightening of monetary policy. In this respect Canada seems to display a perverse reaction. The remaining five countries (France, Italy, Japan, Sweden and Germany) apparently ignore movements in the inflation rate in adjusting their monetary policy. Changes in the external deficit have a significant effect on money supply growth wth in Australia, Belgium, Canada, Germany, Japan, and the United Kingdom and no effect in the other four countries. These response patterns to external deficits indicate that reserve changes are either not serilized at all or only partially serilized.

This completes a characterization of monetary policies and attention is now turned to an examination of the relationship between those policies and bank constitutions summarized in Part 2.

3. Relationships Between Constitutions and Policies

The classification of Central Bank constitutions employed has two dimensions, the first concerning whether there exists a legislated objective concerning price stability or not, and the second concerning the independence of the Central Bank both from government intervention in monetary policymaking and from government influence on the appointment of the bank directorate. On the matter of the legislation of a price stability objective, only a weak test can be performed since only one country, the Netherlands, is in that category. It would be desirable to have countries which differ from the Netherlands in other respects concerning the degree of independence in order to get an independent and more powerful test on the role of legislating a requirement for the Central Bank to pursue price stability. However, weak though the test is, it is possible to compare the performance of monetary policy in the Netherlands with that in the other countries in the same 'independence' category. Making that comparison it is clear that the Netherlands has the lowest inflation rate in that group and has a relatively low degree of variability. Unfortunately, there is no reaction function study available for the Netherlands to examine its responses to inflation and other macroeconomic variables. It is clear, on the limited data available, and on the basis of this admittedly weak test, that there is a positive association between the legislation of a price stability objective and the achievement of a relatively non-inflationary and low variability monetary policy.

Most of the cross-country variability in Central Bank constitutions concerns the degree of independence of the Central Bank from government. First, consider the relationship (if any) between independence and the average inflationary record. In the category in which the bank makes policy and there is some element of independence from government in the appointments of Directors, both countries (Germany and Switzerland) rank 1 and 2 on the anti-inflationary monetary policy criterion. In the two other categories, where the bank is independent in the making of monetary policy but in which the government appoints all the Directors and in the case where the government is involved in all aspects of bank policymaking, there does not appear to be a significant break in the rankings. The 'independent' Fed, in the United States, appears very low down in the ranking (position 9) and cannot be distinguished from those Central Banks which are fully dependent on government. Thus it appears that the critical characteristic of independence as far as inflation is concerned is not independence from government in the making of monetary policy but independence in the monetary policy is *combined with some diffusion of power concerning the appointment of bank directors.*

Secondly, consider the relationship between independence and the variability of policy. It appears that there is no association between any of the categories of Central Bank constitutions and the variability of policy, and that, as far as achieving a stable monetary policy is concerned, there is nothing in the way in which Central Bank constitutions are written that leads to low variance outcomes. This is perhaps not surprising in view of the large potential for individual governor/director preferences and personal strengths and weaknesses to influence policy in a genuinely independent bank (see Friedman (1962)).[11]

Next consider the relationship between independence and policy reactions. This can be applied only to ten of the twelve countries. There is apparently a distinct difference between the first and third categories. The German Central Bank which is independent in both respects, does not apparently expand money supply growth in response to unemployment or inflation. It permits external deficits to have some partial effect on the rate of money supply growth but acts to counter fiscal policy. In the third category, the totally subservient Central Banks, there is a strong (though not uniform) tendency for monetary policy to react to unemployment and also in two cases to financing fiscal deficits. The only cases in which a standard counter-cyclical Keynesian monetary policy reaction to unemployment is not obvious are those of France, Japan and Sweden. Thus again there seems to be a distinction between the types of policy reactions emerging from the genuinely independent German Central Bank and the rest. The United States clearly belongs in the same category as the subservient Central Banks, helping to finance government deficits and reacting in a counter-cyclical manner to unemployment and inflation.

The above findings and results are easily summarized. First, there is weak evidence that a legislated objective of the single-minded pursuit of price stability is associated with the achievement of a lower average rate of inflation than in comparable cases where no such objective is legislated. Secondly, there is strong evidence that full independence (in the sense of independence both in policymaking and in the appointment of directors) is associated with a low rate of inflation but not with a more predictable monetary policy. Further, there is weak evidence that the fully independent Central Bank's monetary policy is used primarily as an anti-inflation weapon and not to stabilize real output and employment. Thirdly, monetary policies do not appear to differ significantly as between independent Central Banks and government-dominated Central Banks where the 'independent' Central Bank has a directorate entirely appointed by government.

IV. A NEW MONETARY CONSTITUTION FOR THE EUROPEAN COMMUNITIES

Attention is now turned to the task of drawing out from the foregoing its implications for the design and establishment of a new monetary constitution for the EC.

First, it is clear that if a monetary constitution for the EC is required which will deliver a monetary policy geared to counter-cyclical Keynesian-style stabilization measures, then any unified monetary constitution would have to await the establishment of a federal parliament and federal government to whom the European Central Bank would have to be subservient. There would be no need to have detailed day-to-day government intervention in the making of monetary policy but it would be necessary to at least have complete government control over the appointment of governors/directors of such a Central Bank.

If, on the other hand, it is sought to achieve stable monetary policies and stable and low inflation rates then there is no reason at all why a unified monetary constitution should await full political union. Indeed, stable monetary policies may be enhanced by political decentralization. However, the lessons contained in the empirical patterns found in the previous section suggest that designing a monetary constitution which delivers stable monetary policy is not at all straightforward. The lessons derived from Switzerland and West Germany suggest that establishing a Central Bank which is independent of government both in day-to-day policymaking and in the appointment of directors does appear to deliver a low average inflation rate. However, there is no guarantee that that inflation rate will have a low variability. Something more is needed, then, than simply establishing a fully and genuinely independent Central Bank if the objective is low *and stable* inflation.

It seems hard to disagree with Friedman's rejection of commodity standards as the solution and, in the absence of any alternative suggestion, hard to reject Friedman's plea for the legislation of a single, simple, achievable monetary growth objective for which the Central Bank is made fully responsible. The legislation of an *inflation rate objective* raises too many objections concerning its attainability since, from year to year, many factors move the price level in a manner making it an unsuitable variable to specify as the object of direct control. For this reason, the objective would, of necessity, have to be specified in terms of some monetary aggregate. It would be foolish, however, in embracing a legislated rule, to expect too much from the rule. First, it must be remembered, as noted by Viner (1962), that any attempt to legislate more than one rule will lead to all the problems that we already have with monetary policy. Two rules give rise to a potential for inconsistency and, in that event, discretion would have to be exercised. There is no way therefore in which a multi-variable objective function for the Central Bank can be legislated without at the same time giving the Central Bank discretionary authority. The second limitation of a rule arises from Viner's other observation, namely that the rule itself might be changed with too great frequency. As Buchanan has noted, what is required is:

> . . . a 'constitutional' attitude; that is to say, people must agree on the basic rules that define the operation of a monetary system and then agree to abide by these rules as adopted. The attitude of which I speak is one that prevents continual tampering with the rules as adopted. This constitutional attitude seems to me to be one of the most difficult of human behavioral characteristics to adopt or even to explain and to understand. Since the Enlightenment, men have refused to acknowledge the validity of any absolutes either in terms of ethical principles or in terms of social institutions, ideas, law, social structures: all have been subjected to discussion and to question and through these to deliberately organized modification and change. Chaos is likely to result if changes made too quickly are not for rational reasons. Until and unless we know what changes are in fact best it is far better to accept certain relatively absolute absolutes both in ethics and in the rules defining the social order and we cannot really know what fundamental constitutional changes are needed until we are able to observe the working of a given set of institutions over time through a long succession of events. The willingness to do this, to play a series of games by the same rules, in order to evaluate properly the rules themselves, is the essential attitude that is required. The need for this attitude is not of course confined to the monetary problem. The monetary problem does serve however to point up sharply the general relevance of the attitude that is more generally required for the maintenance of orderly civilized life. . . . With the emergence of a genuinely constitutional attitude, there are many possible monetary systems that would work well that would ensure an adequate degree of monetary predictability. Without the emergence of this attitude there is no monetary system that will work well and continued monetary chaos of sorts can be expected to prevail. (Buchanan (1962), pp. 182-183.)

It is probably well to bear in mind Buchanan's words both in advocating and adopting a monetary rule, for those who advocate such a rule are in no way suggesting that paradise is around the corner after such a rule has been adopted. All that is being asserted is that it would not make matters worse and might very well make them better.

The suggestions which emerge then from the foregoing *a priori* and empirical investigation are that, if the objective is to achieve monetary stability, there should be established a European Central Bank which has a clearly legislated single attainable objective of achieving a growth rate of the aggregate money supply (approximating to the rate of real growth of output). This would produce movements of the price level of some negligible magnitude depending on the income elasticity of demand for the new monetary aggregate.

It is of some importance, however, to ask the further question: what should become of the existing Central Banks of the members of the EC? In dealing with this question it should be borne in mind that a Central Bank has two distinct functions. Its first is in the area of monetary policy-making and its second is in the area of the regulation and control of the banking and finance industry. The advocated monetary rule would limit the operations of national Central Banks in the first area. However, it would place no restrictions on their regulatory function. Indeed these functions would be enhanced. The most appropriate procedure would appear to be to form a European Communities Reserve System (ECRS) along the lines of the Federal Reserve System in the United States of America, making the Board of Governors of the ECRS responsible for the achievement of the overall money supply growth target. They would achieve this by open market and rediscount policies implemented by the member banks and in particular those in the major financial centres such as London and Frankfurt. The existing national Central Banks which probably would retain their national titles in order to emphasize stability and continuity and would be the agents of the Board of Governors in the implementation of and attainment of the broad monetary policy objective.

As regards banking and finance system regulation, each national Central Bank would police, monitor and regulate the finance industry in its own country. There would not even be a need to homogenize all the rules and regulations concerning domestic banking although some homogenization would no doubt emerge. However, the amount of taxation imposed on banks via required reserve ratios, interest rate ceilings and other regulations could be a matter for national decision. There would of course be the border tax problem but that is no bigger a problem in banking than in any other area.

Precisely when in the process towards monetary union the ECRS should be established would depend on the way in which it is sought to establish union. If the parallel currency approach advocated by the All Saints' Day Manifesto group was to be adopted, there would be a strong case for setting up the ECRS at the same time as the establishment of the Europa. In that event it would be necessary to specify some transition rules for the operation of the ECRS different from that of maintaining a steady growth rate of the European monetary aggregate. In the transition the ECRS would have to manage the purchasing power guarantee of the Europa. Its task would be to collect together the various price indexes for the purpose of establishing a monthly exchange rate between the Europa and the basket of national currencies. Further, it would be necessary to write into the constitution of the ECRS, detailed arrangements concerning the procedures for replacing national currencies with the Europa and also to pre-specify the conditions under which the ECRS would switch from providing a purchasing power guarantee of the Europa to controlling the aggregate monetary growth rate.

APPENDIX 1 – CENTRAL BANKING LEGISLATION

The major summary source for central banking legislation on Australia, Canada, the United Kingdom and Japan is *Central Banking Legislation*, edited by Hans Aufricht, The International Monetary Fund, Washington, D.C., 1961 (Australia, pp. 5-88; Canada, pp. 89-126; United Kingdom, pp. 185-260; Japan, pp. 425-60). The major secondary source for central banking legislation on Belgium, France, the Federal Republic of Germany, Italy, the Netherlands, Sweden and Switzerland is *Central Banking Legislation*, vol. II: *Europe*, edited by Hans Aufricht, The International Monetary Fund, Washington, D.C., 1967 (Belgium, pp. 59-106; France, pp. 175-250; Federal Republic of Germany, pp. 251-302; Italy, pp. 421-64; the Netherlands, pp. 465-500; Sweden, pp. 663-704; Switzerland, pp. 705-46). There are several alternative sources for the United States of America but the one which we have used is *Documentary History of Banking and Currency in the United States*, introduced by Paul A. Samuelson, edited by Herman E. Krooss, vol. 4, New York, 1969.

The only major changes in legislation not included in the volumes by Aufricht taken account of are those concerning Canada following the so-called Coyne affair and France (1973). Full details of the legislative changes in Canada can be found in the *Revised Statutes of Canada*, 1970, Chapter B, and for France in 'Textes Concernant La Banque de France' (Loi du 3 janvier, 1973 et Decret du 30 janvier, 1973), available from Direction Generale des Services Etrangers, Banque de France, 39, rue Croix-des-Petits-Champs, Paris 1er. The rest of this Appendix summarizes the main statutes concerning the establishment of Central Banks in the twelve countries featured in the study.

1. Australia

The Commonwealth Bank Acts of 1948, 1948, 1951 and 1953 are the relevant Central Bank legislation in force up to January 1960. Since that date, the Reserve Bank Act of 1959, which established the Reserve Bank of Australia, has been in force.

2. *Belgium*
'The Banque Nationale de Belgique was established in 1850 by virtue of a law of May 5, 1850. The Bank is currently governed by Royal Decree Number 29 of August 24, 1939 as modified by amendments adopted in 1944, 1948, 1957 and 1959, often referred to as the Organic Law of the National Bank of Belgium.' (Aufricht, 1967, p. 59)

3. *Canada*
The Bank of Canada is governed by the Bank of Canada Act, the original statute being enacted in 1934 and amended in 1936, 1938, 1952, 1953, 1954 and 1967.

4. *France*
'The Banque de France was established by law of the 24th Germinal XI (April 14, 1803). The basic statutes (statuts fondamentaux) of the Bank of France was published by decree of January 16, 1808. The most recent major codification available in English is that connected with the nationalization of the Bank on December 2, 1945. Collectively the various statutes establishing and modifying the rights and duties of the Bank of France are known as the Codified Statutes of the Bank of France (Codification des textes concernant la Banque de France).' (Aufricht, 1967, p. 175). The latest modifications are contained in *Textes Concernant La Banque de France*, Loi du 3 janvier, 1973, Banque de France, Paris.

5. *West Germany*
'The Deutsche Bundesbank is governed by the Law Concerning the Deutsche Bundesbank of July 26, 1957 (Gesetz über die Deutsche Bundesbank, July 26, 1957)'. (Aufricht, 1967, p. 251)

6. *Italy*
'The Banca d'Italia was established by law number 449 on August 10, 1893 and of the agreement between the Bank and the Minister of the Treasury dated October 30, 1894 and approved by decree number 533 of December 10, 1894. The Bank of Italy is at present governed by a royal decree of June 11, 1936 as amended and by Articles 3 and 20-24 of the Banking Law of 1936 (Statuto della Banca d'Italia approvoto con il Regio Decreto 11 guigno 1936, n 1067).' (Aufricht, 1967, p. 421)

7. *Japan*
The Bank of Japan is governed by law number 67 of February 24, 1942 as amended by subsequent legislation. The version given in Aufricht which has been used for the present study is a translation supplied by the Bank of Japan and includes amendments up to and including law number 135 of May 27, 1957. Some subsequent updating may be required but has not been attempted.

8. The Netherlands
'The Netherlands Bank (de Nederlandsche Bank N.V.) was founded by virtue of a decree of March 25, 1814, frequently referred to as the "Octroi of 1814." The principal law governing the legal status and functions of the Bank, prior to the adoption of the Bank Act of 1948 was the Act of December 22, 1863. The Act used in this study is the Netherlands Bank Act of 1948 (Wet van 23rd April 1948, houdende nieuwe bepalingen nopende het Statuut van de Nederlandsche Bank N.V.).' (Aufricht, 1967, p. 465)

9. Sweden
'The Sveriges Riksbank was founded in 1668 as a state institution (note that the Sveriges Riksbank is the world's oldest central bank). The Bank is now governed by the Sveriges Riksbank Act of June 30, 1934 as subsequently amended (Lag for Sveriges Riksbank (Act Number 437) June 30, 1934).' (Aufricht, 1967, p. 663)

10. Switzerland
'The Swiss National Bank was established by virtue of the Federal Law of October 6, 1905. The Bank is presently governed by the Federal Law on the Swiss National Bank of December 23, 1953 which should be read in conjunction with Article 39 of the Federal Constitution as amended in 1951. (The official title of the Law is Bundesgesetz über die Schweizerische Nationalbank vom 23 Dezember 1953.)' (Aufricht, 1967, p. 705)

11. The United Kingdom
'The Bank of England was founded by the Charter of the Bank of England of 1694. Its rights and duties have been amended through various Acts dated 1696, 1708, 1709, 1716, 1741, 1800, 1833, 1844, 1870, 1892, and it is presently operated under the terms of the Bank of England Act of 1946 and the Charter of The Bank of England of 1946.' (Aufricht, 1961, pp. 185ff)

12. The United States of America
The central banking system of the United States of America – the Federal Reserve System – was established by the Federal Reserve Act of December 23, 1913. (*Statutes at Large*, XXXVIII, 251 (Krooss and Samuelson, 1969) and pp. 2436-2470.) The major subsequent amendments were in the Banking Acts of 1933 and 1935. (Krooss and Samuelson, pp. 2725-2769 and 2874-2940)

APPENDIX 2 *Policy Reaction Functions*

Study	Period	Dependent variable	Fiscal Deficit	Real Output fall/ Unemployment rise	Inflation	External Deficit
AUSTRALIA						
Jonson, P.D., 1974 p. 268	1959(3) to 1971(4)	Bond Rate Aggregate	. .	–**	0	+**
		Statutory Deposit Ratio	. .	–**	0	0
Lewis, M.K., Table 2	1956 to 1970 (qtly)	Index of Monetary Policy Intentions	. .	+**	–*	–**
BELGIUM						
Villanueva, D.P., 1972, p. 20	1957(2) to 1968(4)	Discount Rate	. .	–**	+**	+**
CANADA						
Gordon, R.J., 1977, p. 50	1958(3) to	Money Supply Growth	0	0	0	0
Reuber, G.L., 1964, p. 123	1949 to 1961 (qtly)	Money Supply Growth	. .	+**	+**	. .
		Nominal Net Cash reserves	. .	0	+**	. .
		Real Money Supply	. .	+**	0	. .
Wogin, G., 1976, p. 6	1926 to 1972 (qtly)	Money Supply Growth	+**	+**	. .	. .

Study	Period	Dependent variable	Fiscal Deficit	Real Output fall/Unemployment rise	Inflation	External Deficit
FRANCE						
Gordon, R.J., 1977, p. 50	1958(3) to 1973(1)	Money Supply Growth	0	0	0	0
GERMANY						
Gordon, R.J., 1977, p. 50	1958(3) to 1973(1)	Money Supply Growth	–*	0	0	–**
ITALY						
Gordon, R.J., 1977, p. 50	1958(3) to 1973(1)	Money Supply Growth	0	+*	0	0
JAPAN						
Gordon, R.J., 1977, p. 50	1958(3) to 1973(1)	Money Supply Growth	+**	–**	0	–**
SWEDEN						
Gordon, R.J., 1977, p. 50	1958(3) to 1973(1)	Money Supply Growth	0	–*	0	0
UNITED KINGDOM						
Fisher, D., 1970, p. 214	1951( ) to 1964(4)	Bank Rate	..	–**	+**	+**
		Speical Deposits	..	–**	+**	0
Gordon, R.J., 1977, p. 50	1958(3) to 1973(1)	Money Supply Growth	0	+**	0	–**
Nobay, A.R., 1974, pp. 318-9	1959 to 1969	Bank of England's Security Portfolia	..	+**	..	–**

Study	Period	Dependent variable	Fiscal Deficit	Real Output fall/Unemployment rise	Inflation	External Deficit
		Special Deposits	..	–**	..	–**
		Authorities' Desired Bank Advances	..	–**	..	..
		Bank Rate	..	..	..	–**
Pissarides, C.A., 1972, p. 251	1955(4) to 1968(4)	Bank Rate	..	–**	+**	+**
UNITED STATES OF AMERICA						
Barro, R.J., 1977, p. 3	1941 to 1976 (yrly)	Money Supply Growth	+**	+**	0	0
Gordon, R.J., 1977, p. 50	1958(3) to 1973(1)	Money Supply Growth	0	0	0	0
Havrilesky, T., 1967, p. 302	1952 to 1965 (qtly)	Total Reserves, adjusted for legal reserve requirement changes	..	+**	–**	0
Wood, J.H. 1967, p. 153	1952 to 1963 (qtly)	Quantity of government securities held by Federal Reserve	+**	+**	–**	0

Code:

..	indicates that the variable was not tested	**	indicates significant at 5 per cent level
+	indicates a positive significant coefficient	*	indicates significant at 10 per cent level
–	indicates a negative significant coefficient	0	indicates an insignificant coefficient

FOOTNOTES TO CHAPTER 8

1. The movements of the seven independent national currencies against the US dollar from 1970 to August 1977 are as follows:

National Currency Per US Dollar

		1970	August 1977	Percent Change Against US $
Belgium-Luxembourg	Franc	50.000	35.566	+ 28.87
Denmark	Kroner	7.500	6.025	+ 19.67
France	Franc	5.554	4.895	+ 11.87
Germany	D-Mark	3.660	2.315	+ 36.75
Italy	Lira	625.000	882.250	– 41.16
Netherlands	Guilder	3.620	2.449	+ 32.35
UK-Ireland	Pound	0.417	0.575	– 27.89

International Financial Statistics, vol. XXX, no. 10, October 1977 Par Rate/ Market Rate (line rf) for each country (Period Averages).

2. B.I.S. data reported in David F.V. Ashby (1976).
3. See Parkin (1972, 1976).
4. See Basevi *et al.* (1975).
5. For a fuller account of this work, see Parkin and Bade (1977).
6. Appendix 1 provides a brief summary of the major statutes which have been drawn on and provides detailed references to the major secondary sources used for each of them.
7. See in particular, Nordhaus'(1975) and Gordon (1975).
8. It may be objected that this misrepresents the Bundesbank Law which states '§3 "The Deutsche Bundesbank shall regulate the volume of money in circulation and credit supplied to the economy . . . with the aim of safeguarding the currency . . ." The phrase 'safeguarding the currency' no doubt is intended to mean 'avoiding inflation'; however, it is imprecise and could equally well mean 'avoiding inflation on a scale such that the currency ceases to be used as money'; hence the decision to classify the Bundesbank as not having a well-defined objective.
9. The data on aggregate money used were all taken from *International Financial Statistics*, vol, XXIX, no. 5, May 1976, Annual Data 1951-1975. A subsequent revision will attempt to use data on a more consistent and comparable basis form original sources.
10. Studies for these countries may well exist but have not been located.
11. It may be that the use of the coefficient of variation has biased the measure of variability against low inflation countries. In a subsequent paper, other measures of variability will be considered to check the sensitivity of this result to the particular measure used here.

REFERENCES

Aufricht, H., *Central Banking Lagislation* (Washington, D.C.: The International Monetary Fund, 1961).
Aufricht, H., *Central Banking Legislation, Volume II: Europe* (Washington, D.C.: The International Monetary Fund, 1967).
Barro, R.J., 'Unanticipated Money, Output and the Price Level in the United States', Rochester University, mimeo, July 1977.
Bartley, T.J., 'Giblin and the Commonwealth Bank', in *Giblin, The Scholar and The Man*, D. Copland (ed.) (Melbourne: Cheshire, 1960).
Fisher, D., 'The Instruments of Monetary Policy and Generalized Trade-off Function for Britain, 1955-1968', *Manchester School*, vol. 38, 1970, pp. 209-22.
Friedman, M., 'Should There be an Independent Monetary Authority', in *In Search of a Monetary Constitution*, L.B. Yeager (ed.) (Cambridge, Mass.: Harvard University Press, 1962), pp. 219-43.
Friedman, M. and A.J. Schwartz, *A Monetary History of the United States 1867-1960*, National Bureau of Economic Research (New York: Princeton University Press, 1963).
Gordon, R.J., 'The Demand for and Supply of Inflation', *Journal of Law and Economics*, vol. XVIII, December 1965, pp. 807-36.
Gordon, R.J., 'World Inflation and the Sources of Monetary Accommodation: A Study of Eight Countries', *Brookings Papers on Economic Activity*, 1977, No. 2, pp. 409-77.
Havrilesky, T., 'A Test of Monetary Policy Action', *Journal of Political Economy*, vol. 75, June 1967, pp. 299-304.
Hodgman, D.R., *National Monetary Policies and International Monetary Cooperation*. (Boston: Little, Brown, 1974).
Jonson, P.D., 'Stabilization Policy in Australia: An Objective Analysis', *Manchester School*, vol. 42, 1974, pp. 259-76.
Krooss, H.E., and P.A. Samuelson, *Documentary History of Banking and Currency in the U.S.A.*, vol. 4 (New York: McGraw-Hill, 1969).
Lewis, M.K., 'Targets, Indicators and the Insider Lag of Australian Monetary Policy', mimeo.
Nobay, A.R., 'A Model of the United Kingdom Authorities' Behaviour 1959-1969', in *Issues in Monetary Economics*, H.G. Johnson and A.R. Nobay (eds.) (Oxford: Oxford University Press, 1974).
Nordhaus, W., 'The Political Business Cycle', *Review of Economic Studies*, vol. XLII (2), April 1975, pp. 169-90.
Parkin, M., 'World Inflation, International Relative Prices and Monetary Equilibrium Under Fixed Exchange Rates'. Ch. 13 in Robert Z. Aliber (ed.), *The Political Economy of Monetary Reform* (London: Macmillan, 1977).
Parkin, M. and R. Bade, 'The Relationship between Central Bank Constitutions and Monetary Policies', typescript, October 1977.
Pissarides, C.A., 'A Model of British Macroeconomic Policy, 1955-69', *Manchester School*, vol. 40, 1972, pp. 245-59.
Reuber, G.L., 'The Objectives of Canadian Monetary Policy, 1949-61 Empirical "Trade-offs" and the Reaction Function of the Authorities', *Journal of Political Economy*, vol. 72, April 1964, pp. 109-32.

Villaneuva, D.P., 'Statistical Analysis of Discount Rate Policy in Belgium, 1957-68', *European Economic Review*, 1972, pp. 199-208.

Wilson, J.S.G., 'France', in *Banking in Western Europe*, R.S. Sayers (ed.), (Oxford, 1962).

Wogin, G., 'Rational Expectations and the Natural Rate of Unemployment Hypothesis', *Carleton Economic Papers*, no. 77-08, Carleton University, Ottowa, 1976.

Wood, J.H., 'A Model of Federal Reserve Behaviour,' in G. Horwich (ed.), *Monetary Process and Policy: A Symposium 1967.*

Yeager, L.B. (ed.), *In Search of a Monetary Constitution* (Cambridge, Mass.: Harvard University Press, 1962).

Committee on the Working of the Monetary System: Report Cmnd 827 (London: HMSO, 1959).

Revised Statutes of Canada, 1970, vol. 1, Ottawa, 1970.

COMMENT ON PARKIN

Garrett F. Murphy

I begin with two points on the introduction and first section of Michael Parkin's paper, in which he describes the existing monetary constitution of Europe. One point is a detail, the second is more substantive.

First, the detail: the European Unit of Account announced at the outset as having a place in the Community-wide content of the current monetary constitution has no place in it. The only monetary unit now in use in the EEC is the European Monetary Unit of Account (EMUA) – a gold-based unit which is defined in practice by the pivotal exchange rates between the 'snake' currencies and which serves as a basis for accounting interventions and settlements of credits between central banks and the European Monetary Cooperation Fund (EMCF). The role of the unit is not significant outside that field.

Second, and more important, I think, for any question of transition from existing arrangements to a future monetary constitution, is the assertion that the Community-wide content of the existing arrangements is limited to a statement of intent in the Rome Treaty about the role of EMU and the existence of the EMUA which I have already discussed.

In fact the existing monetary constitution contains more than this. It contains the following Community elements:

1. Decisions of the Council of Ministers on relationships between central banks, including the establishment of the Committee of Governors of Central Banks of the European Economic Community.
2. The Monetary Committee which was provided for in the Rome Treaty. It includes officials from treasuries and central banks and its function is to advise the Council.
3. A relationship between central banks through initiatives of the Commission and decisions of the Council which provide mandates to central banks to deal in common with or give advice on specific problems.
4. The European Monetary Cooperation Fund – with a Board of Governors of Central Banks – and the intra-Community credit 'snake' mechanisms associated with it. This institution is also linked to the Council and the Commission which proposed its statutes.

I introduce these elements of the existing monetary constitution of the Community for completeness sake and for further reference in a few minutes when I come to say something about transition from the present position – a point explicitly excluded from the paper under discussion. I also introduce these elements to bring out a point which relates to the analysis in the paper of the independence or otherwise of central banks from Government. Clearly, in the framework which I have described for the Community there is little or no independence for central banks from the political process.

Nevertheless, I would not like to over-emphasise the new Community elements in the monetary constitution because, apart from foreign-exchange arrangements, they have had little or no content to date, either for the securing of coordination of monetary policies in the Community or their replacement with common policies.

The remainder of Michael Parkin's paper deals with two areas:

1. How does the design of monetary institutions affect the achievement of the desired characteristics of monetary policies?
2. An outline of a possible monetary constitution for the Community.

The bulk of the paper reports empirical results relating to national monetary constitutions and the relationship between these constitutions and national monetary policies. I am somewhat unhappy with all of this area, as was the other discussant. However, I don't want to go over ground which he has already covered or to get into too much detail. Therefore I will just mention a few of the main points which caught my attention.

The paper acknowledges, but perhaps does not emphasise sufficiently, its concentration on the written constitutions, to the exclusion of the practice of central banking. This is understandable since the alternative, an examination of practices, would be an enormous task; nevertheless it would be the more interesting one.

I am even less happy about the use which is made of data on monetary constitutions and their relationships with monetary policies. In particular, one notes a single observation per country of percentage variation in exchange rate in the period 1952-75. I wonder whether this is a reasonable measure of inflation over the period or a basis for drawing conclusions about central banks' behaviour? I also raise the general question of how much reliability can be placed on comparisons of data to which no probability statements are attached. Turning to the policy reaction functions, I note that most of the studies quoted cover periods terminating in 1973 or before. This is important for policy reaction since, for example, modern ideas about monetary aggregates could only be expected in recent years. Finally – on technical issues – I note that the adjectives 'predictable' and 'invariable' are used interchangeably in some parts of the paper in relation to monetary policies. I would have thought that consistent response or variability in relation to some other more predictable economic variable would be a better test of predictability than a simple coefficient of variation for money supply growth rates.

The last section of the paper deals with a new monetary constitution for Europe. The empirical section which preceded it studied the 'Independent Authority' versus 'Day-to-Day Political Interference' cases but had no monetary rule case to study. Thus, this last section proceeds to advocate a monetary rule on an *a priori* approach, assuming the goals of low and stable inflation. On that basis there is little to argue about. Yes – a single rule, if any rule. Multiple and potentially conflicting objectives have no place in rigid systems. But, no to the assertion that the rule *would* not make matters worse and might very well make them better. If the 'matters' are stable monetary policies and stable inflation rates there is a good chance that they would improve. But the matters preferred by EEC countries studied in the empirical section of the paper are predominantly counter-cyclical monetary objectives.

I note in passing that the monetary constitution proposed says nothing about exchange-rate policy vis-à-vis the rest of the world, though clearly fully flexible exchange rates are implied. This is important, because in recent years it is certain that a primary concern (which could probably be defined in a reaction function) of monetary authorities has been exchange rates and changes in the levels of official external reserves.

I have two further points on the thrust of the final section of the paper. I said at the outset that the existing monetary constitution – as expanded by my addition of EEC elements – has some importance for transition to any new constitution. The point needs some elaboration. In 1972 when the 'snake' was set up there was little or no EEC framework within which attention was being given to monetary targets and the coordination of policies and instruments. Since then, a technical base has been growing at experts level, and at the political level a sufficiently wide mandate has been given to the relevant institutions to cover further work. These steps should lead, indeed they are leading, to the idea of constitution in Buchanan's sense of playing a series of games by the same rules. The process of agreement on the rules is very slow and political will is weak. There is also an inevitable intellectual lag in the acceptance of developments in monetary theory which are of comparatively recent origin. I stress this present position because it is clear that governments and central banks require some time within the Community to reach consensus on what they are doing now and on what they should be doing with monetary policies. If that consensus cannot be reached then the prospects of a major political jump to a legislated monetary rule for the Community as a whole are remote.

COMMENT ON PARKIN

Norbert Kloten

The central focus of Parkin's paper is of vital interest to the European Communities. There are indeed common relationships between the conduct and the institutional framework of monetary policy. And any suggestions for a new monetary constitution for the Community must be based upon empirical analysis. To this extent, I agree fully with the purpose and the approach of Michael Parkin's contribution.

Nevertheless, I feel urged to ask whether: (i) the empirical methodology is appropriate; (ii) the results obtained can be accepted; (iii) the findings alone offer a sufficient base for outlining a new European Monetary Constitution; and (iv) the suggestions made are convincing.

Concerning the methodology, Parkin himself speaks of a 'ruthless simplication process' employed in his paper. No one will object to his attempt to abstract and to simplify, but the means and ways of any analysis should be free of procedural weaknesses and factual shortcomings. I restrict myself to a few examples, concentrating by and large on the German case.

I must briefly point out that some clarification might still be useful in the description of how members of the German Central Bank Council (Zentralbankrat) are appointed. According to the 1957 law concerning the Bundesbank, the final authority to appoint a new member rests with the President of the Federal Republic (Bundespräsident), who chooses among candidates nominated by the Federal Council (Bundesrat). Although the Laender Governments, represented by the presidents of the State Central Banks (Landeszentral-banken), have the prerogative only to suggest the names of candidates, in practice the Federal Council has always accepted these suggestions. On the other hand, although the Federal Council is required to consult the Central Bank Council on its nominations, in some cases it has even ignored the fact that the Central Bank Council had rejected a nominee by a majority vote.

By the way, the size of the directory (decided by the Federal Government) is by custom restricted to eight, thereby limiting in practice the total number of members of the Central Bank Council to nineteen. This example shows that it is quite tenuous to base the chosen classification purely on the legal statute. Indeed, an empirical study should not neglect 'custom and practice'. This applies also to the question of the degree of autonomy or dependence of the Central Bank authorities. The appointment procedure and the participation of the Government in the Council's activities tends to lead to a pattern of behaviour unforeseen by Parkin. Thus, his belief (reflected in

Table 8.2 and in some of his conclusions) that the legislated objective of the German Central Bank is too vague to actually influence policy is not well founded.

Although the German legal formula 'to secure the currency' is vague indeed, it is commonly interpreted as a mandate to maintain stable purchasing power of money or at least to curb the inflation rate. The formula seems in practice more valuable (reliable) than the more sophisticated Dutch one, because it specifies a definite priority when several policy objectives are in conflict. Any reference to a 'country's welfare' is open to political and, often enough, arbitrary interpretation. A comparison of the conduct of monetary policy and inflation rates in the two countries gives evidence of that.

To give a second example, it would appear to be true, when viewed from the perspective of the level of employment, that the German monetary authorities practically did not respond at all toward movements of real economic activities until the spring of 1974. In a country with full employment or even overemployment for more than a decade, one could hardly have expected any other result. However, looking at a different indicator, it can be seen that this was true in the 1967 recession, whereas things have changed since the autumn of 1974. In other words, monetary policy has reflected both the slowdown of production and the high unemployment rate. What matters here is the objective which determines the monetary target and serves *ex post* to rationalise any apparent overshooting.

This critical remark is not restricted to the time period dealt with in the Parkin paper. An empirical analysis addressed to these issues should not and cannot neglect the most important experiences of the last years. Furthermore, the average figures for the period 1952 to 1975 by no means reflect the typical features of the sub-periods in a proper way. The most important feature which is observed, is the upswing of inflation rates from the midst of the 1960s on. When in the spring of 1973 the fixed-rate system was followed by floating exchange rates, monetary policy changed substantially, not only in Germany, but in other countries as well, notably in the United States and Switzerland. Since then, independence of monetary policy has been associated with a low rate of inflation (pointed out in the paper) and with a more predictable monetary policy (association denied in the paper) thanks to explicit monetary targets.

To sum up, I hesitate to accept the empirical findings, partly derived as they are, from 'arbitrary classifications' and based upon statistical indicators which are not really convincing, thus leading to a ranking which is not fully in line with the facts. Thorough case studies of relevant countries, based on the interrelations which matter and including a comparison of the dependencies which count, might have yielded better results.

Having said this, I would like to emphasise that I agree completely with Parkin on many observations and judgements, even though his empirical findings are not general enough and sufficiently well verified to justify the writing of a new European Monetary Constitution. Furthermore, it seems to me that the proposals in the paper are not really linked with the results of the empirical analysis. They appear to be based primarily upon respectable socio-philosophical considerations *à la* Buchanan and a conception of monetary policy which is, with good reasons, advocated by many highly regarded economists.

Unfortunately, Parkin offers no organisational alternatives to the one proposed. The empirical findings and the more fundamental philosophical arguments ought to have warranted alternatives reflecting different European political scenarios.

Parkin advocates a 'clearly legislated single attainable objective', that of achieving a fixed growth rate of the money supply, while he rejects any reference to the price level. The latter is certainly not a suitable variable 'to specify as the object of direct control'. I think it more useful for Europe to recommend the general use of the money supply as an indicator of monetary policy even though countries might not be prepared to accept binding monetary growth rates. If there exists an adequate 'constitutional attitude' (Buchanan), a policy resembling a system of 'rules' will probably be effective; if there is no such attitude, then the political forces, the parties and the social groups will not be willing to submit themselves to the dictate of an all-determining quantity. Parkin states indirectly that in the case of such a clearly prescribed objective it is of no major importance to elaborate the appointment procedures of, for instance, the governors of an European Communities Reserve System or to list the duties of the board members. Parkin suggests, finally, that if there is an agreed-upon monetary rule, then there is no need 'to homogenise the rules and regulations concerning domestic banking'. Here again I doubt whether things are so simple and whether one can restrict oneself to an extreme solution and refrain from suggesting intermediate solutions. In any case, including the extreme, I dare to say that in a common European money and capital market, it is arbitrary to adapt the given national organisational patterns and the banking procedures in this way or any other. Money and capital are very mobile. Consequently, there will be need for common minimum supervision requirements, for common principles of credit policy, and for common special and liquidity standards.

PART V: CONCLUSIONS

9 Prospects for Moving to Monetary Union: Concluding Thoughts

POLLY REYNOLDS ALLEN

The recent renewal of official interest in European monetary union made the topic of this conference timely and pertinent. European monetary union has been a goal of the EEC since the Werner Report in 1971, but during the ensuing years progress toward monetary union has been slow, if not at times retrogressive. In the last few years there has been growing recognition of several problems inherent in a monetary union among diverse economies, and suggestions have been made for alternative approaches to monetary union. This conference has directed attention to a number of these issues. Among the diverse opinions voiced and topics discussed, there appeared to be a consensus among conference participants on three underlying presumptions.

It was generally accepted that European monetary union is eventually a desirable goal. This was the conclusion of Christie and Fratianni in their paper, following a summary of the various benefits and costs of monetary union. While monetary union itself is still considered by some to be controversial, there was no argument among conference participants about the appropriateness of an eventual union, even by those who opposed any such move in the near future.

The second area of agreement concerns the role of inflation. It was conceded that the EEC is seriously in need of monetary reform, through reduction in the growth of money supplies and a lessening of rates of price inflation. Inflation was seen as bringing no long-run gains of increased output and lower rates of unemployment. Yet, while the inflationary countries in the EEC by now have used up almost any short-run gains from inflation, there remain serious transitional costs in getting rid of that inflation. This is because of the difficulties of removing inflationary expectations. The rates of inflation differ considerably among countries of the EEC, and these differences present a problem for the transition to monetary union.

Thirdly, everyone agreed that earlier efforts of the EEC to move toward monetary union have not been successful. Specifically, attempts by the EEC countries to limit exchange-rate variations through the snake arrangement and to coordinate national economic, particularly monetary, policies are no longer seen as workable means of achieving the requisite conditions for monetary union. Other means of making the transition to monetary union must be found if the goal is to be reached.

Beyond these three general presumptions, a variety of viewpoints were expressed on most issues. For example, it was asked whether there should be a move toward European monetary union in the near future; whether fiscal and political union must accompany monetary union; and whether a European parallel currency, such as proposed in the All Saints' Day Manifesto, is a desirable means of moving toward monetary union. Among the critics of the parallel-currency concept, opinions ranged from a concern that it would not be generally accepted to a fear that it would be accepted too rapidly in the most inflationary countries.

Rather than discuss each paper, I shall summarize the major conclusions and issues that came out of the conference and give my reaction to the major points. The issues are organized under three general topics. There is first the nature of a monetary union and the need for a monetary constitution. Secondly, there are the possibilities for structuring and managing the period of transition to a monetary union. Finally, as a major subtopic of the transition possibilities, there is the proposal to introduce a European parallel currency with constant purchasing power – the Europa.

I. THE NATURE OF MONETARY UNION AND THE NEED FOR A MONETARY CONSTITUTION

It is almost universally agreed that monetary union would involve a loss of national control over the issuance of money. This power would be given to some central decision-making body. There would be no possibility of exchange-rate changes within the union, which probably would be guaranteed by a single union currency. More difficult to answer are questions about the nature of this union monetary authority, regarding its power, responsibility, and mandate. There are also important questions about the amount of fiscal and political unification and centralization that must accompany a monetary union. The two issues are closely interrelated, for the type of mandate given to the monetary authority will greatly affect the need for political and fiscal unification.

Very little work has been done on the question of a constitution or mandate for a European monetary authority, perhaps because of the difficulties of coming to agreement on such an issue. Parkin's paper addresses this question.

Countries must agree on the type of monetary policy they want before committing themselves to a monetary constitution. Some serious doubts about the feasibility of monetary union for Europe have stemmed from perceptions that the EEC countries may not be able to agree on monetary policy because they have different preferences for inflation. Different national inflation rates could not be achieved simultaneously in a monetary union. If it is true that there are no long-run gains from inflation and that Europe is in need of monetary reform of its inflationary policies, then there is no basis for preferring inflation, and this argument against monetary union disappears. With no long-run gains from inflation, the union monetary authority should follow a policy that is non-inflationary over time. Agreement on this issue does not answer the questions of how much discretionary power should be given to the union monetary authority or of whether union monetary policy should be used in the short run to combat cyclical movements in the economy.

Parkin comes down firmly in favour of limiting monetary policy to the long-run task of maintaining price stability. He favours a legislated monetary-growth rule as a mandate for the union monetary authority. I shall not discuss the arguments for and against the use of monetary policy as a stabilization tool. Rather, consider what a decision on this issue for the EEC would imply for the possibilities of European monetary union in the near future.

If monetary policy is to be used as a short-run stabilization tool, then it needs to be coordinated with fiscal policy. In such a situation, the discretionary actions of the monetary authority inevitably would involve political decisions. Alternatively, if the union monetary authority were subjected to a legislated rule, defining the rate of growth of the union money supply, there would be little political content in the decisions of the monetary authority. There would be virtually no need, in making the operational decisions of monetary policy, to take account of fiscal policy or of current stabilization requirements.

Whatever the mandate of a union monetary authority, a move to monetary union would have implications for the effectiveness of fiscal policy as a stabilization tool at the national, as compared to the union, level. Some fiscal centralization probably would prove desirable in any monetary union.
In addition, a monetary constitution that gave considerable discretionary power to the union monetary authority would have to be accompanied by concurrent centralization of significant fiscal and political authority. This would enable coordinated political-economic decisions to be made on the same hierarchical level. By contrast, a legislated monetary-growth rule would make possible (although not necessarily optimal) a monetary union without significantly greater political or fiscal centralization than now exists in the EEC.

It follows that proposals that focus exclusively on a move to *monetary* union in the near future may be reasonable, *if* the accompanying monetary constitution provides for a legislated rule for money growth. Such proposals are too narrow and probably premature, if the monetary authority is to be given stabilization responsibilities and discretionary power.

Parkin asserts that, upon assignment to the union monetary authority of the responsibility for controlling the union money supply under a legislated rule, all other banking regulations and activities could continue as the responsibilities of the national central banks. He is probably correct that a workable monetary union could incorporate and retain existing national institutions and financial structures, and that their variety across the EEC would suggest and even require different regulations in different countries. These regulations should not be left completely to national central banks, however, for they could be used to influence the distribution of the union money supply and variably insulate some countries from the effects of union monetary policy.

There needs to be a clear vision of the nature of a monetary constitution for European monetary union before significant steps are taken toward monetary union. Such an agreement could provide considerable guidance on the most workable transition measures. Furthermore, prior commitment to a monetary constitution would assure that the EEC did not find itself developing a momentum toward monetary union without the necessary consensus to take the final step.

II. STRUCTURING THE TRANSITION TO MONETARY UNION

Coordination of Policies and Exchange-Rate Alignment

The efforts to coordinate monetary policies and to reduce exchange-rate variations between the European currencies, through intervention in the foreign-exchange market in the 'snake' arrangement, have obviously not succeeded in either of their specific goals or in bringing the EEC closer to monetary union. In trying to find alternative means of moving to monetary union, it is useful to determine why the previous policies have not worked.

Klein points out in his paper that any such attempts at cooperative policies, in the absence of a dominant currency, are probably destined to fail. Arrangements with a single dominant currency have more potential for stability and success, because there is no question about which countries must adapt their policies to make the arrangement work. The task of accommodation always falls, under such arrangements, to the governments of the minor currencies. They will continue to adjust their policies as long as the arrangement appears beneficial. The earlier EEC arrangements, by contrast, called for coordination of all countries' policies in the direction of rather vague goals. The uncertainty as to whose responsibility it was to compromise domestic policies and as to what could be the distribution of costs and benefits, made it risky for a country to shape national policies in the union interests.

Purchasing Power Parity as a Guide to Exchange-Rate Determination.

While the arrangements by the EEC to minimise exchange-rate flunctuations proved unworkable, there remains an unwillingness to let the private foreign-exchange markets solely determine exchange rates. One proposal for a response to the large exchange-rate fluctuations and to differing national rates of price inflation has been a purchasing-power-parity rule of exchange-rate intervention. Such a policy, instead of trying to minimize exchange-rate variations, would attempt to maintain real exchange-rate equilibrium while allowing for changes that reflected different inflation rates. Such a policy was proposed in the EEC's OPTICA 1976 Report. Basevi and De Grauwe's paper develops an explicit model in which to evaluate the merits of the OPTICA proposal.

The main arguments for a purchasing-power-parity rule of exchange-rate intervention stem from empirical observations, with theoretical support, that exchange rates can overshoot their equilibrium levels in response to financial flows. The resulting inflationary pressures of the additional depreciation, combined with downward price ridigity and accommodating monetary policies of governments, can add to the inflationary spiral.

Basevi and De Grauwe's model helps to clarify the underlying rationale for the proposal of purchasing-power-parity intervention and some of the inherent limitations of the proposal.

The model was criticized for its static approach to what is essentially a dynamic problem – one of inflation, depreciation, and expectations over time. On practical grounds, there were strong assertions that implementing purchasing-power-parity intervention in recent years would have prevented desirable exchange-rate changes that in fact occurred.

There are sufficient criticisms, both theoretical and practical, of purchasing power parity as a measure of exchange-rate equilibrium, that one is tempted to reject a proposal for intervening to maintain purchasing power parity. Yet, the widespread dissatisfaction with the exchange-rate variability produced by uncontrolled markets inevitably leads to foreign-exchange intervention. As a rough approximation of equilibrium, the guidelines of purchasing power parity remain somewhat appealing, particularly between countries where the real disturbances appear to be few.

Purchasing-power-parity intervention has been recommended as a way of preventing adverse exchange-rate changes and their side effects, and not explicitly as a means of transition to monetary union. It could also serve the latter purpose in two ways. Most important, the elimination of all real exchange-rate changes would impose on the countries one of the 'costs' attributed to monetary union. A move to monetary union would primarily involve, then, the further costs of aligning inflation rates. If purchasing-power-parity intervention succeeded in limiting the rates of inflation in the depreciating countries, the inflation differentials would also be reduced, which should help ease the way to monetary union.

Direct Move to Monetary Union

A third means of moving to monetary union, discussed by Christie and Fratianni, is a discrete move at some point to a central monetary authority and a new European currency, which would replace existing national currencies. Such a proposal does not specify how well aligned the participating economies must be, what the constitution for the monetary union would be, or how much political and fiscal unification should accompany this move. It does point out that a complete move to monetary union avoids some of the problems and costs that arise in a gradual transition.

In a full monetary union, the countries would no longer have the balance-of-payments constraints among themselves that they face as independent monetary authorities. Automatic adjustment would gradually diminish intra-union imbalances in the absence of further real disturbances. There would be no need to reinforce this adjustment because of lack of reserves. Regional redistribution policies might allow imbalances to continue for some time, implying ongoing transfers between countries. As a result of removing the reserve constraint, the burden of economic adjustment under a monetary union may not be as great as when countries maintain pegged exchange rates without giving up monetary independence.

There are, of course, risks of moving too suddenly to monetary union, such as when economic and political conditions exact costs greater than the benefits or before governments and publics are willing to live with the implications of monetary union.

The fourth transition proposal – for a European parallel currency – constituted a major topic of the conference. I devote a separate section to this proposal.

III. EUROPEAN PARALLEL CURRENCY – THE EUROPA

Characteristics of the Europa

The introduction of a parallel currency with constant purchasing power, the Europa, and its implications were the subjects of the papers by Vaubel, Laidler and Klein, and also of much of the discussion. It is interesting to consider how such a Europa would compare with two alternatives that could have similar virtues – a privately created parallel currency with constant purchasing power or the adoption of an existing strong currency, such as the deutschmark.

Robert Triffin suggested that a privately issued parallel currency is an alternative possibility for the evolution of a European currency and for transition to European monetary union. Although Triffin did not include the indexing provision, a private parallel currency could include the provision for constant purchasing power, making it more comparable to the proposed Europa. With small changes in regulations, private banks could be allowed and encouraged to denominate loans and bond issues and to offer demand deposits with a guarantee of constant purchasing power across Europe (calculated by some agreed formula). Such deposits would be equivalent to domestic-currency demand deposits that pay a rate of interest approximately equal to the rate of inflation. Since private banks generally are not allowed to issue currency, these private 'Europas' would be available only in deposit form. This should not be a serious limitation on the currency functioning as

The major difference between a privately issued Europa and an official Europa would be in the incidence of the costs. There are two basic costs in establishing a new currency of constant purchasing power – the start-up costs of building a reputation for, and confidence in, the currency, and the loss of seigniorage.

There are a number of costs in establishing any new currency – costs of disseminating information and building a reputation and costs of establishing the currency on a sufficiently large scale, with sufficient participants for the new currency to function as an effective transactions medium. Individual private banks may not be willing to bear such start-up costs. They may find it more costly than would governments to establish the necessary reputation for the currency and the desired scale of use. Klein's paper emphasises that these costs of establishing 'brand-name' capital for any new currency may be considerable.

Secondly, there is the loss of seigniorage on an indexed currency. With an official Europa, it is the government that forgoes seigniorage (an implicit inflation tax). The burden is borne by taxpayers. With a privately issued Europa, the banks would continue to pay the implicit inflation tax on their required non-interest-bearing reserves of the domestic currency. Some seigniorage gains normally accrue to the banks, because of their monopoly rights to issue demand deposits in the domestic currency, on which they pay little or no interest. A choice by the banks to issue demand deposits denominated in a currency of constant purchasing power would mean relinquishing their share of the seigniorage, while continuing to pay the implicit inflation tax on their domestic-currency reserves.

With encouragement, the private banks might come to some agreement on a standard unit of account that would minimise inflation risk, to be used for issuing bonds, for settling accounts among themselves and possibly for issuing demand deposits. It seems unlikely that a currency of constant purchasing power would be issued privately, because the costs to the banks would probably exceed their return.

A more likely alternative to the Europa would be the gradual adoption of a strong national currency as a European currency. There would, of course, be unwanted political implications in a national currency becoming dominant. Indeed, it is the opinion of some that one of the reasons for encouraging the introduction of the parallel Europa is to prevent any voluntary move toward making the deutschmark the dominant currency in Europe. In addition to the political implications and the related issue of who controls the money supply, there are economic differences between the adoption of a parallel currency and the adoption of a dominant national currency.

For purposes of comparability, imagine that the German inflation rate were to go to zero, giving the deutschmark constant purchasing power over a basket of German goods, and that governments of other countries were to permit the circulation of the deutschmark. A significant shift into deutschmarks, for example by Italians, would create an excess supply of liras. The lira prices of the deutschmark and of goods would rise as a result. The anticipation of capital gains on the deutschmark should reinforce this movement from liras into deutschmarks, creating a potentially unstable situation, where demand for liras disappears and lira prices explode.

The introduction of the parallel Europa effects quite a different process. A shift by Italians out of liras into Europas does not create an excess supply of liras, for the Europas can be obtained only by offering liras in exchange. Italians are not giving up liabilities of the Italian central bank in favour of the liabilities of another central bank, as in the case of a switch into deutschmarks. Rather they are switching the form in which they hold the liabilities of the Italian central bank. The lira-deutschmark exchange rate is not altered by this change of money holdings from liras into Europas, nor are the lira prices of goods driven up. From another point of view, there are no balance-of-payments effects in shifting from domestic currency into Europas, as there are when shifting from one national currency to the other. The unstable element that comes from mounting expectations of capital gains does not exist with the adoption of the Europa.

The Europa as a Means to Monetary Reform

The constant-purchasing-power Europa has been proposed as a means of attaining monetary reform in Europe, while avoiding the transitional stabilization costs that seem unavoidable in domestic-currency monetary reform. The reasoning is that there would be no inflationary expectations for the Europa. The arrangements guarantee constant purchasing power during the parallel-currency stage, and there can be no history of inflation of Europa prices, because the Europa has no history. The removal of inflationary expectations should enable countries to attain a stable price level without transitional periods of declining output and rising unemployment.

Three qualifications need to be made of this claim. If vestiges of money illusion still remain in some areas, with accompanying short-run gains from inflation, then there will still be some transitional costs in reducing the rate of inflation. Secondly, the constant-purchasing-power guarantee of the Europa might not be believed. The exchange-rate guarantee would remain only as long as the Europa was a parallel currency. When the Europa replaced the national currencies, its purchasing power would depend upon a policy-determined supply, which might be inflationary. While the Europa itself has no history, the issuers of the Europa do. People may not believe that the European monetary authorities will behave any better with a central currency than they did with the national currencies. It is the cost of creating such credibility that Klein discusses. Parkin's recommendation for a monetary constitution with a legislated rate of money growth is relevant in this regard. Such a constitution could do much to achieve the necessary confidence in the new Europa. Thirdly, the loss of the implicit inflation tax by the national governments would impose additional financing problems upon the governments. Such a burden upon fiscal policies could prove to be deflationary, causing transitional stabilization problems. This concern is expressed in Laidler's paper.

A Gradual, Voluntary Move to Monetary Union

The second major advantage claimed for the Europa is as a means of moving gradually and voluntarily toward a single European currency and monetary union. There was considerable disagreement at the conference about how rapidly such a Europa would be adopted, in which countries, and for which purposes. Vaubel concluded that the Europa would be attractive, initially, as a standard of value, then as a store of value, and only last as a medium of exchange. He pointed out that the Europa would be particularly useful in those countries that were most open and engaged in large international transactions. The Europa would also be attractive in countries whose inflation rates are the highest.

Some participants voiced serious concern that the Europa would be adopted virtually overnight in countries with high inflation rates, such as Italy, removing any of the advantages of gradualism. The high-inflation countries tend to be the peripheral economies with low productivity, those economies that are seen as benefiting least from monetary union. The increased pressure for real-wage equalization is predicted to result in unemployment and migration out of these areas. Vaubel argues, however, that the peripheral countries have demonstrated a preference for inflation, and that they will not so rapidly adopt the Europa. He concludes that the new currency would first be adopted in the open, central economies.

The high degree of wage indexation in the high-inflation, peripheral economies suggests that workers in these countries may not prefer inflation. The inflationary preferences of these countries may be more on the part of the governments. To the extent that such governments are highly dependent on the implicit inflation tax, a rapid move to a constant-purchasing-power currency could indeed prove costly.

The possibility of too rapid an adoption of the Europa reinforces concerns about the sudden loss to governments of the implicit inflation tax. While it was agreed that monetary reform is needed and that governments should not continue to solve their financing problems through inflationary policies, an abrupt change was seen as presenting transitional problems. Many governments have heavy financial commitments and large deficits. Particularly in a period of economic recession the sudden increase in the tax burden could prove highly disruptive.

Not everyone felt that there would be rapid adoption of the Europa in certain countries. Some participants expressed the opposite concern – that the Europa would not be accepted, that there would be no move toward monetary union, and that the credibility of monetary union would be damaged by such a false start. Klein takes this position in his discussion of the costs of establishing the 'brand name' capital necessary for a successful currency. Laidler suggests that governments would have to do more than merely agree to support the value of the Europa. He points out the need for governments themselves to adopt the Europa for the denomination of government bonds and for the calculation and collection of taxes. Otherwise, the costs to private firms and institutions of using the Europa, even as a standard of value, would be very high.

The prospect of rapid adoption of the parallel Europa raised another, more general, issue – a question of indeterminacy of a parallel currency whose constant purchasing power is calculated in terms of domestic price indexes. Under the proposed arrangement, as a domestic currency is increasingly replaced by the parallel Europa and as goods in that country are priced increasingly in Europas rather than in the domestic currency, the price index needed to calculate the exchange rate of the Europa becomes meaningless or nonexistent. At some point, as the domestic currency disappears, the exchange rate between the Europa and the domestic currency becomes meaningless. It was concluded that the gradual, voluntary adoption of the Europa as a parallel currency could only be taken to a certain stage (where there was less than total adoption of the Europa), at which point the Europa would officially be designated the official currency of the country, replacing the domestic currency. The supply of the Europa as the official currency would be determined by a central EEC monetary authority.

There is no way of controlling the rate of adoption of the Europa or of assuring that it would be adopted at the same rate in all countries. Thus, the switch of the Europa from a parallel currency to an official currency would not necessarily occur at the same time in all countries. It might have to be made in some countries soon after the introduction of the new Europa. It is essential, therefore, when the Europa is first introduced, that countries commit themselves to a monetary constitution for the EEC. They must agree that they will make the move to monetary union at whatever time is indicated by the voluntary adoption of the parallel currency.

IV. CONCLUSION

The historical experience with new currencies is small and has never occurred under comparable economic and institutional circumstances. Thus, the proposal for the introduction of a parallel currency with constant purchasing power is a step into the unknown. This suggests the desirability of moving cautiously and maintaining flexibility. While governments cannot predict or directly control public response to a new parallel currency, there are numerous means available to them for either encouraging or limiting its adoption. For example, widespread government adoption of the new currency would certainly encourage its use, while regulations limiting its use or the imposition of negative real interest rates could prevent too rapid adoption.

What is required is a true will on the part of the participating governments to move to a monetary union and to guarantee the success of the new currency. This commitment must include an agreement on a monetary constitution for the new monetary union and a willingness to give up the implicit inflation tax. If such political will is present, the Europa, as a parallel currency of constant purchasing power, offers a reasonable and promising means of moving to monetary union, with the additional benefit of reducing the transitional costs of monetary reform.

10 Political Epilogue

SARAH HOGG

The nine signatories to the All Saints' Day manifesto published in *The Economist* in 1975 appeared to possess all the faith in the possibility of human progress characteristic of sainthood. But the realities of the time were not such as to encourage optimism. For the fostering of the stunted seedling of economic and monetary union, the climate – political as well as economic – could hardly have been less balmy.

The first great attempt at union – the fixing of intra-European exchange rates in a floating world – had been defeated. In 1975, when payments imbalances and inflation differences between the economies of the European Economic Community were at their largest, any such giant leaps forward towards monetary union looked economically as well as politically impractical. Though countries which fell out of the snake could (as France did) attempt to rejoin it at a lower parity, the lesson was becoming plain. Those who locked their currencies into the joint float did not, and could not, throw away the key. The snake was degenerating into a mechanism for achieving very short-term stability between a few North European currencies, useful for trade but no longer a clear route to final union.

So, *faute de mieux*, the millimetre-a-month approach (so ably described by Herbert Christie and Michele Fratianni) came to be emphasised by those who had not abandoned all hope of eventual union. Market barriers were gradually dismantled (with one disguised step backward for every two forward) but otherwise progress was imperceptible.

This was the declared reason for the All Saints' Day manifesto; but also the obstacle to it. Progress appeared to be blocked by a paradoxical political reaction to any plan for advancement. As a destination, EMU had been endorsed by all member governments; only the gradualist route being followed was proving painfully slow and yet politically painful. But the suggestion of a new gradualist route, offering the momentum of market forces in place of politically-exhausting discretionary decisions, was greeted as some kind of con-trick: an attempt to back Europe into monetary union without the step-by-step consent of governments. A gradualist route to union provides an escalator, rather than an empty lift-shaft, making it easier to take the initial step; but the complementary virtue of the parallel currency scheme was that progress then became automatic. That meant that governments, once embarked, could not step off the escalator; so its gradualism did not lessen their suspicion of its final destination.

The truth was that Europe's governments possessed too few of those to whom Mr. Roy Jenkins, president of the European commission, said his Jean Monnet lecture, delivered in October, 1977, was addressed: those who 'expect to be convinced of the practical benefits of any move forward'. So: 'the politics of monetary union' stood 'immobilised in scepticism'.

The history of the two years between the manifesto and the Leuven conference, which came shortly after Mr. Jenkins had attempted to launch a new debate on union with that lecture (and with proposals put to the rest of the Commission shortly before), certainly seemed to justify his pessimism. The snake had shrivelled still further into a skinny Germanic reptile. The co-ordination of fiscal and monetary policies amounted not to negotiated convergence but to a civil exchange of figures. A division was yawning between the West German government on the one hand and a growing camp of other member governments on the other, on the need for co-ordinated fiscal action to bridge the gap between growth targets and dismal growth forecasts for Europe in 1978. If there was less international heat over divergent monetary policies, this was because monetary policy in many slump-scared countries appeared to be slipping into neutral, with monetary targets for 1978 not very different from the previous year's.

The only political question aroused by Mr. Jenkins's initiative at first appeared to be how quickly, and how savagely, it would be rebuffed; and how much his personal prestige and influence would be damaged by being seen to bang his head against a brick wall. Mr Jenkins could, and did, argue that crabwise progress is better than none: and that member governments had been made readier to agree small sideways steps (e.g., the new borrowing facility) by the consciousness that they were dragging their feet down the main road to union. But the new five-year programme directed towards union that was endorsed at the December summit meeting of the Nine seemed only to confirm the sceptics' power, and Mr Jenkins's impotence.

The first instalment, an 'Action programme for 1978' was finally published by the Commission in April, 1978. Convergence, harmonisation, communication and co-ordination of policies were its themes; bolder ideas were given graceful recognition but no central place. The basic premise remained what it had been before Mr Jenkins's initiative: that no progress to union could be made until the economies of the Nine were on convergent growth paths; and that only better co-ordination of nationally-determined policies could get them there.

Yet at the moment this disappointing document was published, the sceptics appeared to have been overtaken by events. The German response to the reflationary pleas of its neighbours (and of the United States) had been a reciprocal plea for currency stability. Between Christmas, 1977, and mid-April, 1978, the yen had risen about 10.5 per cent against the dollar, the Swiss franc by about the same percentage and the deutschemark by nearly 7 per cent. Snake currencies had been dragged up with the deutsche-mark, the other major European currencies had risen against the dollar but fallen against the snake (although sterling had fallen even against the dollar, from its pre-Christmas high).

Mr Jenkins had urged currency instability as a reason for seriously reconsidering monetary union. His theme had been that both the dangers of 1978 (the risk of slump, the violence of currency gyrations, the depreciation of the world's major reserve asset) and its sunnier prospects (the coming-together of inflation rates among most of Europe's major economies, and the narrowing of payments imbalance) made union look simultaneously more attractive and more possible. That laid him open to the criticism that he was marshalling immediate and short-term problems in support of a very long-term reform. Actions to avert slump needed to be taken today, or better yesterday; designs for monetary union could be realised only the day after tomorrow.

And yet suddenly, an embryonic European currency looks a short-term possibility. The thirst for currency stability was generating a series of ideas for relinking the snake's expatriates, within looser margins. The Belgians had one, West Germany's Herr Schmidt another, the Commission was brewing a third. In April, 1978, these ideas were still circling; but critical to each was the role of the European unit of account.

The first issue in the construction of a new 'boa' was the looseness with which the new target zones for the lira, French franc and sterling were defined. Too narrow a margin would obviously lead to excessive and unrewarding intervention; but loosely-defined target zones might come to mean as little as the International Monetary Fund's rules for exchange rate management. The resistance of the British might reduce bolder plans to one in which zones were defined only negatively (i.e. governments merely undertook not to intervene to drive their currencies outside their zones). That would make a boa no more than a political gesture: part of 1978's horse-trading of policies between those urging reflation and those demanding stability. But if Europe could bring itself to agree on something stronger, the guts of the new schemes would be in the role envisaged for FECOM

If a proportion of national reserves were (as originally planned for the snake) to be pooled and held by FECOM and if it were to issue European units of account, backed by these reserves, in settlement for intervention by central banks; then Europe would be some way towards the creation of a community-wide currency and a central bank. Only some way: the EUA would cease to be a mere calculation, and become a reserve currency; but it would display most of the deficiencies of the Special Drawing Rights. It would be less attractive to hold than the strongest of Europe's currencies (unless the interest rate were, unlike the SDR's, to be fixed by other than the obvious averaging method, in order to compensate for this). And it would be a far cry from the aims of the All Saints' Day manifesto, for a Europa available not just to central banks but to all Europe's citizens, protected against inflation and brought into circulation simply by the domestic demand for it.

Yet this change of mood, so dramatically marked by the difference in political attitudes to Mr Jenkins's initiative and to exchange rate plans floated only six months later, served to show that scepticism, if a natural state of political attitude towards union, is not set, like concrete, right around the prospects of progress. In 1978, the Nine (except Italy) had all left the nightmare peaks of inflation for an assortment of foothills. But because the exchange-rate mechanism was not working well to reflect this convergence, governments were keener to help co-ordination on its way. Suddenly, more of Europe's policy makers 'expected to be convinced of the practical benefits of any move forward'. Some of those (Herr Schmidt for one) most dubious about Mr Jenkins's unfurling of the banner last October were to be found marching beneath it in April. The rapidity with which mood can change makes serious discussion of the kind that took place at Leuven suddenly urgent, lest the evaporation of scepticism leave a vacuum.

If reserve assets are held and managed centrally, it becomes politically less easy to unlock exchange rates unilaterally (i.e., changes in target zones would need real international negotiation). Should FECOM remain a committee of central bank governors? As an embryonic central bank, it immediately raises the issue of Europe's final monetary constitution. Other, even more politically-sensitive, questions discussed at Leuven follow rapidly. First, the parameters within which national monetary policies might be required to confine themselves: then, the point at which the European central bank assumes responsibility for European monetary policy. Under what rules should a European central bank operate? How would the banking systems of the Nine adjust, and how would a European central bank adapt them, or itself, to achieve the results it wanted within very different national contexts? Then, last but politically most important of all, how much freedom can be left to member governments to determine their own fiscal policies, when their overall budgetary balance would have to be agreed on a European basis? How far could regional policy compensate for the effects of union on Europe's low-productivity areas: i.e., how should the gains from currency unification (low transactions costs and risks, and the possibility of sustaining a payments imbalance for the area as a whole greater than the sum of sustainable national deficits) be distributed to offset the disadvantages suffered at Europe's economic peripheries?

These questions have been brought suddenly closer by enthusiasm for exchange rate co-ordination. So, therefore, the claims of a parallel currency approach to ease transition provide no longer a trip through dreamland, but answers to real political questions. When the Manifesto was launched in 1975, it was a counter-inflationary candle in a dark world, an act of faith in Europe's ability to achieve union and price stability, liable to the practical scepticism accorded all acts of faith. In 1978, the destination of EMU had suddenly been brought this side of dreamland by the attraction of a first step. A parallel course for the remaining n-minus-one required not faith, but argument; the proceedings of the Leuven conference were projected from theory into tomorrow's world.

Index